CITY ON FIRE

Antony Dapiran is an Australian author and lawyer and longtime resident of Hong Kong. One of the world's leading observers of Hong Kong politics, he has written about the protests for many publications, including *The Atlantic, The Guardian, New Statesman,* and *The Australian Financial Review,* been interviewed by national television networks such as the BBC, CNN, and the ABC, and been quoted on the subject by leading media outlets around the world, including *The Times, The Wall Street Journal, The New York Times, The Washington Post,* and the *Financial Times.*

ANTONY DAPIRAN

CITY ON FIRE

THE FIGHT FOR HONG KONG

SCRIBE

Melbourne • London

Scribe Publications
2 John St, Clerkenwell, London, WC1N 2ES, United Kingdom
18–20 Edward St, Brunswick, Victoria 3056, Australia
3754 Pleasant Ave, Suite 100, Minneapolis, Minnesota 55409, USA

First published by Scribe 2020

Typeset in Garamond by the publishers
Printed and bound in the UK by CPI Group (UK) Ltd, Croydon CR0 4YY

Scribe Publications is committed to the sustainable use of natural resources
and the use of paper products made responsibly from those resources.

9781950354276 (US edition)
9781913348113 (UK edition)
9781922310002 (Australian edition)
9781925938241 (ebook)

Catalogue records for this book are available from the National Library
of Australia and the British Library.

scribepublications.com
scribepublications.co.uk
scribepublications.com.au

CONTENTS

A NOTE ON LANGUAGE

Unlike standard Mandarin Chinese (or *Putonghua*), for which mainland China adopts the Hanyu Pinyin system of romanisation, there is no universally agreed-upon romanisation system for Cantonese, the variant of the Chinese language spoken in Hong Kong and more widely across China's Guangdong province. A number of romanisation systems for Cantonese have been developed over the years, each with their own benefits and weaknesses. In this book, I have chosen to adopt the most modern, and relatively widely accepted, Jyutping system of romanisation (but omitting tone indicators for the sake of concision). This should enable the Anglophone reader reasonably to approximate the Cantonese pronunciation of Chinese as it is spoken on the streets of Hong Kong, provided that the reader bears in mind one important rule: in Jyutping, the letter 'j' is pronounced as 'y' (consistent with the International Phonetic Alphabet).

That said, I have occasionally used Hanyu Pinyin (again, omitting tone markings) when referring to mainland names or places, or when quoting phrases originally spoken in Mandarin.

Monetary amounts in the text are stated in Hong Kong dollars. At the time of publication, approximate currency-conversion rates were as follows:

- Australian dollars: $1.00 was equivalent to HK$5.00
- British pounds: £1.00 was equivalent to HK$10.00
- US dollars: $1.00 was equivalent to HK$8.00

PREFACE

The question of what to call the protest movement that began in Hong Kong in June 2019 has been a vexed one for writers and commentators. The protests were initially referred to as the 'Anti-Extradition Bill Protests', reflecting the cause that was the catalyst for the movement. However, the protesters' demands quickly expanded beyond just the extradition bill, and the protests continued long after the bill was suspended and then withdrawn. 'Hong Kong's Summer of Discontent' seemed an appropriate name, but summer soon gave way to autumn and then to winter, with no end to the protests in sight.

The protests that Hong Kong witnessed in 2014 came to be known as the 'Umbrella Movement', and in 2019 commentators again looked for a similar icon that might lend its name to the movement: some (including the present author) proposed the 'Hard Hat Revolution', after the distinctive yellow hard hats worn by protesters that became emblematic of the movement's visual identity. Others advocated for 'Water Revolution', in homage to the protesters' Bruce Lee–inspired 'Be water!' philosophy. Both seemed a touch contrived.

Neither 'Anti-government protests' nor 'Anti-China protests' seemed sufficiently specific, and as the months wore on many also pointed out that the events of 2019 seemed to have long outgrown the descriptor of 'protests'; this was a city-wide uprising. However, to call it the 'Hong Kong Uprising' (or variants on that term) surely risked being melodramatic.

In the end, simplicity seems to be the most appropriate course. The Maoist-inspired protests that rocked Hong Kong in 1967 came to be known simply as the '1967 riots'. It would appear that, at least for now, the '2019 protests' is the appropriate term, especially for use in a book that covers events current to and concluding with the end of that calendar year.

As we move into 2020, protests are still continuing in Hong Kong, and the movement that began in 2019 may yet find its historical destiny — and its name. But that will be the topic for another book.

CITY OF TEARS

Tear gas rounds describe a graceful arc as they drop down out of the blue sky, trailing feathery tails of smoke like streamers. The shells hit the road with a ping, and sparks fly as they skip gaily along the asphalt. As they roll to a stop, the shells hiss like an angry snake, dense smoke pouring out of the top of the small aluminium canister, and soon the street is enveloped in clouds of smoke.

The most important thing to understand about tear gas is that it is not a gas. It is a substance, a sort of powder, delivered in the form of smoke from a burning tear gas shell. That powder is 2-chloroben-zylidene malononitrile — known as 'CS' — a compound developed and tested at the United Kingdom's notorious Porton Down military facility. As the tear gas canister burns, which it does for around one minute, it spreads smoke containing tiny particles of CS that spread and stick: to clothes, to skin, to surfaces.

If you get caught in a cloud of tear gas, the first thing you feel is a stinging in your eyes — a feeling akin to handling raw chilli peppers and then touching your eyes. You will reflexively close your eyes as they begin to stream with tears. Next, you will feel the burning in your nose and throat. You will choke and cough as the tear gas attacks your mucous membranes, and you will be gripped with the sense that you cannot breathe. At the same time, you will feel your skin prickling like a bad case of sunburn. Finally, if you are unlucky enough to get a real lungful, you will be overcome with nausea; you will start to gag and spit, perhaps vomit. But most important, from the deployers' point of view, will be your psychological reaction to tear gas. Tear gas obliterates the solidarity of the crowd. When you are hit with tear gas, no longer are you a member of a group gathered together with a common purpose. You are alone, your mind blank, all prior thoughts replaced with only one: the need to get away. Eyes closed, coughing, choking, blinded, and stumbling, you will run.

As well as having a psychological effect on those being gassed, tear gas also has a psychological effect on those deploying it and those looking on, either in person or through the media. By creating a scene of violence and chaos, tear gas works to objectify the crowd, turning it from a group of human beings into a seething, writhing mass. Tear gas also helps to turn a protest into a riot — and therefore makes it a legitimate target for further state violence.

Understanding this perhaps helps to explain why Hong Kong police deployed so much tear gas on the citizens of the city in the course of 2019, often when the crowd was not violent, not charging police lines — sometimes even when the streets were totally empty. It helped to justify the police's own actions: ordered to deploy force against the people, tear gassing those people turned them from fellow Hong Kong citizens, with whom they might sympathise, into an objectified other, into criminals.

The physical effects of tear gas wear off fairly quickly after you leave the tear gas environment. Rinsing out your eyes with water helps, as does a gentle breeze to blow the CS crystals off your skin and clothes.

Within half an hour, your breathing will return to normal. But you need to remain vigilant. Tear gas hangs in the air for long after the smoke is no longer visible. If you are wearing protective gear and manage to avoid exposure during the initial burst, but then make the mistake of later touching your clothes and then touching your face, you will inflict the CS upon yourself.

The danger of real physical harm from tear gas comes not from the gas itself, but from the canisters used to distribute them. Tear gas canisters are fired from Federal Riot Guns at a muzzle velocity of around eighty metres per second. That's less than one-tenth the speed of a regular bullet, but still enough to cause serious injury, especially if the metal canisters — which, with a 40mm diameter, are significantly larger and heavier than a bullet — strike the head or face. The other risk of injury is from burns: tear gas canisters are incendiary devices, and often burst into flame upon hitting the road, sometimes burning hot enough to melt the bitumen.

Shortly before Hong Kong police fire the first rounds of tear gas, they will raise a black banner that reads: 'Warning. Tear Smoke.' Sometimes.

Sometimes they will do that. At other times the black banner will be raised shortly after the tear gas is fired, as a kind of afterthought. Sometimes it will not be raised at all. But when they do raise that black banner, it seems almost quaintly polite, like a remnant of Britishness left over from the old colonial police force.

If you are not close enough to see the flag, you can wait further back and listen for when those towards the frontlines call out, '*Hak kei!*' ('Black flag!') Or listen for the crack and pop as the tear gas is fired into the crowd. It sounds almost celebratory — like firecrackers, or a champagne cork — and your instinct may even be to greet it with a cheer.

In the absence of the black flag, a more reliable indication is to watch for when the police put on their own gas masks. In the hot, humid Hong Kong weather, they will only do this when it is absolutely necessary. And when it is necessary for them to put their masks on, you had better make sure you have your mask on too.

American conglomerate 3M makes a variety of equipment that provides protection against tear gas. Hong Kongers are familiar with the various models of 3M personal protective equipment, and can speak about the relative merits of the half-face respirator — probably the most popular model among Hong Kong protesters, easy to don and remove, but only effective if you wear it with proper, non-vented eye goggles, another 3M product — as compared to the full-face respirator — more effective, but less convenient. These respirators have clip-on filters, and Hong Kongers tell you that you will want the multi-gas/vapour cartridges together with the P100 particulate filters, which will help to filter out the CS particles as well as pepper spray. The particulate filters are bright pink in colour, a signature feature of Hong Kong protester attire.

On 28 September 2014, in the event that prompted the beginning of the Umbrella Movement occupation, Hong Kong police fired eighty-seven tear gas shells at the crowds. It was the first time that tear gas had been used against Hong Kong people in almost fifty years,[1] and it would be the only occasion in the course of those protests on which tear gas was used, such was the public outrage it provoked.

On 12 June 2019, the first occasion on which police fired tear gas during that year's protests, they fired over fifty rounds. During the day that saw the siege of Chinese University in November, police fired over 2,330 rounds in the course of a single day, approaching two rounds for every single minute of the day.

By the end of 2019, over the course of seven months, Hong Kong police had fired over 16,000 rounds of tear gas onto the streets of Hong Kong.

Hong Kongers have a way to describe those days when the police unleash round after round of tear gas on Hong Kong's districts. They call it an 'all-you-can-eat tear gas buffet'.

Yet it seems to say something about the nature of Hong Kong that the police should so assiduously keep track of, and faithfully update the public on, these numbers. It also says something about the nature of Hong Kong that one of the greatest outrages, from the public's point of view, arose when it was discovered that at least some of that tear gas had been used beyond the latest date recommended for use by the manufacturer. The idea that police were tear gassing them was bad enough, but that they were doing it with expired tear gas just seemed to add insult to injury.

Tear gas is a chemical weapon, first used in World War I to flush troops out of the trenches. As the world came to understand the horror of chemical warfare in the aftermath of the war, tear gas, along with other chemical weapons, was banned under the Geneva Protocol of 1925. However, its use was permitted for domestic law enforcement, a position that remains under the more recent Chemical Weapons Convention of 1993.

In the colonies — places such as India, Palestine, and parts of Africa — the British opted for tear gas to avoid using lethal force against local populations, and to preserve their reputation as benevolent colonisers.

And if the Hong Kong Police Force's 'Warning. Tear Smoke' banner seems like some quaint colonial vestige, that's because it is. In the 1930s, as the British government's Colonial Office and the War Office grappled with how to reconcile the use of tear gas on civilian populations when it was banned for use in war, the War Office felt the position could be justified by 'a declared intention to use tear gas and adequate warning given to opponents'— thus the black flag was born, and with it, in British minds, the morally justifiable path to the use of tear gas on civilian populations in the colonies.[2] It was also the British who insisted on using the term 'tear smoke' rather than 'tear gas', the latter being felt to be a 'much more alarming term' rather too suggestive of the poison gas attacks of World War I.

However, it was some time before the British government became comfortable using tear gas on British soil. Tear gas was used on British civilians for the first time at the start of the Northern Ireland Troubles, when the Royal Ulster Constabulary fired tear gas in the Battle of Bogside in August 1969, deploying over 1,000 rounds over the course of two days.

The controversy surrounding the use of tear gas in the Bogside prompted an independent enquiry, the Himsworth enquiry, into the possible toxic effects of CS gas. The Himsworth report concluded that CS gas was safe within certain prescribed dosage levels, and the report has since been used to justify the use of tear gas against civilian populations across the globe. That justification, observed Anna Feigenbaum, the author of a book on the subject of tear gas, is based on the assumption that 'protesters are always supposed to be able to get away from the smoke, and the smoke is always supposed to be able to evaporate and be ephemeral. The problem,' she added, 'is that in Hong Kong neither of those things is true.'[3]

Hong Kong's streets are narrow and congested. When tear gas is fired, it hangs in the stagnant passages between the buildings in the humid, subtropical air. The people, trapped on streets that are challenging to navigate even under normal conditions, find their escape blocked by protester barricades — built to slow the advance of police — and by police cordons and check lines. Police have also fired tear gas into dangerous locations such as bridges and walkways, and inside underground Mass Transit Railway (MTR) stations. Tear gas has been fired in Hong Kong's residential areas — the most densely populated in the world — with canisters landing on balconies, outside the windows of aged-care facilities, and even inside people's homes. Families, the elderly, and children have all been affected, innocent victims of the clouds of gas unleashed upon the city, exposing them to higher concentrations and over periods of time far greater than was contemplated by those studies that consider tear gas to be 'safe'.

It has been estimated that hundreds of people around the world have died as a result of the use of tear gas or its effects. Medical researchers conducting a systematic review of injuries and deaths caused by tear gas and other chemical irritants observed that the use of tear gas can undermine freedoms of expression and peaceful assembly, 'by causing injuries, intimidating communities, and leading to escalations in violence on all sides'. They concluded: 'Although chemical weapons may have a limited role in crowd control ... they have significant potential for misuse, leading to unnecessary morbidity and mortality.'[4]

As the 2019 protests unfolded in Hong Kong, the world's leading medical journal, *The Lancet*, published a letter from a group of Hong Kong academics complaining of a lack of government attention to the health effects of tear gas and a failure to advise the public on how to protect their health and decontaminate their surroundings. They wrote:

> The ongoing situation in Hong Kong calls for a reflection of the appropriateness of tear gas utilisation for crowd and riot control in densely populated urban areas when minimum efforts have been made to provide decontamination guidelines and health protection to bystanders, affected communities, and stakeholders. The Hong Kong SAR Government should invest in tear gas-related health surveillance and long-term environmental monitoring.[5]

Just as the physiological effects of tear gas wear off fairly quickly, so too do the psychological effects. Tear gas teaches resiliance — and resistance. The crowd, once it loses its fear of tear gas, comes back more determined than ever. Hong Kong protesters became so adept at countering tear gas that it quickly lost its effect as a 'force multiplier' — that is, as a tool to panic and disperse a crowd and so increase the effectiveness of other force such as rubber bullets or baton charges. Instead, the Hong Kong protesters just donned their gas masks and goggles, picked up their umbrellas, and fearlessly stood their ground.

Yet the tear gas kept coming, in amounts such that it went far beyond its intended purpose, to disperse a crowd, and became a punitive measure, an offensive weapon, used not to de-escalate but to punish.

Author Simon Winchester, describing the Ulster Troubles, wrote about the effect tear gas has on a crowd. Its deployment by the British army, he said, turned 'what had been a tenuously bonded ... mob of hooligans and housewives' into 'a choking, screaming, radicalised and almost totally solid political group'. Tear gas, Winchester wrote, had 'enormous power to weld a crowd together in common sympathy and common hatred for the men who gassed them'.[6]

The same effect was seen in Hong Kong in the protests of 2019. I have watched as wave after wave of tear gas was unleashed upon crowds of protesters. The crowd would break and disperse momentarily, and then, as the tear gas started to dissipate, the crowd would reform, chanting as they advanced again on the police lines, 'Heung gong jan, gaa jau!' Literally, 'Hong Kongers, add oil!', a rallying cry that could be roughly translated as 'Go, Hong Kongers!'

The experience — and spectacle — of tear gas came to define life in Hong Kong in 2019, whether fighting it at the frontlines, choking on it or dodging it while engaged in a lawful protest, planning one's journeys and schedules to avoid it, watching images of it billowing on television screens, or just talking about it. Children in Hong Kong playgrounds played 'police and protesters', and talked about tear gas as casually as children elsewhere might talk about sports or computer games.

After the protests of 2019, Hong Kongers have a new saying, and a new aspect to their identity: 'You're not a real Hong Konger if you haven't tasted tear gas.'

1

A DEATH IN TAIPEI

In 2018, Valentine's Day coincided with the Lunar New Year holidays. To celebrate, a young Hong Kong couple — Poon Hiu-wing, aged twenty, and her boyfriend, Chan Tong-kai, aged nineteen — decided to go on a long-weekend getaway to Taipei.[1]

The couple had met while working together in a shop in July 2017. Both were also students: Poon was studying at a local vocational education institute, and Chan was studying an associate degree in business at the Hong Kong Polytechnic University. They soon became romantically involved. In November, Poon wrote on her Facebook page: 'He says I am his first and last girlfriend!'[1]

Poon told her mother a few days before her Lunar New Year trip that she would be visiting Taiwan with a friend, but did not tell her mother who she would be travelling with. Poon also had another secret: in December, she had informed Chan that she was five weeks' pregnant.

Poon and Chan travelled to Taipei on 13 February and checked into the Purple Garden Hotel. They were scheduled to return to Hong Kong on 17 February.

Taipei is a favourite weekend getaway for Hong Kongers. Poon and Chan spent three days exploring Taipei: Valentine's Day on Wednesday, Lunar New Year's Eve on Thursday, and Lunar New Year's Day on Friday. What might they have done during those three days? Like so many other visiting Hong Kongers, Poon and Chan would probably have visited the famous Shilin Night Market, which was just four stops on the subway from the Purple Garden Hotel. Strolling under the strings of red lanterns and Lunar New Year decorations, perhaps Chan and Poon might have snacked on local Taiwanese delicacies such as oyster omelettes, grilled sausages, or sweet taro desserts, and bought some of Taiwan's famous *Fenglisu* pineapple pastries to take back to family and friends in Hong Kong. They likely joined the throngs shopping in the bustling, neon-lit Ximending commercial district, and perhaps took time out to visit one of the numerous hot springs resorts in the hills surrounding Taipei.

We know that on the night of Friday 16 February, as families across China were celebrating the first day of the Lunar New Year, Poon and Chan visited a night market, where Poon purchased a large pink suitcase in which to pack her shopping from the trip. China Central Television (CCTV) footage showed her pushing the empty new suitcase into the hotel lobby and upstairs to their room. Back in the room, Poon and Chan argued about how the luggage should be packed. According to the account Chan later gave police, they made up and had sex. At 1.21am in the early morning of 17 February Poon sent a WhatsApp message to her mother saying she would be returning to Hong Kong later that night.

Then, at around 2.00am, according to Chan, they fought again, and Poon revealed that an ex-boyfriend — not Chan — was the father of the baby she was carrying. Poon also showed him a video of her having sex with another man. Chan allededly flew into a rage, hitting Poon's head into a wall, dragging her onto the floor and struggling with her for ten minutes, strangling her until she was dead. He stuffed her body into the pink suitcase, and went to sleep.[2]

Early the next morning, Chan disposed of Poon's belongings at garbage-collection points near the hotel. Surveillance-camera footage then showed Chan, at around half-past eleven, dragging the pink suitcase out of the lobby of the Purple Garden Hotel, alone. He boarded the subway and travelled fifteen stations away before finally disposing of Poon's body in bushes in a park near Zhuwei Station on the northern fringes of New Taipei city. Surveillance-camera footage again showed Chan returning to the Purple Garden Hotel at half-past six that evening, this time without the pink suitcase. Chan used Poon's ATM card to withdraw 20,000 New Taiwan dollars, then went to the airport and caught a flight home to Hong Kong late that night.

Back in Hong Kong, Chan used Poon's ATM card to withdraw a further HK$19,200. Meanwhile, after Poon had failed to return home, her parents became desperate. Poon's father asked Chan about her whereabouts. Chan said only that they had had an argument and gone their separate ways, and then ignored her father's further attempts to contact him.

Poon's mother reported her missing to Hong Kong police, while her father travelled to Taipei to contact the authorities there. A month after their daughter had checked into the Purple Garden Hotel for her final, fateful stay, Poon's parents checked in themselves, searching for clues to their daughter's whereabouts.

As suspicions mounted, Hong Kong police interviewed Chan on 13 March at Tsuen Kwan O police station. In that interview, Chan confessed to killing Poon, gave his account of the events surrounding the murder, and disclosed the location of the body. That evening, Hong Kong police passed on the information to police in Taipei.

When they heard that the body was somewhere near Zhuwei station, local police in Taipei were not surprised. Local residents had complained of a rotting stench in the area some three weeks earlier, but police despatched to the scene at the time had been unable to find anything. Late in the night of 13 March, a team of Taipei police descended on the scene again, and as they searched through the bushes they shouted out into the night, 'Miss Poon, please quickly let us find you and send you home!' — a traditional Taiwanese custom to communicate with the spirit of the dead. They soon discovered her badly decomposed remains concealed beneath a tree. An autopsy would later confirm that Poon had been four to five months pregnant.

And that, normally, is where the story would end: a young life tragically cut short, a crime of passion, the usual tabloid fodder. Poon's social media selfies were splashed across the internet. One newspaper showed a grainy CCTV image of Poon pushing her newly purchased pink suitcase into the hotel with the caption: 'The deceased Poon Hiu-wing seen entering her hotel in a CCTV image, pushing a large pink suitcase: she never would have dreamed that it would become her own, mobile coffin.'[3]

Yet there is a direct path from that hotel room in Taipei to tear gas and bullets on the streets of Hong Kong. Poon's death would set in train a series of events that would throw Hong Kong — and possibly China — into its greatest crisis since the Tiananmen Square incident of 1989. Hong Kong in 2019 became a city on fire, and this was the spark.

As I look at the photograph of Poon and Chan now — captured together in a selfie, with the pouting, self-conscious pose typical of their generation — one thing strikes me: they look just like the thousands of other young Hong Kongers I saw on the streets during the long hot months of 2019, clad in black, chanting slogans, facing off against police behind the burning barricades.

I can't help thinking: *If this protest movement had happened without Poon's death, without Chan's crime, they would have been out there on the streets, too.*

———

Chan Tong-kai had confessed to Poon Hiu-wing's murder, but it soon became apparent that Chan's case fell into a legal lacuna. Under Hong Kong law, a suspect could only be charged with murder if the crime had occurred in Hong Kong. Chan could only face trial for murdering Poon in the place where the murder happened: Taiwan. However, Hong Kong law also only permitted the extradition of criminal suspects to face trial in the twenty jurisdictions with which Hong Kong had entered into extradition agreements. Taiwan was not one of those jurisdictions. And so Chan's case was stuck.

In December 2018, prosecutors in Taiwan issued an arrest warrant for Chan, and the same month Chan pleaded guilty to money-laundering offences in Hong Kong related to his use of Poon's ATM card, and was remanded in custody. The charges bought the authorities in Hong Kong and Taiwan some time while they tried to find a resolution to Chan's case. In April 2019, Chan was sentenced to twenty-nine months' prison on the money-laundering charges; after taking into account time served and good behaviour, he was due for release in October.

Poon's parents began a campaign demanding justice for their daughter's death, writing numerous emotional letters to the chief executive of Hong Kong, Carrie Lam. 'The parents of the victim have not stopped writing letters to the government. There were five addressed to me,' said Lam in February 2019. 'They were still writing this January. If you have read these letters from Mr and Mrs Poon, you would also feel that we must try to help them.'[4]

Sensing an opportunity both to win justice for Poon's family as well as please her political masters in Beijing, Lam, working together with her secretary for security, John Lee Ka-chiu (a former police officer), settled on a plan to resolve Chan's case: Hong Kong's

Fugitive Offenders Ordinance, the law governing extraditions, would be amended to have the geographic restriction removed. The result would be that suspects could be extradited from Hong Kong to face trial anywhere in the world, including Taiwan — and including mainland China.[5]

In February, the government's Security Bureau submitted their proposal to amend the law to the Panel on Security of Hong Kong's legislature, the Legislative Council (also referred to as LegCo). On the same day, Poon's mother appeared at a press conference — her identity disguised behind a baseball cap, sunglasses, and surgical face mask — flanked by politicians Starry Lee and Holden Chow from pro-Beijing political party the Democratic Alliance for the Betterment and Progress of Hong Kong, or DAB. She delivered an emotional plea. 'The whole ordeal has left a hole in my heart, and I can't sleep well at night,' she told reporters. The amendment to the law, she said, 'is the only way justice can be served and until then, my daughter cannot rest in peace'.[6]

The fact that the proposal opened up the possibility of extradition to mainland courts immediately raised alarm. In defence of the proposal, the government pointed to a number of procedural safeguards: following an extradition request, a hearing in a Hong Kong court would need to decide whether the defendant had a case to answer. (However, the case would not be tried on the merits.) The proposal would also apply only to a specific list of crimes, which were required to be criminal offences both in Hong Kong as well as in the requesting jurisdiction (the so-called dual criminality requirement), with political offences explicitly excluded. Finally, the chief executive would have a final veto power over any extradition requests.

Critics, however, were not convinced. The list of crimes in the proposal included not just serious offences such as murder, other crimes of violence, and drug offences, but also offences as diverse as perjury and obstruction of justice, criminal damage or mischief, immigration offences, gambling, prostitution, and fraud. Critically, the law also covered those aiding and abetting any of the listed offences, extending the scope even further. The dual criminality requirement and exclusion of political offences were cold comfort, knowing that the mainland authorities rarely explicitly charged dissidents or political targets with such offences, preferring instead to pursue them for corruption, tax evasion, vice offences, or other unrelated crimes, all of which were also crimes in Hong Kong. In addition, critics scoffed at the idea that a chief executive veto would ever be deployed if Beijing demanded an extradition. What hope did Hong Kong, a part of the Chinese state, have when even other sovereign states were not comfortable that they could enter into an extradition arrangement sufficiently robust to resist political pressure from Beijing? It was not lost on Hong Kong's democrats that numerous countries with common-law legal systems such as Hong Kong's — liberal democracies such as the United States, the United Kingdom, and New Zealand — had not entered into extradition agreements with China. The Australian government had signed an extradition treaty with China in 2017, but was forced to abandon the treaty when it became clear parliament would block its ratification.

Critics of the bill were also incensed that the government sought to short-cut the traditional legislative process, giving the proposal a public consultation period of only twenty days. Carrie Lam used Chan's case to justify her haste. 'If we act too carefully, and slowly consult society or issue consultation papers, then I am afraid we would not be able to help with this special case,' she said.[7]

The government apparently did not foresee any adverse public reaction to the proposal, with the 'Public Reactions' section of the Security Bureau's paper to the government's Executive Committee reportedly consisting only of a short paragraph that raised no red flags.[8]

Lam may have been thinking that the extradition bill controversy would play out like another recent controversy that had similarly raised the passions of the broad alliance of Hong Kong's pro-democracy political parties known as the pan-democrats, as well as those of the legal community.

The West Kowloon high-speed rail station was the Hong Kong terminal of a US$10 billion project connecting Hong Kong to the rest of China's nationwide high-speed rail network. China billed its high-speed rail as one of the 'Four Great Chinese Inventions of Modern Times' (alongside online payment, bike-sharing, and online shopping; never mind that — unlike the 'classic' Four Great Inventions of the compass, gunpowder, paper, and printing — none of these four things was actually invented in China). With average speeds reaching 350 kilometres per hour, connecting to the rail network would be revolutionary for Hong Kong, significantly cutting journey times to mainland cities.

In 2017, as construction on the station neared completion, the Hong Kong government began considering the related customs and border-control arrangements. The government wanted to make journeys as quick and convenient as possible, but was forced to reckon with the obstacle that Hong Kong and the mainland are separate immigration and customs territories under the One Country, Two Systems arrangement that was the basis on which Hong Kong was returned to Chinese sovereignty in 1997. Different visas are required for Hong Kong and the mainland, and travellers crossing the border must undergo immigration and customs checks.

In July 2017, Lam's government announced a proposal that border control and customs facilities for both Hong Kong and the mainland would be co-located within the West Kowloon station in Hong Kong. The proposal involved stationing mainland border-control, customs, and security agents on Hong Kong soil. The government also proposed that mainland law (including criminal law) would apply on the 'mainland side' of border control within the West Kowloon station, as well as on board all trains passing into and out of Hong Kong from the mainland, even when those trains were within Hong Kong's borders.

Pro-democracy advocates were concerned that the presence of mainland security agents inside the West Kowloon station would be effectively a Trojan horse enabling those agents to operate more freely within Hong Kong. Furthermore, the arrangement explicitly gave mainland security officers the power to arrest, detain, and transfer people from the mainland-controlled areas of West Kowloon station across the border and into the arms of the mainland justice system.

Lawyers' groups, such as the Hong Kong Bar Association and the Progressive Lawyers Group, argued that the proposal threatened human rights in Hong Kong and violated the Basic Law, Hong Kong's constitution, which provides that mainland law should not apply within Hong Kong territory.

The government responded with a fudge: it argued that by formally 'leasing' the portion of Hong Kong on the mainland side of border control within West Kowloon station to the mainland, it was no longer Hong Kong territory and therefore the Basic Law did not apply. The government argued that the arrangement was in any event necessary and desirable to enable mainland border control and customs procedures to be completed together with those from Hong Kong in a 'one stop' arrangement that would avoid the need for further clearances at the border, improving the efficiency and speed of journeys ultimately for the convenience of all travellers. The Hong Kong government's proposal was approved by a decision of the National People's Congress Standing Committee, or NPCSC, in Beijing in December 2017.

The Bar Association said that it was 'appalled' at Beijing's decision, arguing that it amounted to:

> an announcement by the NPCSC that the [proposal] complies with the Constitution and the Basic Law 'just because the NPCSC says so'. Such an unprecedented move is the most retrograde step to date in the implementation of the Basic Law, and severely undermines public confidence in 'one country, two systems' and the rule of law in the HKSAR [Hong Kong Special Administrative Region].[9]

The government ignored these objections and pushed ahead with its proposal, using its pro-Beijing majority to force the necessary legislation through a rowdy session of LegCo in June 2018. At a stroke, a piece of Hong Kong inside the West Kowloon station was transformed into a piece of mainland China.

However, after the West Kowloon station opened in September 2018 and began operating, fears appeared to subside, and the issue faded from public view. Perhaps people genuinely enjoyed the convenience of high-speed rail travel to the mainland. Lam was reassured that the pan-democrats' bluster could easily be overcome.

However, the extradition bill, unlike the high-speed rail station, offered no benefits to Hong Kongers. It was a decision made apparently to the detriment of Hong Kong people and entirely in the interests of Beijing. For this reason, many suspected Lam was doing it at Beijing's behest. Lam, and Beijing, both insisted otherwise. 'The central government gave no instruction, no order about making this amendment,' China's ambassador to the UK, Liu Xiaoming, told the BBC. 'This amendment was initiated by the Hong Kong government.'[10]

But while Lam's plan was not instigated by Beijing, they surely welcomed it. Hong Kong had long been a haven for corrupt officials and businessmen from the mainland and their ill-gotten gains, as well as a refuge for political dissidents who continued to be a thorn in Beijing's side. Tiananmen exile Han Dongfang, for example, had been based in the city since 1993, operating China Labour Bulletin, an NGO advocating for labour rights in the mainland.

Yet Lam ignored the obvious warning signs. Public concerns about mainland security agents on Hong Kong soil inside the high-speed rail station were one thing, but nerves in Hong Kong had also been rattled by two other recent and dramatic cases.

In the first case, five men associated with Causeway Bay Books mysteriously disappeared between October and December 2015.[11] The bookstore and its owner, publisher Mighty Current Media, specialised in books on Chinese politics, in particular salacious accounts of the private lives of China's leaders, which were banned on the mainland but extremely popular with mainland visitors to Hong Kong. One of the five booksellers, Swedish citizen Gui Minhai, was abducted from his holiday home in Pattaya, Thailand, while another, UK citizen Lee Bo, disappeared off the streets of Hong Kong after making a book delivery in a remote district on Hong Kong Island.

All five later emerged in custody in the mainland, and were said to be under investigation, variously in connection with a ten-year-old hit-and-run traffic offence allegedly committed by Gui or for selling banned books illegally by mail order into the mainland, and appeared in televised confessions. (Opponents of the extradition bill were quick to point out that Gui would likely have been extradited under the proposed law, notwithstanding the various checks and balances, since his traffic offence was not political and also met the dual criminality requirement.) Mainland investigators demanded that the booksellers hand over the records of their mainland-based customers.

Speaking in June 2017, shortly before she assumed office as chief executive, Carrie Lam was hardly reassuring when, in response to a question about the missing booksellers, she said, 'It would not be appropriate for us to go into the mainland or to challenge what happens on the mainland. That has to be dealt with in accordance with the mainland systems.'[12]

The second case involved mainland billionaire businessman, and Canadian citizen, Xiao Jianhua.[13] Xiao was known as a banker to China's princeling class, with close connections to many of China's most senior leaders, and was reported to be involved in deal-making with the family of China's head of state, Chairman Xi Jinping. For some years, as rumours of corruption swirled around him, Xiao had based himself out of a suite occupying an entire floor of the serviced apartments attached to the Four Seasons Hotel in Hong Kong and avoided travelling to the mainland. But in January 2017, Xiao's luck finally ran out. Late on a Friday night, a group of unknown men gained access to Xiao's suite, overcoming the eight female bodyguards Xiao kept by his side. When questioned, the men told the Four Seasons' security staff that Xiao was unwell and needed medical attention. Xiao was drugged, placed into a wheelchair, with his head covered by a blanket, wheeled out of the front door of the Four Seasons, and bundled into a waiting car. Later, Hong Kong authorities stated vaguely that Xiao had left Hong Kong through 'one of its boundary control points'. It is understood that Xiao remains in mainland police custody.

Given the awkward publicity these cases had attracted, the prospect of having a legitimate channel through which to bring these fugitives back to the mainland to face trial without having to resort to kidnapping was surely appealing to Beijing. Indeed, *Reuters* reported in December 2019 that frustrations in the wake of the Xiao case had led the Chinese Communist Party's powerful anti-corruption body, the Central Commission for Discipline Inspection, or CCDI, to push for just such an extradition mechanism.[14] The revelation undercut the narratives from both Lam and Beijing that the extradition bill was entirely of Lam's devising, and that Poon's murder was the primary motivation. Yet it remained the case that the murder would provide the political pretext for fulfilling the CCDI's long-held wish.

However, precisely because of the risks it posed to those accused of corruption on the mainland, the extradition bill also raised concerns among the usually reliably pro-government business community. If even a billionaire like Xiao was not safe, were any of them? These anxieties were perhaps best expressed by pro-business Liberal Party leader Felix Chung Kwok-pan, a legislator representing the textiles and garment sector, who, in a moment of candour, told *The New York Times*, 'When we started to open up factories in China, the overall rule of law was not so mature. A lot of things had to be done by special ways, through corruption, bribery or whatever.'[15]

To be sure, there were other options besides Lam's proposal. Instead of amending the law on fugitives, the government could have chosen to amend the law on offences to the person, giving the Hong Kong courts jurisdiction over murders committed outside Hong Kong. The Hong Kong Bar Association suggested that a one-off ad-hoc agreement could be reached with Taiwan with respect to the Chan case. Chan could also have been persuaded to surrender himself to the Taiwanese authorities — something he might have been prepared to do in exchange for Taiwanese prosecutors agreeing to waive the death penalty for his case.

Nevertheless, the government dismissed all of these options, instead attempting to amend its proposal to make it more palatable to the business community. Nine white-collar crimes were removed from the list of forty-six extraditable offences, and the threshold required for extradition was increased such that it applied only to offences punishable by three years in prison, instead of the previous one year. Bribery, however, remained on the still-broad list, as did aiding and abetting any of the listed offences. The proposed bill was introduced into the legislature at the beginning of April 2019.

The first indications that community sentiment was beginning to build in opposition to the extradition bill came in late April, when a Sunday-afternoon protest march organised by the Civil Human Rights Front, an umbrella group of Hong Kong pro-democracy NGOs, attracted a surprisingly large crowd of around 130,000 people. It was the largest turnout to a protest since the Umbrella Movement protests of 2014: the crowds of people filling the backstreets of the Causeway Bay shopping district, where the march was scheduled to begin, surpassed even the expectations of organisers.

Lam and her government blamed public opposition on a simple lack of comprehension. They bemoaned the fact that the Hong Kong people did not properly understand her proposal or the mainland judicial system. The reality was that they understood it all too well. As renowned China legal expert Jerome Cohen put it: 'Nobody who knows about PRC legal system wants to be exposed to it.'[16] Even Wang Xiangwei, a former editor-in-chief of the *South China Morning Post* and known for his pro-Beijing stance, was critical of what he called 'China's opaque and corruption-ridden law enforcement and judiciary system'.[17]

As April moved into May, time was ticking away towards the government's deadline to get the extradition bill passed before the legislature's July summer recess. The pro-Beijing and pan-democrat parties in the LegCo became embroiled in procedural skirmishes over the committee process to scrutinise the bill, with each side calling their own meetings and disputing the legitimacy of the opposing camp's meetings. These disputes deteriorated into physical scuffles, with punches thrown as one meeting descended into chaos, leaving a legislator hospitalised and three others injured.

The government responded by dissolving the bills committee altogether, bypassing the usual scrutiny and public hearings, and pushing the bill directly to the full council for debate and vote. 'The bills committee has lost its function to scrutinise the bill, and I see no other way out in the current situation,' said secretary for security John Lee.[18] Pan-democrats decried the government's flouting of legislative procedures and conventions, while even the pro-Beijing parties expressed regret that the usual detailed scrutiny of the bill would not occur.

Then came two dramatic interventions from outside Hong Kong. First, Taiwan stepped in and undercut Lam's rationale for the bill by announcing that it would not seek Chan's extradition even if the bill passed, citing potential threats to the safety of Taiwanese citizens travelling to Hong Kong if the law came into effect. Then, on 17 May, Beijing's representatives in Hong Kong summoned over 200 pro-Beijing business and political leaders to a meeting to request their backing, and Vice-Premier Han Zheng as well as another Politburo Standing Committee member, Wang Yang, spoke publicly in support of the bill. As another Liberal Party leader, Michael Tien, said afterwards, 'If you do business in China, although you may have worries, when the absolute top leader asks for your support, what do you say?'[19]

With Beijing's support secured, Lam pressed ahead, scheduling the second reading debate of the bill for Wednesday 12 June.

Yet momentum was continuing to build against the bill. The normally conservative Law Society, representing the city's solicitors — the branch of the legal profession with more direct exposure to mainland business interests than the barristers represented by the Bar Association — made a statement calling for the bill to be delayed to enable further consultations. Foreign chambers of commerce began to voice their concerns about the bill and the truncated legislative process. They, and foreign governments, had become alarmed when they realised that the extradition bill would apply not only to the thousands of their members and citizens resident in Hong Kong, but also to anyone passing through Hong Kong.

On Thursday 6 June, in a move timed to build momentum for a large public protest planned by the Civil Human Rights Front for the following Sunday, the city's legal profession held a silent march of protest. This was one of several such marches the profession had held since the handover, each at crucial times when the city's rule of law appeared to be under threat from Beijing's interference.

The first such march took place in 1999. That year, less than two years after the handover, Beijing's National People's Congress had exercised its power to overrule Hong Kong's highest court and interpret the Basic Law. It was the first time that Beijing had exercised this extraordinary power, and the moment had come much earlier in the post-handover era than the legal community had been led to expect. A silent march was the legal profession's dignified response to Beijing's intervention.

I had arrived in Hong Kong at the beginning of that year, following two years' study at Peking University, to begin work as a graduate lawyer in one of the international law firms in Central. Joining that march, with all of us sweltering in our dark suits as we walked solemnly towards the Court of Final Appeal building that June evening, I felt for the first time a sense of community in my new home, as well as the realisation that there were important issues of principle being contested in the streets of this city. Little did I realise how the moment would come to foreshadow — if not define — my life here. That sense of community would be reinforced during my time spent among the tents and at the frontlines of the Umbrella Movement fifteen years later. And twenty years later, here I was, marching with my fellow lawyers once again.

The June 2019 lawyers' silent march was the largest yet: some 3,000 representatives of the city's legal profession took part, marching from the historic Court of Final Appeal building in Central to government headquarters in Admiralty to express their disquiet at the government's proposal. There were no placards, no banners, no chanting of slogans — just thousands of people, dressed in dark suits, pacing solemnly and silently, a funeral cortège for Hong Kong's rule of law. The most senior members of the profession were there — Queens Counsels, former public prosecutors, politicians, senior corporate lawyers — joined by barristers and solicitors at all stages of their careers. We all had a very personal stake in the issue: we depended for our identity as Hong Kong legal practitioners upon the fact that, under One Country, Two Systems, Hong Kong retained its own legal system and courts, separate and distinct from those on the mainland. It was an arrangement that had suited both sides well.

I had spent twenty years advising mainland companies, including many state-owned companies, on raising money and listing on the Hong Kong Stock Exchange. Chinese companies relied upon the capital raised in Hong Kong from international investors, who in turn took comfort in Hong Kong's separate legal system and rule of law. In the extradition bill, Hong Kong's lawyers could now foresee the beginnings of a gradual diminution of the very rule of law upon which Hong Kong's success — and our own role within it — was built.

The legal profession also viewed the extradition bill, and Beijing's tightening control over Hong Kong, within the context of a broader crackdown on human rights lawyers in the mainland that, beginning in June 2015, had seen over 300 lawyers and activists detained, and many given lengthy jail sentences. The profession had long spoken out in support of the values of the rule of law and human rights. Now those issues felt closer and more urgent than ever before.

At the end of the march, the LegCo member representing the legal profession, barrister Dennis Kwok, told the media: 'We call on this government to withdraw the extradition bill. This is the clear and almost unanimous belief of the legal profession.'[20]

As I walked with them, the air stifling on that early June evening before the Dragon Boat Festival public holiday, there was a sense that something was building. This was not just another issue destined to fade away into the mists of indifference. Things were turning.

2
THE MARCH OF ONE MILLION

The protest march on Sunday 9 June would follow the traditional route for Hong Kong protests: beginning at Victoria Park in the Causeway Bay shopping district, and winding west for four kilometres through Causeway Bay and Wan Chai to end outside government headquarters at Tamar Park in Admiralty, adjacent to Central, the financial district, a walk that would take around forty-five minutes on a normal Sunday afternoon. On this Sunday, that same walk would take hours. As the early summer afternoon blazed hot and humid, throngs of protesters, all dressed in white — the colour symbolising mourning in Chinese culture — descended upon Hong Kong Island. Protesters had to disembark from the MTR several subway stops away from the starting point, such were the crowds. Buses from Hong Kong's outer suburbs were jam-packed, and there were lengthy queues for those wanting to cross by ferry from Kowloon to the island.

The protesters' demand was summed up in a three-character slogan emblazoned on the red placards they carried: *'Faan sung Zung!'* A direct translation of the phrase would be 'Oppose sending to China', but, digging a little deeper, there was a darker core. *'Sung Zung'* is a homophone for the phrase meaning 'to see off a dying relative'. (It is also, incidentally, a homophone for the phrase 'to give a clock', which is why a clock is always considered an inauspicious gift in China, effectively wishing death upon the recipient.) The slogan was thus a grim pun, death embedded within it, and could be understood to mean 'Oppose sending us to our death' — whether by extradition to China, or through the death of civil liberties in Hong Kong.

Protesters marched peacefully and with good humour, despite the hours-long wait in the crammed streets. One protester showed significant resilience in wearing, despite the humidity, a Winnie the Pooh costume-head topped with a Qing Dynasty style empress's crown, an allusion to the popular joke that 'new emperor' Chairman Xi Jinping resembled the Disney version of that famous bear.

And the Hong Kong people had some reason to expect that their will would be respected: they had in mind a specific historical precedent. In 2003, a protest march held in strikingly similar circumstances had ended in victory for the protesters and, ultimately, the resignation of a chief executive.

Hong Kong in 2003 was in a parlous state. Already battered by the Asian financial crisis, the bursting of the dotcom bubble, and the aftermath of the September 11 terrorist attacks, Hong Kong from November 2002 through mid-2003 found itself at the epicentre of a global health epidemic when Severe Acute Respiratory Syndrome (SARS) struck. In Hong Kong 299 people died, and the ensuing panic devastated the local economy, with tourism particularly hard hit. The property market — already spooked by an ill-considered government plan to increase dramatically the supply of affordable housing — collapsed, and unemployment in Hong Kong rose to a historically high level of 8.3 per cent as an ailing economy led to pay cuts and layoffs.

It was into this environment that the chief executive, Tung Chee Hwa, proposed a controversial new law. Article 23 of the Basic Law required the Hong Kong government to enact legislation to 'prohibit any act of treason, secession, sedition or subversion against the Central People's Government'. Six years after the handover, the legislation had still not been enacted, and Tung, perhaps under pressure from Beijing, decided it was time to act. Indeed, it seems likely that, just as Lam was responding to a brief from Beijing to support Chairman Xi's anti-graft campaign, Tung was responding to a brief from then-president Jiang Zemin, who was pursuing a campaign against the Falun Gong religious sect. Banned on the mainland, where they were considered a subversive cult, the Falun Gong operated freely in Hong Kong.

Tung's secretary for security, Regina Ip, led the initiative to enact the Article 23 anti-sedition law, and proposed a heavy-handed law that would have significantly curtailed freedoms in Hong Kong, including by criminalising the publication or possession of seditious publications, and attempting or conspiring to intimidate or over-throw the People's Republic of China government or 'resist the [PRC government] in its exercise of sovereignty over a part of the PRC'. The government also proposed that those laws would apply to any act committed by a Hong Kong permanent resident overseas.

A new civil society umbrella organisation, the Civil Human Rights Front, was formed, with its membership consisting of civil society groups across Hong Kong, from pan-democrat political parties, to unions, to religious associations. The group coordinated activists' efforts to oppose the Article 23 law, and organised a major protest march against the bill.

On 1 July, the public holiday that commemorates the anniversary of the handover of Hong Kong from the United Kingdom to PRC sovereignty, the front page of the anti-establishment *Apple Daily* newspaper screamed, in huge red characters, 'Take to the streets! See you there!'

The Hong Kong Observatory issued its 'hot weather' warning that day with temperatures climbing to 32 degrees Celsius by early afternoon, when the march was due to commence. It quickly became clear that people would not be deterred by the heat: over 50,000 answered the call to march against the Article 23 law. The subway operator, MTR Corporation, put on extra trains to cope with the crowds. As protesters converged on Victoria Park, they gathered under the hot sun, dressed in black in symbolic mourning for Hong Kong, and carried banners stating 'Oppose Article 23' and 'Resign, Tung Chee-hwa'. Some carried effigies of Tung and Ip. Marchers were young and old, and from all walks of life. Parents carried young children on their shoulders. Prominent entertainers and media figures joined the march, as did various professional groups.

The crowd's mood was a mix of jubilation and anger: anger, certainly, at the government, and outrage at the unpopular Ip, who had suggested that people would attend the rally simply because they had nothing better to do on a public holiday. Some chanted, 'We march for freedom, not for fun,' in riposte. But the crowd was also buoyed by the positive sense that people were united.

It is notable that it was the Article 23 legislation specifically — and not merely tough economic times or an unpopular government — that prompted the march. The legislation was seen as an attack on 'Hong Kong core values', those rights and freedoms that Hong Kong has always enjoyed that the rest of China does not: the rule of law, freedoms of expression and assembly, freedom of religion, and clean and (relatively) accountable government. This was what provoked such a visceral reaction from the Hong Kong populace; they were protesting not just against an unpopular piece of legislation or a proposed curtailment of freedoms. They were protesting against a threat to their very identity as Hong Kongers.

The march followed the same route that protesters would follow some sixteen years later, from Victoria Park towards Central. Like in 2019, the crowds in 2003 waited hours for their turn to march, with the numbers so great that protesters were still waiting in Victoria Park to begin their march long after the first marchers had reached Central; the last protesters would not arrive at their final destination until late that night.

The 2003 protest was successful. Ip resigned, and the legislation was withdrawn (and has never been reintroduced). Tung continued to be unpopular, overseeing continuing policy missteps and a still-faltering economy. As a result, 1 July 2004 again saw a significant turnout of protesters demanding Tung's resignation. He finally resigned the following March, two years before his term was due to end, citing personal reasons.

It is worth reflecting that the victory of the 2003 protests directly enabled the 2019 protests to develop in the manner in which they did. The draft Article 23 law covered, among other offences, the commission of 'violent public disorder that would seriously endanger the stability of the People's Republic of China', as well as an attempt to commit sedition or secession by 'serious criminal means', which was defined to include causing serious injury, seriously endangering the health or safety of the public, causing serious damage to property, or seriously interfering with or disrupting an essential service or facility.[1] It is highly likely that acts committed by some of the more radical protesters during the course of the 2019 protests — such as throwing petrol bombs, vandalising property, and disrupting the MTR system — would have been caught by these provisions had they become law.

The Article 23 fiasco in 2003 should have been a hint to Lam and her government of the reaction that her extradition bill would provoke in 2019. The extradition bill, by breaking the firewall between the Hong

Kong and mainland legal systems, posed a similar threat to Hong Kong's rule of law and its rights and freedoms. In the extradition law, Hong Kongers saw the beginning of the death of Hong Kong as they knew it. Perhaps that is why their slogan of '*Faan sung Zung!*' resonated.

And so, as they marched on Sunday 9 June, they hoped that, like in 2003, their government would hear and respond to their concerns.

Towards the end of the evening, the Civil Human Rights Front, which — as it had in 2003 — organised the march, announced that one million people had joined, double the number in 2003 and, at that time, the largest protest march in Hong Kong's post-handover history. Surely the government could not ignore their voices?

At eleven o'clock on Sunday night, as tens of thousands were still completing their march, the government's response came. 'The procession today is an example of Hong Kong people exercising their freedom of expression within their rights as enshrined in the Basic Law,' said the written statement issued by the government, which continued with an air of impatience: 'The reasons why the Government tabled this Bill have been explained in detail on many occasions.'

The final sentence of the statement came as a punch to the gut: 'The Second Reading debate on the Bill will resume on June 12.'[2]

It was a tone-deaf response by any measure. A significant proportion of the city's populace had taken to the streets, and the response was effectively: 'Lam to City: Drop Dead.'

Plans immediately began for protests on the coming Wednesday, 12 June. LegCo president Andrew Leung had announced that he intended to allow just a couple of weeks for debate before pushing the bill to a vote. For the protesters, it was now or never.

The protests would be focused on Tamar Park, adjacent to the government headquarters and LegCo building where the legislative debate over the bill was to take place.

At lunchtime in Central on Tuesday, activists handed out flyers promoting a general strike and protest for Wednesday. Many private businesses announced they would close; even large companies such as the major banks, accounting firms, insurance companies, and others announced that they would allow employees to adopt 'flexible working arrangements' on Wednesday, acknowledgment that employees could choose not to work if they wished, which seemed as close as workaholic Hong Kong could come to sanctioning a strike.

To avoid being accused of organising an unlawful assembly, protest organisers encouraged people to come 'star gazing' in Tamar Park on Tuesday night, and to 'picnic' in the park on Wednesday.

And on the Tuesday evening, people appeared to be doing just that. The atmosphere was calm, although there was a quiet tension in the air due to a heavy police presence, with riot police armed with Perspex shields entirely surrounding the government headquarters. A young woman sat herself on the ground in a meditation pose in front of a bank of riot shields.

Groups of Christian protesters had gathered, some conducting prayer meetings, and others singing 'Sing Hallelujah to the Lord', a mournful hymn in a minor key, sung *a cappella* in the round. They sang for hours at a time, intending, they said, to promote peace and nonviolence. 'Sing Hallelujah,' they sang, lining the footbridges looking down on the stern rows of riot police. 'Sing Hallelujah,' they sang, gathered around candles flickering in the breeze coming off the harbour on the warm summer night as protesters nervously awaited whatever the next day would bring. 'Sing Hallelujah to the Lord.'

3

BLOCKING THE BILL

When I arrived on Harcourt Road outside government headquarters in Admiralty, early in the morning of Wednesday 12 June, I felt as if I had been transported back in time. The scene before my eyes — the entirety of Harcourt Road, an eight-lane highway, completely occupied by tens of thousands of black-shirted young protesters — was exactly as I had seen it in the first days of the Umbrella Movement protests of 2014.

When that movement had ended almost five years earlier, I had assumed that the Hong Kong authorities would never permit a similar scale of protest to break out. The events of 2019 would prove that assumption wrong.

The Umbrella Movement of 2014 had been, at the time, the high point of Hong Kong's long history of civil disobedience: a seventy-nine-day occupation-style protest that brought the city to a standstill.

The background to that movement lay in Beijing's promise to Hong Kong of democratisation, in particular implementing universal suffrage for selecting the chief executive, the post-handover equivalent of the territory's governor.

Consistent with Hong Kong's executive-led system of governance, the chief executive wields significant power — setting government policy, formulating the budget, and introducing legislation into the legislature. She makes key appointments throughout the government, from the ministers or secretaries responsible for key portfolios and government departments, through to the board members of government bodies as diverse as the Independent Commission Against Corruption and the Securities and Futures Commission. She also serves as the chancellor to all eight of Hong Kong's public universities, and controls appointments to their governing councils.

Under the current method for selecting Hong Kong's chief executive, put in place in 2012, an election committee of 1,200 representatives drawn from various industry, business, social, and special-interest groups nominates candidates. The composition of the committee is such that it is dominated by pro-Beijing loyalists. A minimum of 150 votes from the election committee is required to nominate a candidate, and the committee then conducts successive rounds of voting until one of the candidates wins a clear majority. As a result, the most powerful figure in Hong Kong, the chief executive, does not enjoy any mandate from the broader citizenry.

However, Hong Kongers had long held out hope that this would change. The Basic Law promised in Article 45 that the 'ultimate aim' was that the chief executive would be selected by way of universal suffrage, although it did not specify how or when this would occur, stating only that it would be decided 'in light of the actual situation' in Hong Kong and 'in accordance with the principle of gradual and orderly progress'.

In 2007, ten years after the handover and after years of pressure from Hong Kong's pro-democracy activists, Beijing finally issued a ruling that universal suffrage would be implemented for the selection of the chief executive in 2017. That answered the question of 'when'. As to the question of 'how', Beijing announced that it would provide further details of the exact mechanism of universal suffrage in 2014.

A key question in the minds of Hong Kong's pan-democrat politicians was how candidates for that election would be nominated. They had hoped for a mechanism for civil nomination, whereby any member of the community could be nominated as a candidate to participate in the election. The democrats recognised that, as long as candidates could only be put forward by a Beijing-controlled nominating committee, none of their own would ever be able to run.

In an attempt to place further pressure on the government, a hitherto little-known academic, Benny Tai Yiu-ting, a professor in the Faculty of Law at the University of Hong Kong, came up with a plan. In January 2013, he published a column in the *Hong Kong Economic Journal* newspaper proposing that, if Beijing's electoral reforms did not meet expectations, there should be an act of civil disobedience to protest. Inspired by the Occupy Wall Street movement, Tai called his plan 'Occupy Central'. It would be an act of nonviolent resistance, a sit-in of thousands of citizens in Hong Kong's Central financial district, bringing commerce in the city to a standstill until the government met their demands. Tai, together with his collaborators, Chan Kin-man, a Chinese University of Hong Kong academic, and Reverend Chu Yiu-ming, a Baptist minister — who collectively came to be known as the 'Occupy Trio' — formed a group called Occupy Central With Love and Peace to organise their protest.

However, as the announcement of Beijing's official decision on the chief executive election process approached, all indications suggested that Beijing was not in the mood to be accommodating. On 10 June 2014, China's State Council (broadly equivalent to the government's cabinet) issued a white paper entitled *The Practice of the One Country, Two Systems Policy in the Hong Kong Special Administrative*

BLOCKING THE BILL 39

Region.[1] The white paper purported to promote 'a comprehensive and correct understanding and implementation of the One Country, Two Systems policy in Hong Kong', and reflected the latest in official thinking in Beijing towards the governance of Hong Kong.

The white paper made it very clear, if it was not already, that Beijing was far more interested in the 'One Country' side of the equation than it was in helping preserve the distinction between the 'Two Systems'. 'The "one country" is the premise and basis of the "two systems", and the "two systems" is subordinate to and derived from "one country"', the white paper stated. 'The high degree of autonomy of [Hong Kong] is not an inherent power, but one that comes solely from the authorization by the central leadership.' While the white paper did not say anything new, essentially restating the position under the Joint Declaration and the Basic Law, its tone was striking — in particular, the position it staked out that Hong Kong's autonomy was not inherent, but a gift bestowed upon Hong Kong by Beijing. It was a stark reminder to Hong Kong that Beijing was in charge, and that its tolerance was not unlimited.

The white paper also stirred concern in Hong Kong's legal community, with its characterisation of judges as 'administrators', for whom, as for the chief executive, government officials, and members of the Executive Council and Legislative Council, 'loving the country is the basic political requirement'. The statement led to a sharp rebuke from Hong Kong's Bar Association, and when the president of the Law Society instead made conciliatory statements in support of the white paper, he suffered a vote of no confidence from Hong Kong solicitors and was forced to resign.

In the meantime, as the next step of his campaign, Benny Tai's Occupy Central group conducted a referendum on models of universal suffrage, effectively a city-wide public opinion poll that Beijing's spokespeople branded illegal — which was something of an overreaction, given that there was no law against conducting an opinion poll. Tai's referendum offered participants the opportunity to cast their vote in favour of one of three different models for universal suffrage, as well as asking voters whether the LegCo should veto the government's proposal if it did not meet their expectations for an acceptable model of universal suffrage. The poll was conducted online, via a website established by the University of Hong Kong's widely respected Public Opinion Programme, and required verification by reference to participants' Hong Kong ID card numbers to ensure the vote had some degree of reliability, thereby giving it a legitimacy that infuriated Beijing.

Tai had optimistically been hoping that 100,000 voters would participate in the poll. As the poll began, the website was subject to massive cyber attacks — presumably from the mainland — which threatened to cripple the site. Nevertheless, the survey attracted 792,000 votes during the ten days it was open from 20 June to 29 June 2014. That figure represented around 11 per cent of the population, or around 23 per cent of the registered voting population at the time. All of the models voted upon provided for some version of civic nomination. The vast majority of voters also said that the government's proposal should be vetoed by LegCo if it did not meet their expectations.

Anger at the white paper spurred turnout for the annual 1 July protest that year, with a reported 166,000 turning out, the largest since 2004. The march was led by a large model 'white paper' tank, and ended in Central, where student protesters staged an all-night sit-in that they billed as a 'practice run' for Occupy Central. Hundreds were arrested as dawn broke and police sought to clear the road for the opening of the business day.

When China's parliament, the National People's Congress, finally announced the electoral reforms it would permit Hong Kong in a decision of 31 August 2014, it was unsurprisingly a disappointment to Hong Kong's democrats.

Beijing proposed that the following mechanism be adopted for the election of Hong Kong's next chief executive:

- A nominating committee would be formed, similar to the current election committee.
- The nominating committee could nominate only two or three candidates (more candidates than that would confuse voters, said Beijing officials).
- Each candidate had to receive the endorsement of more than half of the nominating committee (a higher bar than the existing 150 out of 1,200 members of the election committee required for nomination).
- All eligible Hong Kong electors could then vote to elect one of the candidates as chief executive.

It was a process clearly designed to ensure that only Beijing-endorsed candidates could run for the office.

As a result of this decision, the Occupy Central group confirmed that they would go ahead with their protest, planned for the 1 October National Day holiday in a clear provocation to PRC sovereignty. The group expected that they would stage their sit-in, be symbolically arrested at the end of their day of peaceful resistance, and as a result raise awareness of the democratic cause.

In the lead-up to 1 October, students staged a week-long class strike, led by the Hong Kong Federation of Students, or HKFS (an alliance of the various university student unions), and Scholarism, a group founded by student activist Joshua Wong. At seventeen years of age, Wong was already a veteran protester and nemesis of the then chief executive, C.Y. Leung.

In 2011, Leung's administration had proposed a compulsory 'moral and national education' curriculum to be rolled out in Hong Kong's schools. The patriotic education program was intended to help young Hong Kongers to meet Beijing's exhortation to 'love the motherland and love Hong Kong', but many parents, teachers, and students were alarmed at what they saw as an attempt to brainwash Hong Kong schoolchildren with biased pro-Beijing information. Wong, just fourteen years old at the time, founded Scholarism to lead a protest campaign against the plan, with the support of a parents' group, the National Education Parents' Concern Group, and the Professional Teachers' Union. The group staged mass protests and a hunger strike outside the government headquarters in Admiralty. In 2012, in a major victory for Wong, Scholarism, and political protest in Hong Kong, Leung's government was forced to withdraw the proposal.

Now, as the city prepared for the Occupy Central protests in 2014, Wong was back in the limelight leading Scholarism, its membership primarily comprising high school students, alongside the university students of the HKFS. The students' week of protest culminated on the night of Friday 26 September, when a group of students led by Wong and HKFS leader Lester Shum scaled the fence of Civic Square outside government headquarters — the site of Scholarism's successful protest against the national education curriculum two years earlier — and began a sit-in. The sit-in carried on throughout the day and into Saturday night, the crowds growing even larger as many members of the local community came down to support the students.

On the morning of Sunday 28 September, as the scale of the protests grew and moved into their third day, Benny Tai announced what many had already recognised was the reality: Occupy Central had begun, several days earlier than expected, and at the government headquarters in Admiralty instead of Central.

As word of Tai's announcement spread, more supporters began to converge on Admiralty to join the protests. Police formed a cordon blocking access to the site, but the crowds grew to overwhelming numbers and spilled over onto the road, quickly flooding eight lanes of highway and bringing traffic to a standstill.

The crowds continued to push up against the police line, attempting to join their fellow protesters on the other side of the barriers. Police repelled them with pepper spray, and then, when that had no effect, they fired tear gas. Through the rolling clouds of gas, a man emerged, defiantly holding two tattered umbrellas aloft. His image was captured by press photographers, and he soon became the movement's icon: Umbrella Man.

Hong Kongers watching the events unfold on live television were outraged. This was a level of police violence not seen in Hong Kong since anti-colonial government riots in 1967, and seemed far disproportionate to the actions of the crowds, who were armed only with umbrellas and cling film. As a result, more protesters flocked to the site. By evening, contrary to police expectations, the crowds in Admiralty were getting larger, not dispersing. At the same time, spontaneous occupations of streets broke out in other key locations in the city: the Causeway Bay shopping district, the tourist hub of Tsim Sha Tsui, and the working-class Mong Kok district. After midnight, the police retreated, ceding the streets to the protesters.

It later emerged that the police withdrawal was at the express orders of chief executive C.Y. Leung. In the subsequent days, as the government attempted to soothe community anger by announcing that the riot police had been withdrawn, daily protests continued, with massive crowds gathering, easily numbering in the hundreds of thousands.

The protests rapidly developed into a full-scale occupation, with tent cities springing up in the three occupied zones of Admiralty,

Causeway Bay, and Mong Kok, blocking many kilometres of the main arterial roads of the city. A tent census at the peak of the occupation recorded over 2,000 tents in Admiralty alone (with hundreds more in the Mong Kok and Causeway Bay occupied zones). An infrastructure grew around these encampments, with supply stations providing necessities, from food and water, to first-aid and personal-care supplies, to camping equipment.

The Umbrella Movement protests prompted an outpouring of creativity, the sites plastered with posters, banners, flyers, graffiti, paintings, sculptures, and installations. This was replicated online in the virtual world, with a constant stream of cartoons, photos, memes, and online humour responding to the latest events.

Art students from Hong Kong Baptist University created a patchwork canopy made from discarded umbrellas damaged by pepper spray and tear gas. The canopy was suspended over the main stage at the centre of the Admiralty protest site. Umbrella Man, a monumental statue over two metres high of a man holding aloft a yellow umbrella created by local artist Milk, towered over the Admiralty site. Made from a mosaic of wooden shingles, Umbrella Man recalled the work of Anthony Gormley in its geometric evocation of the human form. The statue embodied the humanist spirit of the movement, its form modelled on a photograph taken early in the protests of a protester holding aloft an umbrella to provide shelter to a police officer during a downpour.

But the most striking feature of the Admiralty-occupied area was the Lennon Wall, which took its name from a wall of the same name in Prague, which had been a site for subversive graffiti since the death of John Lennon in 1980. The Hong Kong Lennon Wall began with a simple gesture: at the bottom of a plain concrete staircase, winding its way up the outside of the government headquarters building, someone put up a poster posing the question 'Why are we here?' and left a small supply of Post-it Notes and felt-tip pens, encouraging others to leave their response. The multi-hued notes quickly multiplied as both locals and visitors left messages of support, encouragement, and defiance. These thousands of colourful notes formed a vast mosaic, a physical feature in itself, the pieces of paper fluttering in the breeze, the colourful space a luminous beacon at night illuminated under the fluorescent lights. On some nights, adjacent to the Lennon Wall, a device dubbed the 'Add Oil Machine' projected messages submitted via a website from well-wishers around the world, from Vancouver to London, from Ukraine to Gaza to Prague, home of the Lennon Wall's namesake.

The Lennon Wall also recalled another 'wall' that had been a site of political expression: the Democracy Wall in the Xidan shopping district of Beijing, which for a few weeks at the end of 1978 was a site for hitherto unheard-of political expression in Beijing as 'big character posters' were posted at the site expressing a variety of views on political and social issues. After Wei Jingsheng, recalling Deng Xiaoping's policy of 'Four Modernisations', posted a call for the 'Fifth Modernisation' — democracy — the authorities cracked down. Wei and a number of other dissidents were arrested, and the brief flowering of expression at the wall ended. The spirit of the Democracy Wall lived on, however, not only in the Lennon Wall, but at Democracy Walls on Hong Kong university campuses and at the Umbrella Movement–occupied sites.

At the centre of the Admiralty site, an area in the midpoint of Harcourt Road renamed Umbrella Square by the protesters, was a speakers' podium fashioned from stepladders and planks of wood, referred to as the 'main stage'. It was from here that the leaders of the Umbrella Movement — the Occupy Trio and the student leaders, Joshua Wong of Scholarism and Alex Chow and Lester Shum of the HKFS — held court and directed the movement. They gave nightly speeches, rallying the crowd, updating them on the events of the day, cajoling the government, and reiterating their demands. Wong, in particular, emerged as a key figurehead and spokesperson of the movement. The international media were fascinated with this teenager taking on a global superpower,[2] and his image graced the cover of *Time* magazine alongside the headline, 'The Face of Protest'.

The Umbrella Movement found some inspiration in a successful model across the Taiwan Strait. Earlier in 2014, in a course of action that would resonate with events in Hong Kong five years later, the conservative Kuomintang government had tried to push a controversial trade agreement with China through Taiwan's legislature without undertaking a detailed review. In April, student-led protesters stormed the legislature building to protest the agreement, occupying the chamber in what became known as the Sunflower Movement. The protesters eventually ended their month-long occupation after the government granted them certain concessions. Sunflower Movement student leader Lin Fei-fan visited Hong Kong in October that year, addressing the crowds in Umbrella Square and sharing his experience of the Sunflower occupation.

The Umbrella Movement established the respective colours of the two opposing sides of the political divide in Hong Kong. The protesters adopted the yellow ribbon as the symbol of their movement, and yellow became the colour representing their cause, with yellow umbrellas a particularly popular item. In response, those allied with the government and police began wearing blue ribbons to express their support. By 2019, 'yellow' and 'blue' had become established shorthand to describe pro-democracy and pro-government/pro-police sympathies, respectively.

The Hong Kong protesters' greatest public victory in 2014 came almost a month into the protests on 21 October, when the government agreed to participate in a televised debate with student leaders. This recognition of their status as equal interlocutors with the government immediately gave the protesters and their movement legitimacy, and the opportunity to argue their case directly to both the government and the people. Big screens were set up in the protest zones on the night of the debate, and large crowds gathered to watch and cheer on the students.

The government team was led by then chief secretary Carrie Lam, tight-lipped and unsmiling alongside the secretaries for justice and constitutional affairs, as well as two other officials. On the students' side of the table, Chow and Shum led a delegation of five members of the HKFS in their signature black T-shirts. The contrast between the two sides of the table was striking. The five government representatives, all but one of whom had never faced an election in their lives, were wooden and mechanical, putting in a performance that did nothing to ameliorate the public perception of a government out of touch with its people. All of the student leaders, on the other hand, had earned their place at the table through student union elections, and spoke with passion, conviction, and even humour.

During the debate, Lam refused to give any concessions to the students, saying, 'Political reform is a complicated and sensitive topic. The society has very many different views. We cannot do things all over again because only one side of view objects.' She went on to chide, 'You cannot only have idealistic pursuits. You have to be pragmatic.'[3]

The debate ended in deadlock, with Shum summing up the protesters' views in his closing remarks:

Now the government is only telling us to pack up and go home. The whole generation, awakened by tear gas, cannot accept this. We are the generation chosen by the times. I think the same applies to you — you are the officials chosen by the times. Can you be responsible? Or will you be the ones that kill our political future ...?

There were no further talks, and the occupation stretched into November, with little progress made in reaching a resolution. C.Y. Leung refused any further dialogue or compromise, and his disdain for the people's will could not have been clearer than when he told media that if the city introduced universal suffrage, elections would be 'entirely a numbers game' in which politicians would be forced to 'be talking to the half of the people in Hong Kong who earn less than US$1,800 a month', rather than, presumably, just the pro-Beijing business elites to whom he owed his position.[4]

In the meantime, the student leaders began to lose direction and momentum. Their control of the Admiralty main stage was not uncontroversial, as other protesters complained that the leaders' and their marshals' control over who could speak from the main stage was undemocratic, verging on dictatorial. Things came to a head when a group of more radical protesters from the anarchic Mong Kok–occupied site visited Admiralty in an abortive attempted to 'tear down the main stage'.

By mid-November, time finally seemed to be running out for the protesters: a number of taxi and minibus companies successfully took action in the Hong Kong High Court to obtain injunctions requiring protesters to clear blockaded roads in the occupied areas, and authorising bailiffs to request police to assist in enforcing the injunctions.

At the end of November, police supported bailiffs in executing the injunction against the Mong Kok protest site along Nathan Road, and the site was cleared. A week later, on 9 December, at the end of a routine police press conference, a police spokesman announced that the Admiralty protest site would be cleared on the Thursday of that week, 'to reopen the blocked roads so that the general public can resume their normal daily lives'.

This was the end.

Thousands turned out at the main Admiralty protest site for what would be the last night in Umbrella Square. It was a night for nostalgia. Visitors posed for photographs and collected keepsakes. Parents brought their children, one telling me, 'I want them to see this, and remember it, so they know what Hong Kongers are capable of.'

Meanwhile, village residents started the process of packing up, removing supplies and dismantling tents. Late in the night, archivists begin dismantling the Lennon Wall, photographing it section by section, and then each colourful Post-it Note was carefully removed, collated, and stored in archive boxes.

The following day, police and government contractors moved in to clear the main Umbrella Square site. They worked their way through the protest zone, dismantling tents, tearing down banners and posters, heaping all of the debris into piles. Dump trucks and cleaners followed behind the police, sweeping everything up.

By nightfall, the kilometre-long stretch of the highway that had been home to the protesters for seventy-five days had been swept clean, and traffic flowed where rows of colourful tents, banners, and handmade wooden furniture had stood only hours earlier. With the clearance of the small remaining protest site in the Causeway Bay shopping district a few days later, the Umbrella Movement was over.

On that final night of the Umbrella Movement in Admiralty, as most posters and banners were being taken down, a few new ones were going up: 'We will be back!' they read. It became a refrain on that last day, chanted by a few hold-outs as they staged a sit-in, their symbolic final act of nonviolent resistance, and awaited arrest by the police. I couldn't help thinking it was merely an act of wishful thinking. If, after all these months, this occupation ended with nothing, what would it take for people to come back?

Beijing's proposal for chief executive electoral reform was finally presented to LegCo in June 2015. Carrie Lam led the government's efforts to solicit popular support for their proposal, but her 'Pocket It First' slogan was hardly inspiring. The pan-democrats, buoyed by the results of Benny Tai's referendum, were determined to vote against the proposal. The day of the vote ended in fiasco when the pro-Beijing parties, led by the DAB, bungled an attempt to walk out of the LegCo chamber in order to deny a quorum and stall the voting. They miscounted, the vote went ahead, and in the end attracted only eight votes in favour. All of the pan-democrat legislators voted against the proposal, which failed to pass.

In 2017, the twentieth anniversary of the return of sovereignty to China, the election committee of 1,194 voters voted to select the next chief executive of Hong Kong. The election was preceded by a charade of an election campaign, with televised debates, campaign rallies, and advertising posters in MTR stations. Maintaining a pretence of a need to win hearts and minds among the (disenfranchised) population of Hong Kong occurred alongside the dropping of a different pretence: whereas previously any suggestions of Beijing's interference in Hong Kong had been strenuously denied, there now seemed to be no squeamishness in acknowledging that Carrie Lam was Beijing's preferred candidate and that loyalist election committee members were casting their votes for her in accordance with Beijing's directions.

This elaborate piece of political theatre concluded with a live broadcast of the vote count, giving the appearance, if not the reality, of transparency and openness. Given that the outcome was regarded by most as predetermined, the theatricality did point to some recognition from Beijing of the role of public opinion in the Hong Kong political process, and marked Hong Kong's continued distinction from the rest of China: there was little prospect of the next candidate for mayor of Beijing driving down Wangfujing in an open-topped double-decker bus any time soon.

At the end of the process, Carrie Lam was selected as the next chief executive of Hong Kong — not by the votes of the people of Hong Kong, but of 777 members of the election committee.

So it was that, looking down on that crowd as I arrived in Admiralty on the morning of Wednesday 12 June 2019, I felt as if I was seeing the Umbrella Movement suddenly reincarnated before my eyes.

Pan-democrat politician Claudia Mo, who had been one of the last hold-outs to be led away by police from Admiralty in December 2014, summed up the moment triumphantly: 'We said we would be back!'

The protesters were, again, primarily young, and all clad in black T-shirts. Drawing on their experience from the Umbrella Movement, they quickly equipped themselves with protective gear — surgical face masks, goggles, hard hats — in anticipation of police batons, pepper spray, or even tear gas and rubber bullets.

Already the 'supply stations' — just like in the Umbrella Movement — were springing up along the roadside, and being equipped with everything from first-aid supplies to water and snacks. Dozens of umbrellas hung along a railing. Barricades were being rapidly assembled to blockade the streets. Even the Lennon Wall was already being reincarnated at its former site, as the grey concrete wall by the staircase began to be covered in colourful Post-it Notes.

Artist Perry Dino was back. Perry had been a fixture during the Umbrella Movement, painting one complete canvas of the protest scenes every day. In 2019, he was back painting, and he summed up the emotions of the moment well: 'I never imagined this could happen again. When I stepped out of Admiralty Station this morning, tears came to my eyes.'

Unlike during the Umbrella Movement, the protesters had two

advantages that increased their chances of success. In 2014, they were trying to push the government to adopt a 'genuinely democratic' means of electing the territory's chief executive — although specifically which model of genuine democracy, the protesters could not quite agree upon. In 2019, their request was simple: they wanted the government to drop the extradition law. And it is a truism in politics that it is easier to oppose than propose.

The protesters knew that if LegCo were allowed to meet, the pro-Beijing majority would push the bill through. Their protest was the only way the bill could be stopped. Tens of thousands of protesters completely surrounded the government headquarters and LegCo building, chanting, '*Cit wui! Cit wui!*' ('Withdraw!') Police, equipped with riot shields, truncheons, and guns, formed three-deep defensive lines around the building.

Around midmorning, pan-democrat legislator Eddie Chu Hoi-dick appeared among the crowd with a megaphone. He announced that the morning's LegCo meeting had already been cancelled, as legislators had been unable to reach the building to get into the chamber. 'Your protest is already a success!' he said to cheers, and urged the protesters to persist.

As I looked around the crowd, the scene felt reminiscent of the Umbrella Movement, but there was one clear difference: there was no main stage, there was no one with a megaphone directing proceedings, there were no leaders. This seemed to be a sensible decision, given that, at the same moment we stood on that street, the leaders who had stood on the main stage here five years before — Joshua Wong of Scholarism, Benny Tai and Chan Kin-man of the Occupy Trio, and Shiu Ka-chun, who had been the master of ceremonies of the main stage — were sitting in jail for their role in inciting those protests. The HKFS's Lester Shum and Alex Chow had also served jail sentences. And yet, if there were no leaders, how did we all come to be here?

Where did those supply stations come from? It was as if the lessons of the Umbrella Movement had been built into the collective muscle memory of the city: all it took was a flex, and all of the tactics and infrastructure, the shape of protest as a way of being, unconsciously emerged.

The protests were boosted by the power of technology. The online forum LIHKG.com — a sort of lo-fi Hong Kong version of Reddit, where users comment and vote on posts — had become a popular venue for young activists to discuss tactics and exchange ideas, while the chat app Telegram was being used to communicate on the ground. This seemed to be the medium through which the word was spread that something was going to happen at the police barricades outside the government headquarters at three o'clock.

Sure enough, a few minutes after three o'clock, protesters began to charge the police line. The police responded with force — with pepper spray, batons, and then the pop and crack of tear gas shells as the white clouds of smoke drifted over the crowds.

At first, just one or two rounds were fired, and things seemed to calm down. I walked around the block towards the other side of the government headquarters, where more protesters had flooded the roads outside the chief executive's office. But as I was only halfway up the block, I looked ahead and saw more clouds of tear gas billowing, and the crowd turning and running towards me. I had no choice but to be pushed with them and, as we all fled, police continued to fire tear gas into the backs of the retreating crowd. We instinctively bowed our heads, placed our hands on the shoulders of those in front of us, and stumbled, half-blind and choking, desperate to escape.

Looking ahead, I saw that a fire escape at City Hall had been propped open, and protesters were streaming inside. I followed them in, all of us coughing and choking. A bathroom was down the short corridor; next to the door, a cleaner leant on her mop, watching impassively as people rushed into the bathroom to wash their eyes and faces.

Inside the building, as protesters rested and recovered, they looked through the windows at the police outside, uttering exclamations of disbelief at the amount of tear gas being fired. Having recovered somewhat, I went back outside and made my way to the highway bridge overlooking the Admiralty site. The police's clearance operation was continuing. They fired tear gas indiscriminately into the crowd, most of whom did not have any protective equipment beyond paper surgical masks and wet cloths tied around their faces. With each volley of tear gas, the crowd dispersed, then immediately began to regroup and advance again, their spirit indomitable, chanting, 'Heunggong jan, gaa jau!' ('Hong Kongers, add oil!').

Calls went out among the crowd, 'First aid! First aid!' and volunteer first-aiders in high-vis vests arrived to lend their assistance. Some called out for asthma medication, holding their hands up to give a hand signal as if they were using an asthma spray, and the signal was echoed in the crowd around them until someone in the crowd passed a spray back to where it was needed. Looking down from the bridge where I stood, I saw a group of first-aiders surrounding a protester lying on the ground, sheltered from police fire around the corner of a building in the lee of a fast-food restaurant. The protester appeared to be coughing up blood, and onlookers suggested he had been hit with a rubber bullet. Subsequent reports also revealed that a driver for public broadcaster TVB had been hit in the head with a police projectile and was seriously injured, his heart stopping before he was later resuscitated.

Outside CITIC Tower, an office building adjacent to LegCo, protesters found themselves caught between their own barricades and police lines. As police fired tear gas from two directions, giving the crowd no escape path, they tried to flee into the locked CITIC Tower building behind them, breaking down the doors in a near-stampede as clouds of tear gas drifted over them into the office lobby.

In the midst of the tumult, Wu Chi-wai, the chairman of the Democratic Party and a LegCo member, approached the police lines, alone and unarmed, with nothing more than a flimsy surgical mask for protection. 'I want to see your commander!' he called out. Video footage of the incident showed a police commander directing an officer to fire tear gas directly at Wu, as Wu continued to shout out, 'I am a legislator! I want to see your commander!', the tear gas grenades popping and smoking near his feet.

Police began to target the highway overpass on which I was standing. They fired tear gas up onto the bridge, first at one end, and then at the other. The crowd panicked, sandwiched between two clouds of tear gas. For a moment, I was afraid that we would be either caught in a stampede, or that people would be panicked into jumping off the bridge. I spotted a gap through the crowd between the edge of the bridge and a smoking tear gas shell, and ran.

From a clear spot further along the bridge, I looked down on the crowd who continued to be inundated with tear gas. The protesters had quickly learned how to deal with the tear gas cannisters: some were throwing wet towels onto the smoking shells to smother them, and I watched another protester douse a smoking shell with water to extinguish it.

As the protesters retreated from Admiralty, they barricaded themselves inside the nearby Pacific Place shopping mall. Looking across from a footbridge, I saw the facade of the adjacent High Court building engulfed in clouds of tear gas. I could not think of a more fitting metaphor for this day on which Hong Kong's rule of law had become so dramatically and physically contested.

As evening fell, the protesters moved back towards Central. The parallels with the Umbrella Movement ended there: there would be no occupation today. There was no need for it, as the protesters had achieved their aim: the LegCo meeting had been postponed; the bill would not proceed for now. Taking the last MTR trains of the day, the protesters dispersed into the night.

Police arrested thirty-two people as a result of the day's unrest, including a number of wounded protesters while they were in hospital seeking treatment for their injuries. Speaking to the media on Wednesday evening, police chief Stephen Lo described the protests as a 'riot'. Carrie Lam concurred, saying, 'Clearly, this was no longer a peaceful assembly, but a blatantly organised instigation of a riot. This could not be an act that shows love for Hong Kong.'[5]

Activists were outraged at the remarks, not only because they regarded their protest as peaceful and the police use of force as excessive against unarmed protesters, but because there were real legal consequences to the characterisation of the incident as a riot. Under the Public Order Ordinance — a piece of Hong Kong legislation dating back to the colonial era and widely regarded as far out of step with contemporary human-rights standards — rioting is an offence punishable with a jail term of ten years.

That night, TVB aired an interview with Lam that they had conducted that morning at the very same time as protesters were gathering outside LegCo. In the interview, Lam was unrepentant: 'I continue to hold fast to the belief that it is the right thing to do.' If the bill was not adopted, Lam said, 'I cannot promise you, Mr and Mrs Poon, that the criminal who murdered your daughter would get his punishment through the law'.

She also angered many with a tone that they regarded as patronising, depicting herself as a mother figure to a group of spoiled children:

To use a metaphor, I'm a mother too, I have two sons. If I let him have his way every time my son acted like that, such as when he didn't want to study, things might be OK between us in the short term. But if I indulge his wayward behaviour, he might regret it when he grows up. He will then ask me: 'Mum, why didn't you call me up on that back then?'

In a bid for sympathy that appeared unseemly given the events that had transpired that day, Lam said tearfully, 'My love for this place has prompted me to make many personal sacrifices.'[6]

She was immediately accused by Democratic Party lawmaker James To Kun-sun of shedding 'crocodile tears'.

In 2014, the public outrage at police firing eighty-seven rounds of tear gas upon an unarmed crowd of protesters had sparked tens of thousands to flood the streets, and effectively provoked the beginning of the Umbrella Movement. Five years later, on that Wednesday in 2019, police fired 150 rounds of tear gas, as well as several rounds of rubber bullets and twenty beanbag rounds. Yet people seemed to treat the event with equanimity: the use of tear gas had been normalised, if not expected. This time there would be no public outcry, no outpouring of bodies onto the streets that night.

The protest's organisers, the Civil Human Rights Front, had called for another protest march to be held the following Sunday. But, given the muted reaction to Wednesday's events, would people still turn up? Or would they feel that, given one million of them had already marched the previous Sunday to no effect, there was no point marching again? Would they come?

4

THE MARCH OF TWO MILLION

They came on buses from Tin Shui Wai near the Shenzhen border. They came on ferries from Cheung Chau and other outlying islands. They came on trains from Hong Kong's suburbs, Tsuen Wan and Sha Tin. At the Star Ferry pier in Tsim Sha Tsui, people queued for hundreds of metres along the waterfront, waiting to cross the harbour. The MTR system was swamped, station platforms and tunnels clogged with a sea of bodies in black T-shirts. On Sunday 16 June 2019, beyond all expectations, they came.

They continued their death-tinged chant of '*Faan sung Zung!*' — and this time there was an actual death to mourn. The night before, around the same time as chief executive Carrie Lam announced that work on the extradition bill had been suspended in a belated and vain attempt to defuse public anger and prevent another large protest, a young man wearing a yellow raincoat climbed scaffolding outside the Pacific Place shopping mall in Admiralty and hung banners bearing slogans of the movement. It was unclear whether he was threatening, or intended, to jump, but there can be little doubt that what happened next was a tragic accident. Rescue workers on the roof attempted to reach out and grab his arm — was it slick with sweat on that humid

Hong Kong summer night? — but slipped. The young man was suspended in midair momentarily as the rescuers desperately clutched at his T-shirt, which slipped away, and the man plunged several storeys to his death on the concrete below.

The previous week they had been dressed in white, the Chinese colour of mourning. This week they dressed in black, and this time the march was a funeral march.

They carried white flowers — so many that they exhausted the entire supplies of the city's flower markets — and piled them high in a growing memorial outside the Pacific Place mall, the crowd growing sombre and quiet as they passed the spot where the young man had perished, all slogans momentarily silenced. The site outside the mall became a shrine as people piled their flowers in tribute, lit candles and incense, and left messages of condolence.

This mortality-obsessed theme would continue throughout the summer of 2019, and made a sharp contrast to 2014's Umbrella Movement, which was an exuberant affair.

At the main Admiralty-occupied site of the Umbrella Movement, rainbow rows of coloured tents had lined the roads, while cultural expression flourished — every available surface, from walls to footpaths, bridges to traffic barriers, was plastered in banners, posters, flyers, chalk drawings, Post-it Notes, and sculptures.

The mood at weekends felt like a community arts festival: the main stage hosted guest speakers, movie screenings, and performances, and thousands flocked with their families to visit on the sunny autumn afternoons. Musicians played impromptu gigs, dancers performed routines, and there was an array of other events: portrait-sketching, leather work, weaving, origami. Volunteers gave public lectures, and there were discussion groups and nightly 'sharing sessions' where people gathered to discuss the unfolding events.

The infrastructure in what came to be called Harcourt Village developed by the day, as carpenters built increasingly sophisticated staircases over cement road barriers, and makeshift shower tents were set up. And, of course, there was the Homework Zone, which began when a volunteer carpenter hammered together some planks to make a few desks over a traffic barrier so that student protesters would have a more comfortable place to study. From there it grew, every day more furniture being constructed — desks, benches, and bookshelves. Marquees were pitched above the desks to protect students from the elements. Then carpet was laid down, and a diesel generator installed, which enabled lighting for night-time study sessions and free wi-fi. Volunteers provided tutoring, with signs out front advising which tutors were on duty, as well as politely requesting onlookers to avoid photographing students to protect their identities.

The Umbrella Movement quickly fostered what felt like an unprecedented sense of community in a city not previously reputed for its humanitarianism. Protesters and supporters donated water, food, and camping supplies, established first-aid stations and lending libraries, and collected rubbish and sorted it for recycling. The public bathrooms were regularly cleaned by volunteers and equipped with a comprehensive selection of toiletries. This self-regulating society became a mini-utopia, reflecting the hopes of the Umbrella Movement itself, agitating for a more perfect democracy for Hong Kong.

The demonstrations of 2019, by contrast, would reflect a feeling of desperation, as demonstrators said they were fighting for the very life of the city, and a sense of mortality would hang over those summer days. Far from the utopian ideals of the Umbrella Movement, demonstrators were battling what they saw as their city sliding into a nightmare of police brutality, arbitrary detention, and extrajudicial punishment. Raymond Chan, a pro-democracy lawmaker, summed up the prevailing sentiment when he told me, 'If we lose, it may be the end of Hong Kong as we know it.'

This willingness to invoke death so directly — in words and imagery — was significant for a traditionally deeply superstitious culture, in which death-related symbols are anathema. The number four is considered unlucky because it is a homophone for death (many buildings lack a fourth floor, for example), and it is considered inauspicious to stick chopsticks vertically into a rice bowl, because it is reminiscent of incense sticks burning to commemorate the dead. This background gave their *Faan sung Zung!* slogan added bite.

But death was something that protesters now appeared willing to contemplate. Some reportedly even put their last will and testament in their backpacks when they prepared to go to the frontline. On the side of a volunteer first-aider's helmet during one protest, I read the following chilling message, written in neat black felt-tip pen: 'Do NOT resuscitate if severely wounded and unresponsive. Handwritten will in pocket.'

Following that first tragic death at Pacific Place on 15 June, more suicides would follow; some left messages supporting the protests before leaping to their deaths.

And as the summer unfolded, the levels of violence would spiral to deadly new levels.

The difference in tone between the two movements could also be heard through their respective soundtracks.

On that first night of the Umbrella Movement in September 2014, as the clouds of tear gas cleared, I watched thousands of protesters sit on the road facing a squad of riot police and sing the Cantopop anthem 'Boundless Ocean, Vast Skies', made famous by Hong Kong band Beyond. It was an act of courage, of peaceful resistance, and of solidarity, and anyone who lived through those events finds it difficult to listen to the climax of that song's chorus without re-experiencing the emotion of that time.

Music played a central role in the Umbrella Movement. The songs were optimistic and upbeat, reflecting the movement's utopian spirit, summed up in a line adorning a banner in Admiralty taken from another song popular during the movement, John Lennon's 'Imagine': 'You may say I'm a dreamer, but I'm not the only one.'

As well as the Beyond anthem, another song — 'Raise the Umbrellas' — was written especially for the movement by Cantopop composer Lo Hiu-pan, and recorded by a number of pop stars, including Denise 'HOCC' Ho, who would go on to become one of Hong Kong's leading political activists. During Umbrella Movement rallies, Shiu Ka-chun, a social worker who acted as master of ceremonies on the Admiralty main stage, would lead the crowd in singing both songs. The scene, a sea of illuminated mobile-phone lights, often resembled a Cantopop concert more than a political rally.

Even in the rare moments of conflict in 2014, the music was playful. When pro-government antagonists entered the occupied areas and began haranguing the crowd, protesters would surround them and sing 'Happy Birthday', a practice that began thanks to a well-timed accident when one such antagonist in mid-tirade accidentally pressed a button on his megaphone, which triggered a grating electronic-beeped rendition of the song, prompting the surrounding crowd to sing along. The cheerful collective singing of that universally known song during such moments of conflict would serve both to drown out the attacks and to defuse a potentially violent situation with humour and absurdity.

Five years later, music was also central; but, in keeping with the darker tone of the 2019 protest movement, the music also took a darker turn. The old Cantopop ballads of the Umbrella Movement no longer seemed to fit the tenser atmosphere at the frontlines of 2019's protests.

This also reflected a change in the way music was used as a tool of protest. Winnie W.C. Lai, an ethnomusicologist at the University of Pennsylvania who has researched Hong Kong protest music, argued that music had gone from being largely expressive during the Umbrella Movement, a way for protesters to 'feel good among themselves situated in their utopian community', to being more utilitarian. The protest songs of 2019 had 'rather clear functions and purposes that are directly related to the people's political will and action', Lai told me.

This was the case with 'Sing Hallelujah to the Lord', which became an early theme song of the 2019 movement. In addition to the Christian protesters' message of peace and nonviolence, it also had a tactical rationale: religious gatherings are exempt from Hong Kong's laws governing public protests and assemblies, and protesters (probably mistakenly) thought that by singing hymns they might take advantage of the exemption. However, as the months wore on, the song was abandoned at the same pace as was adherence to the policy of nonviolence.

In keeping with the Hong Kong protesters' seemingly limitless talent for satire and memes, there was also room for some musical levity. Remixers deconstructed and autotuned a speech given by entertainment figure Maria Cordero at a pro-government rally, and combined it with the hit song 'Chandelier' by international pop artist Sia, to create an anti-police anthem, the chorus of which roughly translates as 'Ah! Dirty Cops!' The song quickly became an online viral sensation, and at subsequent protests the primal scream of 'Ah!' was met with a crowd responding in full-throated chorus, 'Dirty cops!' providing a moment of humour and catharsis.

Another song, 'Do You Hear the People Sing?', was one of the few songs that seemed successfully to cross over from the Umbrella

Movement to 2019. With massed bodies and voices defending the barricades of the occupied zones during the Umbrella Movement, the song from the hit musical *Les Misérables* was perhaps an obvious choice. In the desperate atmosphere at the barricades of the 2019 protests, the song took on a new urgency — although it was best not to dwell on the ultimate fate of those who defended the barricades in Paris in 1832.

This sombre, almost martial tone was also present in the most significant addition to Hong Kong's protest-music repertoire, 'Glory to Hong Kong', referred to by some protesters as Hong Kong's national anthem. Written by a local Hong Kong composer who identified himself only as 'Thomas', with the lyrics posted and workshopped in the online LIHKG forum, 'Glory to Hong Kong' was reminiscent of national anthems the world over. Within a week or two of the song first making its appearance online — just a month before China celebrated its national day — it was being sung at rallies, soccer matches, and at pop-up protests in shopping malls.

The anthem created a kind of solidarity among protesters, and served to rally spirits, protesters told me, as they sang during protests on Hong Kong's streets.

'This song for me is very meaningful. When I listen to this song, I think, *This is Hong Kong*,' said Rachel, twenty-seven, a social worker. 'When the police beat our students, I feel very helpless. But when I sing this song, I feel very powerful.'

'I feel very proud of it,' said Chong, twenty-six, who worked in sales. 'It makes us feel more united. We feel the common identity of Hong Kongers.'

With lines such as 'Distant clouds will echo still our call to battle; We are fighting for Freedom', and 'Again, our blood will be shed! But "Forward!" our cry rings out!'[1] the song reflects the violent struggles of 2019. But it could also be understood as containing a glimmer of brightness in the dark, as it envisages a rejuvenated, glorious future for Hong Kong.

One Sunday night in the shopping district of Causeway Bay, at the end of a long and particularly violent day of clashes between protesters and police, a young woman stood by the roadside playing 'Glory to Hong Kong' on a harmonica. When I asked what the song meant to her, she replied, 'The song means hope for Hong Kong, and hope in people's hearts.'

It was this same mixture of desperation and jubilation that was in the air as protesters gathered on Sunday 16 June 2019.

Such were the numbers marching that protesters had to disembark from the MTR at Quarry Bay, three subway stations away from the march's official starting point at Victoria Park, Causeway Bay; it was impossible to get any closer. The march began in the early afternoon and lasted late into the night, people waiting patiently in the midsummer heat for hours to take their turn to march, many insisting on undertaking the full march from Victoria Park along the entire route to Admiralty to make sure they were counted in the final crowd figure. All the westbound roads along the north side of Hong Kong Island were closed off to traffic and fully occupied with protesters — never before had Hong Kong seen a protest march of this scale.

Organisers put the final figure at two million people, plus a symbolic one for the fallen protester of the night before; police said the march totalled 338,000 people at its peak, but also acknowledged that their count only covered one route, not the four other roads down which the densely packed crowds also marched. With the participation level reaching over one-quarter of the population, it seemed remarkable that Carrie Lam had succeeded in inciting a level of anger and anxiety in Hong Kongers not seen since 1989, when over 1.5 million residents marched in support of the students in Tiananmen Square.

Yet it should not have been a surprise. There was a reason why this issue galvanised public opinion and provoked a response like no other in recent years, a reason connected with a deep sense of Hong Kong identity.

In the past, Hong Kong had distinguished itself on the basis of its wealth: for decades, its people were rich compared to those of China, which from the late 1970s began struggling to lift itself out of poverty. Many Hong Kongers have memories of going to visit cousins in the mainland in the 1980s, bearing gifts of the latest-model rice cooker, or a television set. However, over the twenty years since the handover from the UK to the People's Republic of China in 1997, as Hong Kong's economy drifted and China's boomed, that distinction failed to hold. Indeed, their respective positions reversed, as the Hong Kong economy increasingly relied on the mainland, whether that was mainland tourists staying in Hong Kong's hotels and shopping in its luxury boutiques, or mainland companies raising funds on the city's stock exchange and keeping legions of professional-service providers profitably occupied.

As a result, Hong Kongers replaced their pride in material success with a pride in Hong Kong core values, those rights and freedoms that distinguished life in Hong Kong from the rest of China. The concept of Hong Kong core values was first articulated by a group of pro-democracy scholars and politicians in 2004, initially to raise alarm at the prospect that those values were being lost. However, the concept was soon co-opted by the government and more widely across Hong Kong society to articulate Hong Kong's competitive advantage vis-a-vis the rest of China, and indeed much of the rest of Asia. Hong Kong core values included clean, corruption-free government; a lively and unfettered media; freedom to criticise the government; the right to participate in the electoral and governing process; observance of the rule of law and due process; an independent judiciary; and, of course, the right to protest. 'Hong Kong core values' became the answer to the question 'What does it mean to be a Hong Konger?'

As with Article 23, the extradition bill was another attack on Hong Kong core values. The two million people gathered on Hong Kong's streets on that summer afternoon were protesting not just against a theoretical risk of extradition to the opaque mainland criminal-justice system; they were protesting a threat to their very identity as Hong Kongers. And by taking to the streets, they were expressing their dissatisfaction by exercising one of those key rights and freedoms: *I am a Hong Konger, therefore I protest.*

Seen in this way, protest became a performance of Hong Kong identity. Among the slogans being chanted that Sunday in June, more than either '*Cit wui!*' ('Withdraw!') or '*Lam-Cheng Haa-toi!*' ('Lam resign!'), was the simple slogan '*Heunggong jan, gaa jau!*' ('Hong Kongers, add oil!'). In the course of 2019, that slogan became a message of solidarity, a call to arms, an expression of shared identity that could just as well be shouted at a protest rally as spoken between friends or even passing strangers in the course of a quotidian interaction.

The Sunday march ended with the crowds of tens of thousands again occupying Harcourt Road in Admiralty. When buses or ambulances wanted to pass along the road, the crowd would part like the Red Sea, and then immediately close again after the vehicle had passed. Mixed with their anger and defiance was a strong sense of solidarity, community, and euphoria.

On the sidelines of the march, singer Denise Ho and her team of volunteers manned booths carrying out a voter-registration drive to encourage especially young, new voters to enrol in order to vote in the district council elections due later in the year.

Over by the chief executive's office, the atmosphere was tense. Some protesters were taunting the riot police lined up behind the fence; a group of Christian protesters stood nearby singing Hallelujah to the Lord. Standing on the highway overpass, looking down on the scene, I chatted to a protester who gave her name as Julie and said she worked in a bank. She told me she had been tear gassed 'at this precise spot' on the bridge on Wednesday. Still, reflecting on the past week's events, she was philosophical: 'We Hong Kongers are getting better at protest. For example, in the past, there was a lot of rubbish left piled around the bins. But now there is much less; we have learned to bring less rubbish and to recycle.'

The day, thankfully, would end peacefully. As night fell and the crowds began to disperse, many protesters sat on the sloping lawns of Tamar Park, enjoying the cool breeze coming off the harbour, the lights of Kowloon twinkling across the water.

5

BE WATER!

In the wake of the two-million-person march, Carrie Lam issued a written apology and, two days later, made a formal apology at a press conference. 'I personally have to shoulder much of the responsibility. This has led to controversies, disputes, and anxieties in society,' Lam said. 'For this, I offer my most sincere apology to all people of Hong Kong.'[1] However, she refused formally to withdraw the extradition bill, reiterating she had already indicated that the bill would not proceed.

In response, the online activists who seemed increasingly to be leading the protest movement issued an ultimatum: if Lam did not formally withdraw the extradition bill by five o'clock on Thursday evening, 20 June 2019, they would escalate their protest actions on Friday, beginning with an action to surround government head-quarters in Admiralty. The ultimatum was issued in the name of the political party Youngspiration, together with an alliance of various online chat groups — possibly the first time that chat groups have formally made demands of a government.

With no response coming from the government by Thursday evening, the following morning's edition of the *Apple Daily* newspaper lent its support with a front-page headline: 'People's Picnic at Admiralty'.

The day began as many other protest days did, with black-clad young protesters gathering at Tamar Park early in the morning. They were given an early victory when the authorities quickly declared the main government headquarters closed.

By midmorning, their numbers swelled and the protest escalated: Harcourt Road was occupied once again, traffic brought to a standstill. Initially, it looked to be the beginnings of another entrenched occupation, but after setting up barricades and blockading the road briefly, the protesters dispersed and moved on. The old 'occupy' playbook had been thrown out the window. Clearly, lessons had been learned.

The Umbrella Movement, inspired by the worldwide 'Cccupy' movements following the Global Financial Crisis of 2008, had adopted the same logic, in the hope that the disruption caused by their occupation would force Beijing — or its proxies in the Hong Kong government — to the negotiating table. However, the chief executive, C.Y Leung, refused to make any concessions, and the protests ended in failure. A static, long-term occupation clearly didn't work.

On this Friday morning five years later, their new strategy became clear: 'Be water!' The saying came from a hometown hero, kung-fu movie star Bruce Lee, who, borrowing from the wisdom of Taoist master Lao Tse, famously said: 'Empty your mind. Be formless, shapeless: like water ... Water can flow or it can crash. Be water, my friend.'[2]

In laying claim to Lee's philosophy, the protesters were also co-opting him to their cause, staking their claim to the beloved Hong Kong star as a kindred spirit who — like them — stood up against injustice. It was a role that Lee depicted in many of his movies: the underdog battling an evil criminal mastermind (*Enter the Dragon*); the scrappy immigrant fighting to protect his girlfriend's family business against gangsters (*Way of the Dragon*). Lee, the protesters seemed to be saying, is on our side.

Following Bruce Lee's edict, the protesters flowed like water. Leaving a blockaded Harcourt Road in their wake, with a few dozen protesters sheltering from the midday sun in the shadow of the overhead pedestrian bridges, the protesters split into several groups. One large group encircled the nearby police headquarters building, and began a siege that would last until late into the night. A number of smaller groups splintered off to carry out targeted wildcat occupations of other government facilities: the taxation and immigration department headquarters in Wanchai, and another key government office building in Admiralty. In each case, they arrived at the buildings in groups of only a few hundred, blocking all entrances, and flooding the escalators and lift lobbies, until the government declared the office closed and dismissed staff for the day. With their objective achieved, the protesters immediately dispersed and moved on to their next target. 'Be water!'

In eschewing the fixed, immobile occupation strategies of the past in favour of this highly mobile, agile style of protest, the Hong Kong protesters had developed a remarkably effective and efficient means of protest. As a result, they showed that a relatively small group of protesters could successfully disrupt the government of a major global financial centre. What's more, the protesters made themselves effectively immune to clearance or arrest: with no entrenched positions and adopting an unpredictable and constantly mobile presence, they would simply disperse and regroup elsewhere later if they met with police opposition.

This very characteristic might explain another term that police and the pro-Beijing press soon developed for the protesters: 'cockroaches'. Critics were quick to call out the dehumanising language, noting that the term was also used by the warring factions in Rwanda, and pointing out — admittedly slightly hyperbolically — that dehumanisation was one of the first steps on the path to genocide. However, one can understand why the metaphor resonated for a frustrated police force: protesters would swarm the streets, yet as soon as the police arrived on the scene — like cockroaches in kitchens across Hong Kong when the light was switched on — they would scurry away before they could be caught, only to remerge as soon as the police departed.

As temperatures rose and frustrations built up over the following months, police officers would take to openly calling protesters cockroaches on the streets in the course of their policing, a sign of how far force discipline had fallen. But on this day in June, as the siege on their headquarters continued, the police remained surprisingly restrained.

A number of novel protest strategies emerged in the course of the day. The protesters surrounding the police headquarters dressed themselves in 'black bloc' attire: entirely black clothing, including long black trousers and long-sleeve black tops, black headwear, and full face masks leaving only their eyes exposed. The tactic, initially adopted by anarchist protesters in the West, was intended to ensure that protesters were indistinguishable from one other, making it more difficult for police to identify individuals for subsequent arrest. In the age of the surveillance state, and in particular sitting on the doorstep of China — which had built itself into the most advanced and complete surveillance state on the planet — the Hong Kong protesters were acutely aware of the risks posed by facial-recognition technologies, and could frequently be heard calling upon onlookers not to take photographs of protests. Black bloc was a measure against that surveillance, stymying attempts at facial recognition.

However, the black-bloc attire had another effect: it was a uniform and, as with all uniforms, had the psychological effect of uniting a crowd of disparate individuals into one coherent team. One could almost visibly see the change that came over these young Hong Kongers as they geared up: pulling on the black face masks, straightening their backs, and sharpening their gazes. The black uniforms gave them a sense of power and purpose, and no doubt served to intimidate their antagonists as well.

Black bloc also created a distinct visual identity for the protesters, in particular when combined with their other signature accessory: the yellow hard hat. The hard hat had been worn by some protesters in the Umbrella Movement, in particular in the face of police baton charges in the rough-and-tumble Mong Kok–occupied area. But in the 2019 protests, they became the de rigueur accessory worn by all protesters, as early as on the first day of clashes on 12 June. The humble yellow construction hard hat soon became a symbol of the protests: featured on posters, worn by commuters on the way to work to express their sympathy with the protesters, and incorporated into memes. A clip from the classic Hong Kong action movie *A Better Tomorrow* was re-dubbed by protesters to depict the iconic character Brother Mark, played by another Hong Kong homegrown action hero, Chow Yun-fat, announcing his intention to join the protesters in the following terms: 'Brother Ho, I want to go buy a hard hat.'[3]

Consistent with their identical appearance, reminiscent of a swarm, the crowd that day also appeared to be operating with a 'hive mind', moving from site to site en masse, sometimes — I learned after asking several of them — without individual members of the group even knowing their ultimate destination.

This led to the 2019 protest movement being characterised as 'leaderless'. This was, on the one hand, a deliberate response to the government's aggressive prosecution of the Umbrella Movement's leaders. Few were willing to take a prominent and public role again, and risk being prosecuted for inciting an unlawful assembly. With no visible leader, there would be no one to imprison.

But the lack of a centralised leadership was also a result of the movement's online, organic tactics. Protesters used online forums such as LIHKG, as well as chat groups on the messaging application Telegram (the largest among such groups had upwards of 200,000 members), which have a 'poll' function, to vote on their next steps — ranging from which buildings to target, to when to move on. Protesters voted on the spot, and acted accordingly. This was supplemented by dynamic small-group discussions on the ground among smaller subgroups of protesters.

In the absence of meaningful democracy provided by Beijing and the Hong Kong governance system, the Hong Kong people had improvised their own democratic institutions. Like Benny Tai's referendum in 2014, LIHKG emerged as a key improvised democratic institution during the course of the 2019 protests. Through this forum, the protesters enacted the kind of participatory democracy they wanted to see introduced. Ideas would be raised in a LIHKG post, and then other participants would respond with their comments as they 'upvoted' or 'downvoted' the various posts. When consensus emerged around a post proposing a particular protest action, it would be acted upon.[4]

As I watched the siege of the police headquarters unfold, I could not help comparing it with the ill-fated 'escalation' in the dying days of the Umbrella Movement. In a final attempt to reinvigorate their protest at the end of November 2014, the student leaders used the main stage to call upon protesters to surround and blockade the government headquarters. However, they were unable to rally sufficient numbers, and the blockade was quickly repelled by police, who then seized the opportunity to take back much of the occupied territory, weakening the protesters' position even further. The action was a failure, and arguably precipitated the end of the Umbrella Movement occupation.

The communication tools available then were no different from those available now; however, the protesters' approach had totally changed. This time, there was no main stage and no one issuing directions over loudhailers. The protesters themselves proposed and voted on their plans, and only those proposals with sufficient support were voted to the top and put into action. As such, the movement may have been leaderless, but it was not disorganised.

Indeed, instead of the term 'leaderless', some preferred the term 'leaderful': everyone had a part to play in this protest movement. Volunteers with megaphones or walkie-talkies may have helped to announce and coordinate, but they were not 'leaders'. As a result, the movement avoided the disillusionment that the strong, centralised leadership of the Umbrella Movement ultimately engendered. Every participant in the 2019 movement felt invested, felt that they had their own contribution to make. Professor Francis Lee of the Chinese University of Hong Kong called it open-source protest. To use another analogy, one might think of it as a WikiProtest: everyone could make their own contributions to an integrated whole that the entire community then benefited from. This movement wasn't lacking in leaders: it was full of leaders. It gave the movement a resilience that the Umbrella Movement lacked.

In the ensuing months, it emerged that the protesters — especially the so-called frontliners — operated in small subgroups or teams (one media outlet used the loaded term 'cells') of around ten members. The members of these teams tended to know each other — they may have been friends, classmates, or colleagues — and always moved as a group, acting together and supporting each other. They would then cooperate with other teams on the frontlines, lending a hand to build a barricade, or lining up alongside other teams to face the police. These teams communicated with each other and coordinated with the wider group, again over mobile chat applications.

The protesters' use of Telegram was so well known that it soon attracted the attention of the authorities. A handful of chat-group administrators were arrested. During the most intense early clashes between protesters and police, Telegram reported that it had been subject to a distributed denial-of-service attack originating in mainland China.[5] On top of this, the massive overload of mobile networks that occurred when tens of thousands of people were standing in the same small area trying to access their devices simultaneously meant that communications quickly became unreliable.

In response, protesters turned to alternative peer-to-peer technologies — in particular, the AirDrop feature with which every Apple phone is equipped. (AirDrop enables iPhone users to send files to each other over a Bluetooth connection, without the need for a mobile network.) Protesters used AirDrop to share messages on the ground in the course of protests, and to spread the word among the broader community. Commuters on the Hong Kong subway system found themselves receiving unsolicited AirDrop messages with slogans promoting the protesters' cause or advertising the next rally. Prior to protests, Telegram chat groups carried a reminder: 'Remember to have AirDrop switched on!' During one protest in Mong Kok, my phone began pinging with incoming AirDrop messages warning of an impending police clearance operation. While in the MTR on the way to another protest in remote Yuen Long, I received AirDrop maps of the proposed protest area, which featured warnings of triad-controlled areas that were not safe for protesters. Towards the end of that same protest, as the protesters were preparing to be water and disperse, my mobile phone suddenly began to receive AirDrops carrying a simple message: 'Leave together at 7:00.'

Back outside the police headquarters that Friday night, the exits to the complex were barricaded by protesters, and the buildings pelted with eggs and graffitied with anti-police slogans. Thousands of police remained trapped inside: it may have been an indication of how sensitive the government and police were to adverse publicity following the clashes of the previous Wednesday that they did not try forcefully to clear the protesters as the night wore on.

Umbrella Movement leader Joshua Wong — who, to the government's great inconvenience, had ended his jail sentence just a few days earlier — was on the scene, and appeared at one stage to take a megaphone and try to rally the crowd, but the authority he had commanded during the Umbrella Movement had evaporated. He was no longer a figurehead to this next generation of protesters, who were too busy voting on their mobile phones to pay attention to him: should they maintain their siege of the police headquarters, or call it a night and head home? One response to the question posted on the LIHKG discussion forum summarised well the playful spirit of the movement, as well as the challenges of policing it: 'I think the best way is when the police are all equipped and ready to storm out, we leave all of sudden and let them watch.'

Ultimately, the protesters — adhering to a new slogan, 'Leave together!' ('*Jat cai zau!*') — voted to leave shortly before midnight.

With their 'Be water!' strategy, Hong Kong's protesters had moved beyond merely massing bodies on the streets; their evolution showed a multi-dimensional approach to protest, a series of individual protesters moving, each with their own unique energy, through space and time to achieve a collective aim. As they did so, they did not meet force with force, but deflected and flowed, yielding when pushed, and pushing when there was no resistance.

The 'Be water!' strategy made for a much more sustainable protest movement. The Umbrella Movement had required significant commitment and personal sacrifice in order to maintain the occupation, with people sleeping in tents on hard concrete night after night, for months on end. The 2019 style of protest was much less demanding of its participants' time and their physical comfort: protesters would join a protest on a weekend, and then go to class or work for the remainder of the week.

In a statement the next day, Saturday 22 June, the alliance of online groups reiterated their tactics: 'We are highly mobile, flexible and proactive ... "100 Flower" guerrilla attacks will be one of our most common methods of resistance. When the enemy attacks, we retreat; when the enemy retreats, we attack.'

Their philosophy came directly from the Taoist classic the *Dao De Jing*, in which Laozi wrote: 'The weak overcomes the strong; the soft overcomes the hard.' Faced with the hard power of state violence, Hong Kong protesters had found a way to turn their comparative weakness to their advantage, in a kind of protest tai chi. A rally might turn into a march; a march might begin in one direction and abruptly change to another direction; the focus of a particular protest action might only emerge in the course of the march itself.

The protesters concluded: '6.21 was just the beginning.' They would go on to make good on their threat. The 'Be water!' model would become the template followed for the rest of the year.

It was one of many Hong Kong protest strategies that were soon taken up by activists around the world, including Extinction Rebellion protesters from Brisbane to London — making Hong Kong into something of a 'Silicon Valley of protest' for a new generation of civil-disobedience innovators. Mao Zedong had once inspired revolutionaries around the world. Now, Hong Kong activists were doing the same.

They were also hoping to bring the world's attention to their own revolution.

They saw the planned G20 summit of world leaders, to be held in Osaka at the end of June, as an opportunity. Though unable to get their struggle onto the formal agenda on the G20 conference tables, they aimed for the next best thing: their breakfast tables. Activists took out a series of full-page advertisements in newspapers across the world to publicise their struggle. They funded the initiative with an online crowdfunding campaign that raised over HK$6.7 million within a matter of hours. Volunteers — again coordinated via an online forum — prepared and proofed the text in multiple languages, booked the advertising space, and delivered the artwork to the newspapers. In the days leading up to and during the G20 summit in the final days of June 2019, striking full-page black-and-white advertisements reading 'Stand with Hong Kong at G20' appeared in newspapers from *The New York Times* to *The Guardian*, *Le Monde* to *Süddeutsche Zeitung*, *The Australian* to the *Asahi Shimbun*, the *Globe & Mail* to the *Seoul Daily*.

It was yet another example of the Hong Kong protesters' creative tactics. Throughout the protest movement of 2019, such tactics in cyberspace went alongside tactics in the physical world of the streets. And a few days after the crowdfunded advertisements appeared, the protesters made another bold move by transgressing into yet another hitherto forbidden space.

6

STORMING THE SYSTEM

Ever since the march to oppose Article 23 in 2003, the public holiday on 1 July marking the anniversary of Hong Kong's return to China has been a traditional day of protest in Hong Kong. Beijing would no doubt prefer that Hong Kongers marked the day with expressions of patriotic joy. Instead, they use it to vent dissatisfaction with the government and voice demands for increased democracy, civil liberties, and other political causes. While the core of the annual protest remains its pro-democracy, anti-government message, the march embraces all manner of political and social causes. Strolling along the route of a typical 1 July protest, one will see street stalls promoting press freedom, academic freedom, women's rights, LGBT rights, seniors' rights, housing equality, various environmental causes (from recycling to anti-nuclear power), and the rights of animals from the Lantau Island wild oxen to the sharks that die to have their fins put on Hong Kong's wedding banquet tables.

In 2019, however, it was to be a 1 July like no other.

The day started early. With Lam due to attend a dawn flag-raising ceremony at the convention centre in Wanchai, protesters tried to picket the venue, but the area was cordoned off and protected by a heavy police presence. Nevertheless, it was deemed unsafe for Lam to watch the flag-raising outdoors in person: she and other dignitaries watched from inside on a closed-circuit television, and raised a champagne glass to toast the event, while police pepper-sprayed protesters a few blocks away.

By midmorning, Harcourt Road was already blockaded by protesters. I saw some sitting under a large blood-red banner emblazoned with the slogan, 'If We Burn, You Burn With Us.' It was a quote from the *Hunger Games* series of movies, and simultaneously an indication of the protesters' 'fight to the death' mentality, their dystopian vision of Hong Kong's future, and their fluency in global pop culture. It would also prove to be a prophetic vision of the months to come.

The protesters had expanded their demands from the previous few weeks. Notwithstanding Lam's reassurance that work on the extradition bill had been suspended, they still wanted the bill formally withdrawn. In addition, the protesters were demanding: withdrawal of the characterisation of the 12 June protest as a 'riot'; an amnesty for arrested protesters; an independent inquiry into police behaviour; and universal suffrage for election of the chief executive and LegCo — the unfinished business of the Umbrella Movement. (The demand for Lam's resignation had been dropped, with many protesters arguing that it made no difference if she resigned, as Beijing would just appoint another puppet in her place.) These demands collectively became known as the 'Five Demands', forming the basis of the entire protest movement, and were summed up in the slogan 'Five Demands, Not One Less!' (*Ng daai soukau, kyut jat bat ho!*).

The march from Victoria Park began in the midafternoon, and turnout was significant — perhaps not the millions of a few weeks earlier, but still many hundreds of thousands — a sign of the depth and strength of feeling within the community. In the midafternoon,

I took a detour away from the main march route and strolled across to Admiralty. On Harcourt Road, there was a sense of urgency in the air as protesters wearing yellow hard hats and carrying umbrellas prepared supplies and built barricades. Yet, on the other side of government headquarters, outside the entrance to the LegCo building, all was quiet. The area was empty, the ground strewn with the refuse of protest — water bottles, torn posters, a few battered umbrellas. At the deserted metal barricades along the front of the LegCo entrance, a couple of large helium balloons suspended a sagging black banner that read '#FreedomHK'.

However, as the afternoon turned to early evening, there was a perceptible shift in mood. People finishing the main march joined the young protesters in Admiralty, the crowd numbers swelled, and protesters moved towards the LegCo forecourt. As I arrived back at the entrance to LegCo, I saw that the police had abandoned the barricades guarding the exterior of the building, and were lined up inside, behind the glass windows and metal shutters. The protesters, meanwhile, had begun an all-out assault on the entrance to the building. They had dismantled the steel pedestrian traffic barriers, and used zip ties to refashion them into triangular units, which they were now using as battering rams against the tough, reinforced-glass exterior of the LegCo building. Metal bars had been ripped from the outside cladding of the building, and protesters were using them to beat at the windows. The crowd was heaving now, roaring and cheering on the frontline protesters.

Something else was happening: as the protesters at the frontlines needed more supplies, they used hand gestures to make their requests. These signs — a gesture over their heads for helmets, holding up hands to their eyes like binoculars for goggles, miming putting up an umbrella — were then echoed through the crowd in the LegCo forecourt and around the corner onto Tim Mei Avenue. From a pedestrian footbridge above, I watched as the hand signs rippled down human chains of protesters stretching hundreds of metres, all the way down Tim Mei Avenue and across the ten lanes of Harcourt Road, to supply stations on the far side of the road near Admiralty Station. There, the hand signals met their response, with the necessary supplies being passed from the supply station all the way back along the human chain to the frontline, either hand-to-hand or with runners running the supplies up between the lines to the cheers of the crowd. It was a formidable logistical operation, breathtaking in its simplicity and effectiveness. A few weeks earlier, I had seen the beginnings of these hand signals among the crowds, and guides had been circulating online to socialise the agreed-upon signals. Now the system had blossomed into its fully realised form.

This hand-signal system would become another key strategy for the protesters as the summer wore on. In numerous protests, supply chains would stretch for multiple city blocks, sometimes tracing complex paths around street corners and overpasses, even stretching over a kilometre in length. The sign language would become so iconic that, later in the summer, at a 'silver-haired' rally of elderly Hong Kongers marching in support of the young generation, the elders were learning and practising the youngsters' hand signals in solidarity. Meanwhile, in London, Extinction Rebellion protesters developed their own hand-signal system, inspired by the Hong Kong protesters.

Back outside LegCo, the tempered glass was proving remarkably resistant to the protesters' improvised battering rams. At one point, a metal trolley laden with garbage bins was run into the glass. From the far side of the LegCo forecourt, I could hear the constant battering and crashing, along with the cheers and chants of the crowd. Closer to the windows, I saw dozens of police lined up inside. They occasionally made announcements over a loudspeaker that the protesters should cease their attack, and warning that anyone coming inside the building would be arrested immediately. At one point, some of the senior pan-democrat politicians tried to intervene to stop the frontline protesters, but were roughly pushed aside. This was no longer their battle.

The assault continued for hours, and what began as small breaches in the tempered glass were gradually enlarged into holes big enough for people to fit through, following which protesters started working to break through the steel shutters. From a vantage point on a hill in the park outside looking down into the LegCo lobby, I was surprised to see that the police had completely withdrawn. The building lobby appeared to be empty. I could not understand this — I recalled that on 12 June, internal police messages were leaked online, stating that the LegCo building was a 'fortress' that was to be held at all costs. And hold it they did, deploying pepper spray and tear gas in the LegCo forecourt on that day. But tonight, they had gone.

At around nine o'clock, word began to spread around the crowd: 'They are in!' From the LegCo forecourt, the crowd looked up to the windows above them: a few figures could be seen shining lights and waving down at the crowd, to cheers and applause. I went back up into the park and, looking down through the multi-storeyed windowpanes into the building, I could see black-clad protesters pouring inside. They sprayed graffiti on the walls and unfurled massive protest banners in the atrium. I had a dull sense of dread. This seemed to have gone too far.

To understand why the protesters targeted the LegCo building, and why they took the actions they subsequently did while inside, it is important to understand something of the political structure in Hong Kong — and its inherent flaws.

As Hong Kong's legislature, LegCo is nominally the body that enacts Hong Kong's laws. However, the power of LegCo to function as a democratically representative governing body is severely circumscribed, both structurally through its composition and through the powers it is able to exercise. In terms of its composition, LegCo comprises seventy members, of which:

- Thirty-five are returned by way of geographic constituencies elected by means of universal suffrage. These seats are similar to parliamentary seats in the lower house of Westminster systems such as that in the United Kingdom or Australia, or to congressional districts in the United States. There were approximately 3.8 million registered voters for geographic constituencies in Hong Kong in the LegCo election held in 2016.

- Thirty are returned by functional constituencies: these are seats representing various industries, professions, or other special-interest groups. These include, for example, seats representing the textiles, transport, real estate, and insurance industries; the medical, legal, and accounting professions; and certain rural residents' groups. Only members of the particular group are permitted to vote for their representative. Thus, for example, only barristers or solicitors may run or vote in the legal profession functional constituency. There were, in total, only 232,498 registered electors in functional constituencies in 2016.

- Five are returned by the district council functional constituency: these seats may only be filled by existing district councillors (members of local councils). Voters not eligible to vote in other functional constituencies may cast votes for these seats.

Thus, everyone in Hong Kong votes for two representatives; however, all those representatives sit in the one chamber.

This system produces a structural bias in favour of the pro-Beijing parties, which, due to the influence of the pro-Beijing lobby among the small-circle functional constituencies, traditionally win almost all of those seats. Together with the additional seats they are able to win in the geographic constituencies, the system ensures that the pro-Beijing parties always win a majority of the seats in LegCo, even though the pan-democrat candidates consistently win around 55 per cent of the popular vote.

In terms of its powers, LegCo enacts laws like any other legislature does. However, its power is circumscribed in one very important way: while the government can freely propose legislation to LegCo, legislators themselves may only introduce private members' bills with the written consent of the chief executive if they are 'relating to government policies'. With any kind of meaningful legislation invariably 'relating to government policies', this gives the chief executive an exclusive right to define the issues for debate. In addition, private members' bills, unlike bills proposed by the government, are subject to a super-majority requirement, needing separate majorities in each of the geographic-constituency seats and functional-constituency seats in order to pass, thereby giving the pro-Beijing parties a veto power through their control of the functional constituencies.

Legislation does nevertheless require a positive vote of a majority of LegCo to pass, even for government-initiated bills. Thus, the government must secure the support of LegCo in order to implement its policies. Legislators have the power to question government officials and require them to justify their policies, meaning that the government is to some degree accountable to LegCo and so, indirectly, to the people.

However, as a result of the electoral system, in effect Hong

Kongers elect the opposition; they do not elect the government. This is because, structurally, the system is designed to produce a result whereby a majority of the popular vote will only ever elect a minority of the seats. In any event, the legislature that they elect:

- does not form or produce government: ministers are not drawn from the legislature (as they are in a Westminster parliamentary system), nor does the legislature vote on ministerial appointments made by the chief executive (as in the United States, where presidential cabinet appointments are subject to Senate confirmation); and
- is not in a position to propose policy or new laws without the support of the government, and is solely in the passive position of debating, and then voting for (or against) laws and policy introduced by the government.

Because of their status as the perennial 'loyal opposition', the only constructive role the pro-democracy parties have to play in the policy-making process is to act as vocal critics of the executive, rather than as an effective check and balance on it.

Yet there was a hope, in the aftermath of the Umbrella Movement, that the pro-democracy forces might finally have sufficient momentum to change this dynamic. On the last day of the Admiralty occupation, I chatted with the chair of the Democratic Party, Emily Lau, on the sidelines of the sit-in that would lead to police arresting 208 protesters at the end of that day. Lau reflected on what might be the legacy of the Umbrella Movement: 'I hope these young people can channel their energy into the electoral system as well, and think about forming or joining political parties. They will have to learn that the movement is more than just demonstrations in the streets.'

Some of the Umbrella Movement leaders and activists took Lau's advice, going on to form several new political parties. Scholarism announced it would dissolve, and its leaders, including Joshua Wong and Agnes Chow, as well as figures from the HKFS, including Nathan Law, formed Demosistō, with the intention of participating in the LegCo elections scheduled for September 2016. Meanwhile, a growing 'localist' or 'nativist' movement led to the formation of a number of other parties, including Youngspiration and Hong Kong Indigenous.

As preparations began for the LegCo elections in mid-2016, the Electoral Affairs Commission, seemingly at the behest of Beijing in response to the rising localist movement, announced a new requirement: all candidates were asked to sign a form declaring their adherence to the principle set out in the Basic Law that Hong Kong is an inalienable part of China. The move was clearly intended to give a pretext for the disqualification of certain of the localist candidates who had included self-determination or even independence in their election platforms, and amounted to a political screening of candidates. The process descended into farce when some of the old-guard pan-democrat politicians refused to sign the declaration as a matter of principle but were nevertheless permitted to run, while some localist politicians, including Edward Leung of Hong Kong Indigenous, signed the declaration but were nevertheless banned by the returning officer, who did not accept the sincerity of their declaration. In total, six candidates were banned from running as a result.

The 2016 LegCo elections attracted what was at the time a record turnout — 58 per cent of registered voters — clear evidence that the Umbrella Movement had energised political engagement among Hong Kong's populace. Pan-democrats won the majority of the popular vote (a record high of approximately 60 per cent). But the functional-constituency system ensured that establishment parties retained majority control of the legislature, with pro-Beijing parties taking forty out of the seventy seats, and pan-democrats the remaining thirty seats (an increase of three seats since the previous election, in 2012).

Most notable was the success of the young politicians from the Umbrella Movement generation. Indeed, localist candidates attracted 19 per cent of all votes cast. Edward Leung's nominated successor, Sixtus 'Baggio' Leung (no relation), won a seat, as did fellow Youngspiration member Yau Wai-ching and another localist candidate, Lau Siu-lai. Demosistō's Nathan Law was also successfully elected. The success of Demosistō and Youngspiration represented a stunning result for the political newcomers and a clear achievement of the Umbrella Movement. Among other successful non-establishment candidates, Eddie Chu, a veteran protester and land-justice activist, attracted the most votes of any single candidate, with Hong Kong media crowning him the 'King of Votes'.

Just when it appeared that the pro-democracy parties were about to enjoy an era of renewed vigour and increased influence, everything fell apart. During the oath-taking ceremonies for the new legislators, the two Youngspiration lawmakers deliberately botched their oaths as an act of protest, mispronouncing 'China' as 'Chee-na' (deeply offensive in China, as it was a derogatory term used by the Japanese occupiers during the war), adding obscenities to their oaths, and displaying 'Hong Kong Is Not China' banners. Lau Siu-lai read her oath with a six-second pause between each word, rendering the oath a meaningless list of words. A number of other pan-democrat lawmakers also enacted less extreme forms of symbolic protest during their oath-taking.

The LegCo president accepted the oaths of all but the Youngspiration duo, and seemed prepared to give them an opportunity to retake their oath properly in order to take up their seats. There was, after all, precedent for them to do so. Veteran activist 'Long

Hair' Leung Kwok-hung and other radical pan-democrat legislators had engaged in symbolic acts of protest during their oath-swearing in previous years, without consequence. However, this time, Beijing and its proxies in the Hong Kong government sensed an opportunity. The Hong Kong government intervened, suing in the courts in an effort to prevent the legislators from being allowed to retake their oaths. In yet another twist, before the court had the opportunity to hand down its decision, the National People's Congress Standing Committee stepped in with an unsolicited interpretation of the Basic Law. This was unusual in itself — in the past, Beijing had only directly intervened in Hong Kong legal matters at the request of the Hong Kong government or courts. An unsolicited interpretation, while a case was still under active consideration by the courts, was an inappropriate interference in the operations of Hong Kong's judicial system.

The content of the interpretation was even more eyebrow-raising. The NPC ruled that the Basic Law requirement for legislators and other government officials to take an oath of office should be understood to mean that they had to take their oaths properly and solemnly; and that if an oath were taken improperly, it could not be retaken and the relevant officer would be immediately disqualified. This clearly went beyond the text of the Basic Law, and amounted to making new legal requirements out of whole cloth. In addition, the interpretation was to be applied with retroactive effect, something widely regarded as anathema in the common-law tradition. University of Hong Kong law professor Johannes Chan called the NPC interpretation a 'vote of no confidence' by Beijing in Hong Kong's independent judiciary.[1]

In the wake of the NPC decision, Hong Kong's High Court confirmed that the Youngspiration duo were disqualified from office. Emboldened by the NPC interpretation, the Hong Kong government took further action in the courts to disqualify four additional legislators for oath-swearing infractions: Lau Siu-lai, Nathan Law, 'Long

Hair' Leung, and architects' functional-constituency representative Edward Yiu. The disqualified legislators were also required to repay all salaries and allowances received by them during the time they were 'illegally' occupying their seats — claims that amounted to millions of Hong Kong dollars.

The outcome was that six duly elected pro-democracy lawmakers had been unceremoniously booted out of office, opening up their seats for by-elections in which the LegCo proportional-voting system would mean that at least one seat would flip to a pro-Beijing candidate. In the subsequent by-elections for five of the seats vacated by the disqualified pan-democrats, two were won back by pan-democrats, but three went to pro-Beijing candidates. (One seat remains vacant while the disqualification is appealed through the courts.) As a result, the pro-Beijing parties controlled forty-three out of sixty-nine seats, but the pan-democrats held on to their 'super minority' block.

So, as the protesters gathered outside LegCo that hot July night in 2019, they would have had a deeply internalised sense of injustice — not only of the flawed system, but of the manner in which even their attempts to work within it had been stymied. Their candidates had been barred from running or disqualified from office, their participation in the formal political process foreclosed, and their efforts of peaceful protest on the streets ignored, leading them to the conclusion that they were left with no choice but to escalate their actions. And the space they were now entering was freighted with this history, as the scene of some of those very injustices.

Reporters followed the protesters into the LegCo building, and images began to appear online of what was going on inside.

As protesters stormed the building, they engaged in what at first glance appeared to be a rampage of vandalism and destruction. Yet, on closer examination, it became apparent that the vandalism was, perversely, extremely disciplined and focused. Protesters deliberately chose symbols of Beijing's power in Hong Kong and of the flawed Hong Kong political system as the targets of their ire. Inside the LegCo chamber, they painted out the words 'People's Republic of China' from the phrase 'Hong Kong Special Administrative Region of the People's Republic of China' in the Hong Kong emblem; they tore up a copy of the Basic Law; and they vandalised the seats occupied by pro-Beijing legislators. They draped the 'Black Bauhinia' flag (the Hong Kong flag reinterpreted from Chinese red to deathly black) near the president's seat, and unveiled black-and-white funeral-style portraits of the city's leaders: Televiosn (Carrie Lam; security minister John Lee; justice minister Teresa Cheng; and police chief Stephen Lo. Most controversially, they displayed the British colonial-era Hong Kong flag, an act that did not sit well with many onlookers conscious of the legacy of colonialism.

Walls throughout the building were covered in graffiti, much of it delivering pointed messages to Beijing: 'Hong Kong is not China yet'; 'China will pay for its crimes against Uighur Muslims'. Other graffiti bore the key slogans of the protest movement.

Protesters also trashed offices and computer equipment, in particular computer equipment in the security office that they thought might contain CCTV footage of their invasion. Yet elsewhere in the building, the protesters were almost scrupulous in the care they took: the library was untouched, and a sign reading 'Please do not damage the books' was posted at the entrance. Protesters taking cans of drink from a cafeteria refrigerator left cash in payment.

Their attack was not an attack on a building: it was an attack on a system. If it was an act of violence, it was an act of retaliatory violence against the continuous acts of systemic violence to which these protesters felt they had been subjected.

Brian Leung Kai-ping, a twenty-five-year-old law and politics graduate about to embark on PhD studies in the United States, was one of the protesters who entered the LegCo chamber that night. In 2014, Leung had skipped his classes at the University of Hong Kong to join the Umbrella Movement protests, and he was editor of the university student magazine *Undergrad* when it was specifically criticised by C.Y. Leung in his 2015 policy address for promoting Hong Kong self-determination.[2] In the febrile post–Umbrella Movement environment, the chief executive's very public criticism served only to raise the profile of an issue that had hitherto attracted little public attention.

Now, at the climax of the evening on 1 July 2019, Leung watched his fellow protesters becoming aimless in their vandalism of the LegCo chamber, and felt that 'the momentum of history was slipping away'. He later explained, 'What I saw was that people were wandering around, people were trying to protest in their own way, by defacing the emblem, doing some sort of graffiti, slogans ... I saw a moral vacuum that demanded someone stand up.'[3]

So Leung stood up. Removing his face mask — ignoring warnings that he was revealing his identity to the surrounding television cameras — he cried out, 'Hong Kongers have nothing more to lose!'

'If we retreat now ... they will film all the destruction and mess inside LegCo, point the finger towards us, and call us rioters,' he told the crowd, urging them to remain in the LegCo chamber.[4] Leung hoped he might inspire the 'peaceful, rational, nonviolent' protesters outside to join them, and to begin an occupation of the legislature like that of the Sunflower Movement protesters in Taiwan five years earlier. Leung then read the Admiralty Declaration, a ten-point manifesto that criticised the 'corrupt government', and called for democracy and universal suffrage, the release of arrested persons, and an investigation of police brutality. He ended with the words: 'Never forget Hong Kong's Bloody June'.

However, Leung's plea was ignored by the crowd — what he was proposing was, after all, a direction contradiction of the 'Be water!' philosophy — and protesters began to leave the building as police announced that they would move in to clear the site at midnight. It seemed that few had an appetite for a bloody showdown. There would be no occupation.

Yet this act of defiance — Leung's courage in stepping forward as the sole unmasked protester — became the defining moment of the night, a galvanising moment that gave the LegCo invasion a sense of purpose that might otherwise have been characterised as a wanton orgy of destruction. It would also cement the bond between the 'frontliner' and the 'peaceful, rational, nonviolent' protest factions. As Leung would later tell *Stand News*, 'It was a beautiful mistake.'[5]

The next day, video would emerge of the last protesters to leave the chamber: one protester insists on staying behind, to face whatever is coming, to the death if necessary. His fellow protesters surround him and physically drag him, screaming, out of the chamber. As they leave, a woman's haunting voice is calling out over the crowd, *'Jat cai zau! Jat cai zau!'* ('Leave together!')

In the aftermath of the LegCo invasion, Lam and her government must have thought they had been handed a public-relations gift. Indeed, the event seemed so convenient to the government that many suspected the police withdrawal had been deliberate, that the protesters had been allowed to break in. As the protesters rampaged through the building, Lam perhaps calculated that public support for the protest movement would quickly dwindle, allowing her to return to business as usual.

If that indeed was Lam's gamble, it seemed to ignore one

important fact: at the same time as the protesters were battering the windows of the LegCo building, several hundred thousand people were peacefully marching just a few blocks away in protest against her government. And those people, and the many others sympathetic to the protest movement, seemed to appreciate the symbolic nature of the protesters' actions. They also understood the injustice of the system that was their target.

In the hours after the attack, renowned Hong Kong author Dung Kai-cheung wrote:

> True, they destroyed things, but they were not rioters. They destroyed things in an orderly way, in a controlled way. Their destruction was a symbolic act, a means of stating their position, a means of expressing their righteous indignation. In the course of doing so, they did not harm a single person ... On the contrary, they were prepared to sacrifice themselves. Should we not reflect upon our understanding of violence? ... Damaging the inanimate objects inside LegCo, is that violence? This is an expression of anger against a useless government, the shameless pro-establishment political parties and an undemocratic system.

Brian Leung expressed a similar view, explaining that the actions of the protesters were aimed at 'telling the public that this was not just mob action but to register the accumulated frustrations of an unfair electoral system'.[6] It was, he said, 'a culmination of desperation and frustration and the cry of democratic freedom from a large group of young people. They have no choice.'[7]

The Civil Human Rights Front and Democratic Party did not criticise the protesters; rather, they called for understanding from the public, placing the blame at the door of the government. There would be no condemnation.

The moment crystallised a deeper principle that had been emerging over the course of the protest movement. Conscious of the internal divisions that had undermined the Umbrella Movement, and of the infighting and factionalism that had plagued the pan-democrat parties in Hong Kong for decades, this movement saw a new emerging solidarity, summed up in the slogan: 'No Splitting, No Cutting Off, No Snitching.'

The protesters recognised that they were divided, broadly, into two camps, the 'peaceful, rational, nonviolent' (*'Wo Lei Fei'*) protesters, and the so-called 'valiants' or 'braves' (*'Jung Mou'*), also referred to as 'frontliners', who were willing to engage in direct and often violent confrontation with police. In the past, these two camps had been critical of one another; such conflict during the Umbrella Movement had led to scuffles over demands to 'tear down the main stage'. The peaceful protesters in the past would argue that those willing to engage in acts of violence would lose both the moral high ground and the support of the wider community, while the valiants would argue that the nonviolent tactics had been ineffective and that the old-guard pan-democrat politicians had failed the young generation.

But now the protesters saw themselves as a collective. There would be no factionalism: no groups would be 'cut off' from the movement. It became a point of common acceptance that if particular groups engaged in acts one did not agree with, one was free not to participate but should not criticise. The protesters began referring to each other as '*Sau Zuk*', a word meaning 'brothers', made up of the characters for 'hand' and 'foot': they saw themselves as the hands and feet of one unified organism. In this sense, to cut off any members of the group would be akin to an amputation of one's own limb. This newfound solidarity came to be seen as one of the key victories of the movement.[8]

A week after the LegCo break-in, Lam made another public appearance in a bid to sooth public sentiment, announcing: 'There are still lingering doubts about the Government's sincerity or worries whether the Government will restart the process in the Legislative Council. So I reiterate here, there is no such plan. The bill is dead.'[9]

It seemed ironically consistent with the death-themed protests that Lam should turn to a mortality-tinged metaphor, something she did both in her English statement and in Chinese, saying that the bill was '*Sau zung zing cam*', meaning that it had 'died a natural death in its bed' — something that online critics were quick to point out did not reflect the true state of affairs, given that the bill effectively had been killed by the protesters.

In relation to the other of the protesters' 'Five Demands', however, Lam held firm. There would be no independent commission of enquiry, she said, arguing that the Independent Police Complaints Council, or IPCC, would take up the role of investigating any complaints about police behaviour. (Critics complained that the IPCC was toothless, with no power to subpoena witnesses.) She also refused to acknowledge that the protests had been characterised as a riot, and said that any amnesty for arrested protesters would be contrary to Hong Kong's rule of law.[10]

Coming in the wake of the attack on LegCo, Lam's announcement seemed to be yet another vindication of the protesters' tactics. The violent clashes during their protest on 12 June had led to Lam announcing the temporary suspension of the bill. Now their LegCo break-in had forced her to confirm the bill was 'dead'.

A piece of graffiti left by the protesters in LegCo made the point unequivocally: 'It was you who taught me that peaceful marches are useless.'

7

'RECLAIM HONG KONG! REVOLUTION OF OUR TIMES!'

The protest march on Sunday 21 July was again organised by the Civil Human Rights Front. The day before, police had issued their letter of no objection (required for public gatherings under the Public Order Ordinance), but had insisted that the march end at Southorn Playground in Wanchai and not continue past Admiralty into Central as planned — a significantly foreshortened route. The decision seemed calculated to lure protesters into breaking the law: there was insufficient space in Southorn Playground and the narrow Wanchai streets surrounding it. Participants would have nowhere to go when the march finished, making their gathering in the streets around the end point of the march a de facto unlawful assembly.

The turnout was, once again, huge — tens of thousands, maybe over 100,000. And when this mass of humanity reached the half-hearted police line at Southorn Playground, the police simply stepped aside, and the crowd continued to stroll past. The march was now illegal.

The police seemed to be prepared for this eventuality. In the days leading up to this protest, two-metre-high water-filled barriers had been placed around Government Headquarters in Admiralty as well as at the Police Headquarters in Wan Chai. Thousands of police were reportedly encamped inside the fortified facilities, awaiting the protesters. Bricks on the surrounding footpaths had been glued down to prevent them from being extracted and used as projectiles, and any remaining metal street barriers not already deconstructed by protesters in previous protests had been removed, and replaced with red plastic tape. Riot police were lined up behind the barriers at Police Headquarters and at LegCo, with police dogs barking from behind the barricades. The authorities clearly did not want a repeat of the 1 July LegCo invasion, and were taking all measures to prevent it.

So it came as something of a surprise when the protesters, upon reaching Admiralty, just continued to stroll right past, flowing like water.

Their first destination appeared to be the Court of Final Appeal in Central, the planned destination of the march before it was nixed by police, but from there a new target seemed to emerge organically from within the crowd: the Central Government Liaison Office, Beijing's representative office in Hong Kong. The crowd moved in that direction en masse, easily 10,000 people or more flowing down the main road through Central towards Sheung Wan, where the office was located, several kilometres away.

The crowd soon reached its destination, an imposing, blue-glass-clad office tower topped with an enormous sphere (which presumably houses all manner of surveillance and communications hardware). The national emblem of the Peoples' Republic of China, resplendent in red and gold, hung over the entrance. There was no police presence outside the Central Government Liaison Office at all, notwithstanding that the building was adjacent to a police station. Apparently, no one in the government or police had had the forethought to protect the building.

The building was quickly surrounded by protesters in black T-shirts and yellow hard hats. There was tension in the air: Hong Kong protesters had never done anything like this before. If storming LegCo was a taboo, this seemed to be a taboo of a higher order. A couple of protesters turned a metal traffic barrier into an improvised ladder, and, scaling it, spray-painted over the lenses of the building's security cameras, to cheers from the crowd. Now emboldened that they were free from surveillance, protesters pelted the building façade with eggs, and sprayed its walls with graffiti, blacking out the official signage and scrawling slogans such as 'Fuck Chee-na', 'Down with the Communist Party', and 'Respond to the Five Demands'. Black paint bombs were hurled at the national emblem, several successfully hitting their target and creating an image that would generate significant outrage in the mainland. This was a direct challenge to Beijing's rule over Hong Kong, an insult aimed right at the heart of Chinese sovereignty.

As rumours spread that police were approaching from the west, the crowd began to fall back again towards Central. The protesters barricaded Central Police Station and graffitied its walls, and then began building barricades at the border of Sheung Wan and Central.

And that is when I heard it. As the crowd massed and heaved, there came a new chant, one I had not heard in the protests previously: '*Gwong fuk Heung Gong! Sidoi Gaakming!*'

'Reclaim Hong Kong! Revolution of our times!'

In 2014, Edward Leung Tin-kei was a disillusioned philosophy major at the University of Hong Kong, struggling to graduate and suffering from depression. When the Umbrella Movement began to unfold, led by his fellow university students, Leung said, 'Suddenly it seemed I had something to do.' The police tear gas on that September afternoon in 2014 shook Leung out of his depression: 'September 28 stirred up so much emotion. It seemed suddenly my life was meaningful ... with a sense of fulfilment. We were standing the ground for the city. Holding on to the values that make this our home.'[1]

Leung became active in the Umbrella Movement and, when it ended in failure, fell into depression once again. As his depression worsened and he began to entertain suicidal thoughts, Leung turned to friends for help. One of those friends was Ray Wong, the founder of Hong Kong Indigenous, one of the handful of localist groups — alongside Youngspiration and the Hong Kong National Party, among others — that sprang up in 2015 in the wake of the Umbrella Movement. In June 2015, Leung joined Wong as a member of Hong Kong Indigenous, shook off his depression, and found a renewed sense of purpose in life.

Hong Kong Indigenous and its fellow nativists kept themselves busy protesting against mainland parallel traders in the far northern districts of Hong Kong, close to the mainland border. Those traders regularly travelled to Hong Kong to make bulk purchases of pharmaceuticals, cosmetics, baby powder, and other goods that were more expensive, in short supply, or of unreliable quality on the mainland, and then resold them across the border. This led to local shopping areas in these districts becoming overrun with stores catering to the traders, pushing out local businesses and reducing their amenity for local residents. In addition, the parallel traders clogged footpaths and subway stations with their overloaded trolleys of goods.

These nativist groups often displayed an anti-mainland sentiment that bordered on ugly xenophobia — for example, by referring to mainland visitors as 'locusts' swarming Hong Kong. Yet Leung sought to position their protests in terms of a threat to Hong Kong identity: 'After 1997 ... we've witnessed the decline of all our core values, living style, and culture. The main influence is from China. They deprive our political rights, they undermine our culture. They want to control every aspect in Hong Kong.'[2] This was a theme that Leung emphasised after causing a minor media storm when he revealed that he had been, in fact, born in mainland China himself, having migrated to Hong Kong as a toddler with his mother. He defended himself against charges of hypocrisy by arguing that it was his defence of 'Hong Kong values, culture, and institutions' that defined him, not his place of birth. He tellingly also added that his mainland immigrant mother could speak Cantonese.[3]

The period following the Umbrella Movement saw numerous localist-inspired protests, some of which ended in violent clashes. The most violent of these would come to be known as the 'Fishball Revolution', and would propel Leung to fame and, ultimately, a prison cell.

The Lunar New Year street market is a longstanding Chinese tradition, and Hong Kong authorities had traditionally turned a blind eye to unlicensed street vendors selling local snacks such as fishballs and stinky tofu during the festive season. However, in Mong Kok on Chinese New Year's Day, 8 February 2016, officers from the Food and Environmental Hygiene Department began patrolling and attempting to shut down the vendors. In response, activists led by Leung's Hong Kong Indigenous party sent out calls to their supporters to convene in Mong Kok to protect the vendors (and the traditional Hong Kong culture they represented), leading to scuffles between the hygiene officers and protesters.

Police were called in and, as more protesters — and more police reinforcements, armed with riot gear — flocked to the area, the mood quickly degenerated into violence and rioting, with protesters and police engaging in violent confrontations. Leung was on the scene, directing the crowd over a megaphone. Protesters set fire to rubbish bins and tore up more than 2,000 brick pavers to throw at police — some of whom were pictured throwing them back. Police responded with batons and pepper spray, and one officer fired two live rounds from his service revolver as warning shots, something regarded at the time as deeply shocking in a city unaccustomed to gun violence. Police estimated that around 700 were involved in the rioting, which lasted for more than ten hours before order was restored. More than eighty police officers and scores of protesters were injured, and eighty-six people were arrested, including Leung.

How did fishballs come to excite such passions? As Hong Kong–born restaurateur Alan Yau, the founder of the Wagamama chain, later explained, fishballs are 'the quintessential Hong Kong street food and — culturally — it represents the Hong Kong working class'. Fishballs, Yau said, 'represent the values of entrepreneurship. Of capitalism. Of liberal democracy. Anthropologically, they mean more than a $5 skewer with curry satay sauce.'[4]

While many in the community deplored the violence, and the two largest pro-democracy parties, the Democratic Party and the Civic Party, quickly condemned the attacks on the police, many involved were unrepentant. 'If history decides we're culpable for the violence, so be it,' Leung told the *The New York Times*.[5] All of Hong Kong's university student unions issued statements in support of the protesters.

Just a few weeks later, Leung, aged twenty-four at the time, ran as a candidate in a LegCo by-election. For that campaign, Leung adopted a provocative slogan: 'Reclaim Hong Kong! Revolution of our times!' Tall, handsome, and charismatic, Leung was a naturally gifted politician, described by fellow traveller Baggio Leung of Youngspiration as a 'genius', even 'another Sun Yat-sen'.[6]

The by-election was ultimately won by pan-democrat Alvin Yeung of the Civic Party. But newcomer Leung shocked the establishment by winning 66,524 votes, over 15 per cent of the votes cast.[7] The result heralded the arrival of a new force in Hong Kong politics, one that sent echoes of panic through the corridors of power. If Leung ran again in a wider LegCo election with its proportional-voting system, he would likely win a seat in the LegCo, something the authorities could not allow to happen.

When Leung attempted to submit his candidacy for the September 2016 full LegCo elections, he was one of the six candidates screened out by the returning officers for his allegedly pro-independence views. Leung signed the required declaration, and argued that he had changed his stance on independence, but the returning officer was not convinced of his sincerity, dredging up a weighty file of press clippings in support of the position.

Leung expressed his frustration at the decision, wondering whether his exclusion from Hong Kong's political process amounted to a permanent ban: 'Do I have to sign a "letter of repentance" and pledge I won't call for independence in front of six cameras and the whole universe?' he asked, adding, 'I have been stripped of my political rights for my entire life.'[8]

Leung nominated Baggio Leung of Youngspiration as his substitute, and campaigned alongside him. On election night, when the formal announcement was made that Baggio Leung had successfully won a LegCo seat, the chants of his supporters filled the tally room: 'Reclaim Hong Kong! Revolution of our times!'

Leung may have felt bitter at having been robbed of his opportunity to sit in the legislature, but worse was to come. In 2018, Leung went on trial on charges of rioting and assaulting a police officer in connection with the events of the Fishball Revolution. He was found guilty, and in June 2018 sentenced to six years' jail, the court justifying what was an extremely heavy sentence on the basis of general deterrence.

While Leung watched the events of 2019 from inside jail, his slogan was embraced by the protesters, and his plight became a *cause célèbre*. Among the slogans graffitied inside the LegCo building on 1 July was 'Free Edward Leung', and in October a crowdfunding campaign to pay the costs of his legal appeal reached its goal within fifteen minutes of being launched, with a total of 1,268 people donating over HK$450,000.

Ray Wong, having sought asylum in Germany after fleeing Hong Kong in the wake of the Fishball Revolution, summed up Leung's significance for the 2019 protest movement when he told *The Atlantic*, 'Edward Leung and Hong Kong Indigenous planted a seed in Hong Kong politics, and now it has started to grow.'[9]

And so, 'Reclaim Hong Kong, Revolution of our times!' The slogan 'features two of the most powerful words in the political vocabulary of modern China', according to Sinologist Geremie Barmé.[10] The word 'revolution' is self-evidently provocative. But the term '*gwong fuk*' (or '*guangfu*' in standard Mandarin), 'reclaim' or literally 'light returns', is rather more complex. As Barmé explains, the expression referred to 'recovering a fallen nation, a rightful restoration or taking back lost territory', and historically was used by revolutionary leader Sun Yat-sen following the fall of the Qing Dynasty, the establishment of the new republican government also being seen as a 'Han Chinese reconquest of a land long dominated by Manchu invaders'.[11] More recently, the term was used by the Nationalist government on Taiwan to refer to their long planned but never realised retaking of the mainland from the communists.[12]

But what was being reclaimed? At its most simplistic level, one might be tempted to render it in a crude contemporary Western parallel as a bid to 'Make Hong Kong Great Again', a sentiment familiar to nativist populist politicians around the world. At the other extreme, Beijing interpreted the slogan in territorial terms, seeing it as nothing less than advocating Hong Kong independence. As with Sun Yat-sen and the Taiwanese Nationalists, Beijing understood this as a bid to reclaim the territory of Hong Kong from Chinese sovereignty. Many in Hong Kong, however, argued that the slogan was not about independence, but rather about reclaiming institutional autonomy, the autonomy promised under the One Country, Two Systems formula of 'Hong Kongers ruling Hong Kong' — a demand for a government responsive to its people and governing with their interests as its foremost priority, rather than a government constantly looking over its own shoulder and trying to please a distant sovereign master.

But perhaps, ultimately, it was none of these things. Perhaps this was ultimately about reclaiming a sense of agency. For too long, Hong Kongers had been objects of the history of others: whether that was British colonial history, in whose narrative Hong Kong was the 'barren island' (in the words of Lord Palmerston in 1841) turned by the British into a global financial centre, or whether it was communist China's history, in which Hong Kong was one more example from the century of national humiliation that the party increasingly used as part of the narrative to legitimise its rule. What Hong Kongers were reclaiming was the subjectivity of their own history.

The chant echoed in the canyon between the buildings, under the looming concrete overpasses: '*Gwong fuk Heung Gong! Sidoi Gaakming!*' 'Reclaim Hong Kong! Revolution of our times!'

As the crowd prepared for the police onslaught, the fully equipped frontline troops — kitted out in their black-bloc attire, yellow hard hats, and face masks — came running in formation through the crowd to face the police lines. The crowd roared in support. With their improvised shields made from road signs and planks of wood, the frontline braves had picked up a new trick from the riot police, who would beat their riot shields with their batons as an intimidation tactic. The protesters began to do the same, beating their shields against the ground or against the barricades, beating the traffic dividers and rubbish bins with umbrellas — a beat that was tribal, raw, a death rattle that rallied their spirits as they faced the police, who now came in full-bore with tear gas and rubber bullets. A violent clash ensued, with bricks being thrown, protesters wielding slingshots, and, for the first time, Molotov cocktails being hurled. A barricade was set ablaze.

I escaped the tear gas down a side-alley to find a *cha caan teng* (local Hong Kon–style café), where the events of a few blocks away were being broadcast live on a television outside. I took a seat at an outside table, ordered an iced tea, and watched the television: as clouds of tear gas billowed on the screen, I looked down the end of the alley to see yellow hard-hatted crowds rushing down the street, away from the same onslaught I was watching on the television. Some of the fleeing crowd rushed up the alley where I sat, as the elderly lady who owned the restaurant laconically wiped down the tables, looking up to watch the crowd rush past.

I went back down into the crowd. Looking ahead towards Sheung Wan, I saw drifting clouds of tear gas, illuminated by flashing police lights and protester laser beams; the protesters had taken to deploying powerful laser pointers, both to distract and annoy police as well as to point at cameras to prevent their photographs being taken — again, their heightened awareness of the surveillance state in evidence.

But now the crowd was shifting again. Word was being passed around, 'Leave together at 11.25! Leave together at 11.25!' People in the crowd took up the call and passed it forward, and the crowd began to fall back in an orderly retreat. As they reached the nearest MTR station entrances, they began dumping equipment and clothing at the station entrances, changing out of their telltale black protester outfits and into ordinary clothes down side-alleys. A lamppost had several coloured T-shirts tied around it, together with a handwritten sign that read 'Change shirt'.

By midnight, the protesters had completely dispersed, and the police lines were left facing an empty road. Outside the MTR stations were piles of hard hats, collapsed umbrellas, broken shields, discarded black T-shirts, and face masks.

I waved at a journalist friend as he passed in a rush. 'Where are you going?' I asked.

'Yuen Long!' came his reply as he dashed down into the MTR station.

The day before, I had decided to attend a pro-government rally organised in support of the police. I did this knowing full well that Beijing had been blaming the continuing protests on the work of hostile 'foreign forces' trying to foment trouble in Hong Kong; indeed, several of my Western friends who had either reported on or attended the protests had already been accused in pro-Beijing chat groups of being covert CIA agents — a charge they seemed to level at any foreigner appearing at a protest.

The rally took place at Tamar Park, the day overcast with dark, thundery skies that matched the mood of the crowd. The crowd was large, easily in the tens of thousands, although the suspicion on the anti-government side had always been that attendees at these protests were paid for their attendance. Certainly, attendance was highly organised and coordinated, a top-down approach to protest compared to the bottom-up, organic nature of the pro-democracy protests. Many protesters on this day had been bussed in, and they congregated under banners representing various mainland friendship and clan associations such as the Hong Kong–Shenzhen Association,

Hong Kong–Zhejiang Province Association, or the Taipo District Clansman Association. They thanked the police officers on duty as they passed by, and told them to 'Add oil!' Some posed for photos with the police, who gladly obliged.

This was a much-bigger-budget production than any of the pro-democracy rallies I had attended, with multiple big video screens, a massive sound system, and rows of portable toilets. Out on the harbour, five fishing trawlers festooned with banners of support ('Protect Hong Kong!') circled and blew their horns: fishermen, along with Hong Kong's rural communities, have traditionally formed part of the pro-Beijing support base.

At the entrances to the rally, participants were handed free copies of the pro-Beijing newspaper *Ta Kung Pao*, its front page containing an aggressively anti-violence message: 'Kick Out Violence!' read the headline — oxymoronically and apparently unironically — with a cartoon of a black-shoed foot kicking a caricature of a yellow-hard-hatted protester through the air, sending him flying across Victoria Harbour.

Much of the crowd appeared to be elderly, and either rural or working class. (A subsequent survey conducted by Hong Kong university researchers would provide data to support this: the majority of those who said they supported the police fell into the 65-plus age bracket and/or had only primary school education.)[13]

If over the last month I had seen protesters fighting to uphold the 'two systems', here, the 'one country' side of the equation was on display. I had the distinct feeling that if Hong Kong was fated to become just another Chinese city — as many had hand-wringingly warned — this crowd would have been just fine with that.

The crowd was also immediately hostile to a foreigner in their midst. Was I another CIA agent there to stir up trouble? The fact that I was taking photographs and messaging on a mobile phone immediately aroused further suspicion. I noticed people around me none-too-subtly taking my photo and distributing it on chat groups. Young rural toughs in blue 'marshals' T-shirts followed me threateningly as I wandered around the rally. I realised that this was the first time I had ever felt unsafe in twenty years in Hong Kong — even after having been caught in a riot-police baton charge in Mong Kok, and being tear-gassed in Admiralty.

The atmosphere was a stark contrast to the cheerful, largely festive feel of the pro-democracy marches. This crowd was filled with self-righteous anger. A speech delivered from the main stage by Arthur Shek Kang-chuen, associate publisher of *Hong Kong Economic Times*, was typical of the day. Shek argued that the protesters deserved a beating, and was eerily specific about how it should be done: with bamboo canes. 'You should say no to those masked, black-shirted people,' he said. 'Do you have a cane at home? Get one, a long one ... Teach your son a lesson.'

His words would prove to be prophetic.

As the retreat from Sheung Wan was underway that Sunday evening on 21 July, the most distressing and violent scenes of the night were only just occurring: in Yuen Long, a satellite suburb in the north-west corner of Hong Kong towards the Chinese border, white-shirted gangs apparently affiliated with triads had attacked commuters coming off the MTR trains at Yuen Long station. They targeted young people in particular, people wearing black T-shirts, and anyone who looked like a protester, but their attacks were indiscriminate as they lashed out at people in the station and even burst into a train stuck at the platform and attacked passengers inside. The vicious attacks hospitalised forty-five people. Many injuries resulted from the weapons the thugs wielded: bamboo canes.

Meanwhile, calls to police went unanswered, and when two

police did appear at the station, they made a quick retreat when they saw they were outnumbered. Riot police only appeared an hour or so later, by which time the gangs had retreated to nearby villages. The commanding officer on the scene was recorded as sarcastically replying to media enquiries about the tardiness of the police response: 'I don't know if we were late … I couldn't see my watch.'[14] Police were later photographed chatting with armed, white-T-shirted men in the area, while they claimed publicly they were not able to find the perpetrators.

This incident would mark another rupture in the relationship between the Hong Kong Police Force and the community, one that had been growing more fractured by the week. The Yuen Long incident provoked a deep and burning fury in the Hong Kong populace.

In the aftermath of the incident, and in the light of his remarks at the Saturday rally, Arthur Shek was forced to resign his directorship of the *Hong Kong Economic Times* group. Another controversial figure implicated in the incident was Junius Ho, a local pro-Beijing legislator known for his divisive and inflammatory rhetoric. Shortly after the Yuen Long attacks, videos circulated of Ho smiling and shaking hands with white-shirted men in the area that Sunday evening, some of whom were identified as being part of the gang. The footage immediately prompted rumours that Ho had instigated the attacks. Ho later gave a press conference saying he had merely been in the area after dinner and did not know or organise the attackers. He added that the attackers were just 'defending their homes', and suggested that blame should lie with pan-democratic legislator Lam Cheuk-ting for 'leading protesters' to the area. Lam had happened to be on the train going home, and was injured in the attacks. A few days later, the graves of Ho's parents were vandalised and sprayed with graffiti such as 'Government-Triad Collusion'.

The next day, Carrie Lam, flanked by her entire team of ministers, gave an ashen-faced press conference. Lam renounced violence on all sides, but provoked ire by denouncing the defacement of the national emblem at the Liaison Office before mentioning the attacks in Yuen Long, appearing more concerned about damaged property than injured citizens. The gathered media were visibly angry, and the press conference became heated as reporters demanded explanations and at least some expression of basic human emotion from the robotic Lam. Nabela Qoser, a Hong Kong–born ethnic Pakistani reporter renowned for her fluency in numerous languages, berated Lam in Cantonese in a phrase that became legendary: '*Gong janwaa, mgoi nei.*' ('Please, talk like a human being!')[15]

Lam and her entourage walked out of the press conference a few minutes later, the press pack continuing to bellow at their backs.

8

THE RIGHT TO THE CITY

'Free Hong Kong! Free Hong Kong!' I looked down from the departure level of Hong Kong International Airport to the arrivals hall below, the vast space filled with thousands of young protesters in black T-shirts, waving signs and chanting, 'Fight for freedom! Stand with Hong Kong!'

This protest, on the Friday night of 26 July, had been organised by airline-industry unions together with online activists under the slogan *'Wo Nei Fei'* ('Fly With You'), a pun in Chinese for the protesters' self-descriptor *'Wo Lei Fei'* ('peaceful, rational, nonviolent').

The protesters greeted arriving passengers with chants and banners in multiple languages, from English to French, and from Spanish to Japanese. They handed out flyers styled as tourism brochures that explained their cause and sought tourists' support. One brochure with the unexceptional cover 'Discover Hong Kong' opened to reveal surprising images of police brutality and triad attacks. Another was a 'tourist map' of Hong Kong highlighting key protest sites, with a caption explaining: 'Here are some sites that best represent Hong Kong, where you can experience the determination of the anti-extradition bill movement.'

They chanted protest slogans and sang 'Do You Hear the People Sing?', the rousing chorus echoing across the arrivals hall. They were also entirely peaceful, nonviolent, and civilly obedient: the protest was in the arrivals area only, passages were left through the crowd to enable tourists to pass safely, and the protesters made no attempt to delay departures or inconvenience passengers.

Flight attendants, pilots, and air-traffic controllers all joined the protest, alongside the young activists who heeded the online calls to travel out to the airport to join the sit-in. I saw that many of the protesters, even though they were not wearing airline uniforms, were carrying telltale black luggage with 'crew' tags, and many still wore their regulation hair and make-up.

A recording emerged of an anonymous Cathay Pacific pilot's in-flight announcement upon arrival in Hong Kong that evening, in which he calmly explained that arriving passengers would see some protesters in the terminal and that they should not be alarmed, and encouraged them to approach and speak to the protesters if they wanted to learn more. He finished his announcement with a phrase in Cantonese: '*Heunggong yan gaa jau! Maansi siusam!*' ('Hong Kongers, add oil! Take care!')[1] The recording quickly went viral.

As a strategy, the airport protest was brilliant. It was visually striking — a mass of bodies in the cavernous airport, a made-for-television moment. And, with its abundant transportation links, the airport was easily accessible to protesters, and also not susceptible to violent dispersal by police: it was hard to imagine police firing tear gas inside a busy airport terminal full of innocent travellers. Both its media-friendly nature and the location meant that the protest was effective in spreading the protesters' message globally. The action centred on the tourism- and trade-focused economy of Hong Kong, exposing its vulnerability and exploiting the global nature of the city to win attention to the protesters' cause. This was to be another of the tactics coming out of the Hong Kong protest laboratory that would be emulated by activists overseas: Extinction Rebellion protesters undertook their own airport protest in London later in the year.

But at the airport, the protesters were also expressing another demand, one that had connections back to the Umbrella Movement: they were staking their claim to their right to the city.

The right to the city was a theory first proposed by French sociologist and philosopher Henri Lefebvre, writing in Paris in the late 1960s, a time of significant social upheaval. Lefebvre bemoaned the collapse of the traditional city, as industrialisation and commodity capitalism engendered urban sprawl, industrial zones, the growth of gated communities, the death of the high street, and the rise of the mega-mall — a result of the twin forces of ghettoisation and gentrification. In the face of this decline, Lefebvre envisioned a revolutionary right to reclaim the city from these forces of commodity capital, a right he declared as the 'right to the city', which, he said, was 'like a cry and a demand ... a transformed and renewed right to urban life.'[2] It was an idea that retained currency fifty years later: many of the twenty-first century's mass social movements, particularly those of the Occupy Wall Street era, could be understood as articulating a demand for the 'right to the city'.

In Hong Kong, the sense of identification with the city runs deep. The space of the city and the space of the political territory known as 'Hong Kong' overlap entirely: Hong Kong is the city, and the city is Hong Kong. In Hong Kong, citizens are referred to in Cantonese as 'si man', a term that contains within it the very word 'city' ('si man' literally means 'city person'), which in Hong Kong's identity politics serves to distinguish the citizens of the city of Hong Kong from the citizens of the wider Chinese nation, officially referred to as gongmin (literally, 'common person' or 'public person'). 'People of the city' thus serves as a label of identity for Hong Kongers. Even the government's branding of Hong Kong placed the city at the heart of Hong Kong's conception of itself: 'Asia's World City'.

However, to assert a right to the city raises an inevitable question: 'Whose rights and whose city?' — the rights of the protesters at their barricades, or those of the citizens who objected to them, or of the authorities who cleared the roads? All of them were exercising their respective rights. Marxist geographer David Harvey has argued that the more important aspect of the right to the city is not merely a physical right of access but a collective right to participate in the continuing production of the urban space, a right to 'reinvent the city more after our hearts' desire'.[3] To see the right to the city in this way neutralises the question of mutually conflicting claims of right of access to the city's spaces, and gives way to an expression of desire rather than a territorial claim, a right of democratic participation. In Hong Kong, a city ruled in effect by an alliance between the local government, the Beijing authorities, and the city's all-powerful real estate tycoons, the system by its very design excludes the people from participating in the production of their urban space.

The concept of urban space was central to the Umbrella Movement, which saw contesting political views represented in space. On the side of the protesters, as an occupation movement, the logic of their protest was centred around space — that is, to occupy and disrupt the space of the city until their demands were heard and addressed. Opposition to the protesters was similarly expressed in spatial terms, through incursions into the occupied spaces or legal action in the courts to obtain injunctions to reopen the blockaded roads. The government remained focused on clearing the occupied spaces, regarding this as equivalent to resolving the political impasse.

Similarly, in 2019, the government spent significant time complaining of the disruption arising from protesters' occupation of space.

———

How could it be otherwise in Hong Kong? As one of the most dense-ly populated cities on the planet, with the world's most unaffordable housing — raising ever-present concerns about land use, property prices, and the real estate tycoons' control of the economy — space is a fraught issue and a source of anxiety for Hong Kong residents. In this context, and with the connection in the political imaginary be-tween public space and public participation in politics harking back to the Athenian agora, it is not surprising that public space becomes a site for political contestation.

Yet in Hong Kong there is a distinct lack of genuine public space: there is no 'public square'. Most of the city's space has been packaged by the government and sold to the real estate developers, leaving Hong Kong's protesters to occupy the roads, footbridges, footpaths, underpasses, and staircases of the city. Navigating this geography — walkways and tunnels, staircases and escalators — can sometimes feel like being trapped in an Escher print.

It is for this reason that Hong Kong's protesters are forced to make their own agora. In the Umbrella Movement, the protesters did that literally by creating Umbrella Square in the middle of occupied Harcourt Road. In 2019, protesters turned to a ready-made public forum: the shopping mall.

Hong Kong has the highest concentration of malls in the world, partly a result of a unique alliance between the government and real estate tycoons in building the city's infrastructure. Hong Kong's subway system is funded by granting the subway operator, MTR Corporation, property-development rights for the land above its sta-tions. MTR in turn partners with the tycoons to build vast residential and commercial developments — shopping-mall podiums with residential and sometimes office towers — directly connected to the stations. Much of the city's population lives on top of, or effectively inside, a shopping mall.

As a result, the mall plays a unique and all-encompassing role in daily Hong Kong life. Malls are shopping destinations for everything from daily necessities to luxury goods; recreation spaces; and the primary places where people socialise with family and friends. Hong Kong apartments are generally too small for entertaining guests: malls host children's parties, graduation lunches, and wedding banquets. And in Hong Kong's humid, tropical climate, the air-conditioned, temperature-controlled atriums, courtyards, and squares in the malls provide respite from the heat and shelter from tropical downpours. Malls are also the passageways through which citizens pass from public-transport hubs to their homes. Many of the malls are required, under the terms of their leases, to keep their doors open twenty-four hours a day for public passage. This contractual requirement is essential: although they masquerade as public spaces, these urban enclaves are privately owned and fall under the control of mall management.

During the protests of 2019, in a unique Hong Kong–style evolution of the right to the city, the malls became sites of contestation: protesters began to assert their 'right to the mall'.

On 14 July, a large protest took place in the Sha Tin district. As riot police closed in, protesters fled through the adjacent New Town Mall packed with shoppers and diners on a Sunday evening, traditionally a family day out in Hong Kong. Police pursued the protesters into the mall, firing pepper spray and beating protesters with batons. Protesters responded by throwing umbrellas and bottles at police. The violence left blood on the mall's polished floors, and police were pictured slipping on slicks of their pepper spray. Meanwhile, Sunday-night shoppers and diners, including families with small children, cowered, horrified by the melee going on around them. The fact that all this occurred with not a single window broken nor a shop looted was testament to the discipline of the protesters: they even cleaned up the mess afterwards.

Mall management subsequently found themselves caught up in the fallout from the incident as protesters blamed them for the clashes, alleging that mall staff had led the police into the mall. The mall management issued a statement denying the charges, but its office nevertheless became a target of further protests.

Other malls took note of the New Town Mall experience. In Sham Shui Po, when riot police pursued protesters who had taken refuge in another nearby mall, staff refused the police entry. After protesters threatened a flash-mob protest targeting malls operated by Wharf, the property developer posted signs in its malls reading: 'We will do our best to ensure customers' safety in the mall. Police, please do not enter unless crimes happen.' The protests were called off.

After protesters had used the Pacific Place mall as a refuge during the clashes in Admiralty on 12 June, online forums had praised the mall's management. During a subsequent 'silver-haired' march of elderly protest sympathisers, Pacific Place staff helped with crowd control to facilitate the elderly protesters' passing comfortably through the air-conditioned space, earning cheers from the crowd. One elderly protester gave a thumbs-up and said to me, 'This is the best mall in Hong Kong!'

However, as Beijing intensified its pressure on businesses to support the government, the mall operators were forced to fall into line. When New World Development apologised to protesters for allowing riot police to use the public toilets in one of their malls, the company drew sharp criticism on social media in mainland China, and was forced to apologise for their apology, stating: 'We are against violence, and support Hong Kong police in carrying out their duties.'

It was yet another manifestation of the age-old conflict between profit and principle, with the malls, many of which rely on revenue from mainland tourists, being pushed to defer to the wishes of their largest market over those of the communities who live their day-to-day lives on top of, and inside, their premises. This dynamic made the malls a microcosm of one of the underlying anxieties driving the protests: the creeping mainlandisation of Hong Kong that had left residents feeling squeezed to the margins of their own city.

Other malls that earned the protesters' ire were subject to destructive attacks. In November, baton-wielding undercover police officers arrested protesters who were vandalising pro-government stores in Festival Walk in Kowloon Tong. As bystanders tried to intervene to prevent the arrests, riot police stormed in and forcibly cleared the mall. In retaliation for mall management's failure to keep out the police, protesters broke into the mall after hours, smashing glass barriers and escalators, and setting a four-metre-tall Christmas tree ablaze. The mall was forced to close for two months to carry out repairs.

Yet, as well as defending — or punishing — the malls, protesters also used them as sites of protest, in sometimes surprising ways. Shopping malls took on a role as mid-march refuges for protesters during the oppressively hot Hong Kong summer days. Many protests began or ended at malls, particularly in the early days of the protests when the MTR had not stopped servicing stations adjacent to protests. This created the unique Hong Kong experience of finding oneself lost in a mall and unable to find the protest. Protesters targeted mall-management or pro-government businesses, but also gathered in malls to conduct mass singings of the protest anthem 'Glory to Hong Kong', reclaiming their right to use these privatised spaces as public squares.

It was just one of the many ways in which protesters subverted the urban infrastructure to put it in service of their protest. Throughout the 2019 protests, protesters 'deconstructed' the city's fabric. Metal pedestrian barriers, ubiquitous along Hong Kong's roadsides, separating footpaths from the traffic, were dismantled and then reconstructed into barricades across streets, or occasionally fashioned into battering rams. Traffic signs were removed and, with the addition of a few zip ties as handles, converted into makeshift shields. As police increasingly deployed water cannons and armoured 'barricade-smashing' vehicles to clear the streets, protesters dug up vast quantities of the city's brick paving — Hong Kong footpaths are generally brick-paved rather than cement — broke them into chunks, and tossed them onto the roads, effectively blocking access for the police vehicles. These broken chunks of brick were also used as missiles directed at police lines. As large patches of sand were exposed along the footpaths where the brick pavers had been torn up, a slogan from another youth rebellion, fifty years earlier, appeared just as apt here: '*Sous les pavés, la plage!*' ('Under the paving stones, the beach!')

And, as in Paris, the response from the government was an attempt at a kind of Haussmannisation of Hong Kong. Just as George-Eugène Haussmann, under the rule of Napoleon III, attempted to frustrate barricade-fighting by carving wide boulevards through the narrow, winding streets of nineteenth-century Paris, so too the Hong Kong government, when it became familiar with the protesters' tactics, begun to take countermeasures, stripping the city of the urban hardware that the protesters so readily recontextualised for the purposes of their barricade resistance. The authorities pre-emptively removed metal road barriers and fencing, replacing them with red plastic tape, and removed rubbish bins from the streets. They laid down glue on footpaths to prevent the removal of brick pavers, and filled in the gaps where the pavers had been removed with roughly poured slabs of plain cement.

Ultimately, the fundamental difference between the Umbrella Movement and the 2019 protest movement revealed itself in the two movements' respective approaches to space.

The Umbrella Movement focused on blocking flows: by occupying the roads, preventing the flow of traffic, people, goods, and, ultimately, capital through the city, they hoped to exert political pressure to achieve their aims. But Hong Kong is a city designed to facilitate just such flows, and by fighting against those flows the protesters were fighting against the very nature of the city — a fight destined to failure. At the same time, their static, fixed-space strategy of occupation engaged only those citizens who chose to enter and engage the protest spaces, limiting the ability of the Umbrella Movement to engage the broader community. It was too late in their campaign before the Umbrella Movement activists attempted to take their cause out into the community by setting up booths in the housing estates, transport hubs, and shopping malls of Hong Kong's satellite suburbs.

The protesters in 2019 understood that, if they were to be more successful in rallying support for their cause, they would need to extend their occupation so that protest spaces metastasised across the city, rather than remaining as isolated enclaves. Rather than trying to block flows, the 2019 protesters, with their 'Be water' approach, flowed throughout the city, engaging the populace where they found them. They shifted the target of their protest actions from the flows themselves to the natural end points of those flows: the terminals. In the terminals of the modern city — the airport, the MTR, shopping malls — the protesters found vulnerable targets that could be paralysed quickly and to great effect, without the need for a permanent blockage.

Towards midnight on that late-July Friday night, the crowds at the airport began to thin out and the chants to die down as protesters left to catch the last trains and buses home. Not long after that, like water, they were gone, and the echoing arrivals hall was empty, save for a few travellers pushing their luggage trolleys beneath the posters and banners still festooning the walls.

9

BLOOMING

If the protesters' urban interventions could be understood as 'rewriting the text of the city', the protesters also wrote texts onto the surfaces of the city. Indeed, during 2019, the surface of the city became a great palimpsest of protest texts.

Hong Kong had historically been a city free of graffiti, a city as *tabula rasa*. The only texts the city bore were the advertising billboards and illuminated bus shelters ubiquitous across the postmodern urban landscape. Even the city's historic neon signs — which once hung so precariously from shop fronts along the 'Golden Mile' of Nathan Road, bathing the night in multicoloured glowing words and slogans — had gradually been removed in the early years of this century.

The Umbrella Movement created a new kind of textual space in Hong Kong. Within the occupied spaces of 2014, it seemed that every available surface — from walls to pavements, from bridges to traffic barriers — bore texts in the form of banners, posters, flyers, chalk drawings, or Post-it Notes.

The very boundaries of the Admiralty protest site were demarcated by texts. On the barricades at the eastern end of the occupied area were large characters reading '*Gwongming Leoilok*' ('Candid and

Upright'), quoted ironically from a police spokesperson who was justifying police actions. At the western border of the site, a large banner read in English 'Welcome to the Hong Kong commune', a reference to historical parallels in Paris. Text also defined the occupied space in three dimensions: in addition to the vertical spaces (walls, columns, traffic barriers) being covered in posters and flyers, the horizontal spaces (road surfaces and footpaths) were inscribed in chalk. At Umbrella Square at the heart of the occupied area, banners were suspended from the pedestrian footbridges overhead, while oversized yellow umbrellas were hoisted around lampposts, defining the volume of the space. Together with the orange glow of the streetlamps at night shining through an often misty humid atmosphere, this created a three-dimensional affective space into which one would pass when entering the occupied areas. The saturation of texts meant that entering an occupied area involved entering into and being embraced by this semantic textual space.

Many of the texts were intertextual or dialogic in nature: quoting, citing, or riffing off official discourse; historical, literary, or cultural allusions; images from popular culture; or even images and texts generated by the movement itself in a self-reflexive turn. This cacophony of voices became a stance of free expression against the unified voice with which the government and Beijing sought to speak; it became a case of democratic dialogue pitted against authoritarian monologue.

But leaving the occupied spaces meant leaving the textual world behind. And when the Umbrella Movement ended and the sites were cleared, so too were these texts. The Umbrella Movement texts were all temporary: the posters were torn down, the chalk washed away. There was little graffiti. After its 'erasure', the Umbrella Movement left few visible traces: it made its absence felt in the empty spaces left behind, dead space replacing the vitality of the once-living occupation villages.

With the protests in 2019, texts once again flourished across the city, but this time in more permanent form. For the first time, Hong Kong became an extensively graffitied city, as protesters left slogans spray-painted on walls, traffic dividers, bus shelters, and road surfaces across the city's districts. A variety of slogans from the movement, in both Chinese and English, were graffitied, but one slogan was by far the most common: 'Reclaim Hong Kong! Revolution of our times!'

One way in which this re-textualisation of Hong Kong occurred was in the resurrection of the Lennon Walls. The Umbrella Movement's Lennon Wall had been in just one location, in Admiralty, but in 2019 Lennon Walls spread across the city. Responding to exhortations to let the Lennon walls *pindei hoifaa* ('bloom everywhere'), any vertical surface in a highly trafficked location — on footbridges and in underpasses, on columns and walls outside stations — became an opportunity for a Lennon Wall. The larger Lennon Walls, such as the monumental Lennon Tunnel at Tai Po, became sites of pilgrimage in their own right, with people travelling from across town to visit.

They were decorated with thousands of Post-it Notes — some used to write small messages, some compiled into impressive mosaics of pixel art — as well as an ever-rotating series of posters, flyers, artwork, and sometimes even installations or works of sculpture. Some art was pre-printed, some hand-drawn, some graffitied directly onto the walls. The walls also served as community noticeboards, featuring advertisements for upcoming rallies or other planned protest actions, information about recent events, and, invariably, various forms of protest propaganda. Posters criticised the government and police, paid tribute to protesters who had lost their lives, and propagated the latest conspiracy theories.

Other posters depicted ever-growing chronologies of key events in the movement, with accompanying photographs. There was a sense that history was being lived, and that protesters were writing the narrative of that history in real time. Lennon Walls were sites where this narrative was inscribed, circulated, and socialised; where events on the streets were given context and meaning.

This conscious control of the historical narrative was also seen in the convening, beginning in early August, of weekly citizen press conferences. These press conferences, announced via chat group and hosted by a rotating cast of usually masked and anonymous activists, were given sometimes overly elaborate titles — 'The Crusade of the Aggrieved: on the treacherous shards of Carrie Lam's lies' or 'Hong Kong's Humanitarian Hellfire: the outcry of the "Water" amid police brutality and moral corruption', to give two examples — but the purpose was quite serious. These press conferences presented the protesters' narrative, as a counter to the official narrative being propagated by daily police media conferences and government press releases. Spokespeople directly engaged with and argued against the government characterisation of events; victims of police violence gave personal testimony; and young protest leaders put forward their political positions. This was another way in which the protesters wrote their own history, and wrote their texts into the mainstream media narrative. Local and international media regularly attended, and reported on, these citizen press conferences.

Following on from a form of cultural production begun in the Umbrella Movement, much of the protester artwork appearing on the Lennon Walls involved self-reflexive images of the protest movement, often appropriating other cultural figures and refashioning them in the likenesses of the protesters (for example, as characters in Hollywood's *The Avengers* or *Star Wars*, or Japan's *Neon Genesis Evangelion*). In producing these images, the protesters were self-mythologising, borrowing from mythologies past and present to build their own identity. Long a place comfortable with multiple identities and code-switching, Hong Kong was uniquely suited to these mash-ups of politics and popular culture. Hong Kong's protest artwork combined references to the gamut of global cultural production, from local Hong Kong cinema to Hollywood action movies, from Japanese anime to classical Chinese mythology, and simultaneously laid claim to all of them as the constituent elements of a unique Hong Kong culture.

Many of these images originated and were disseminated online in the form of memes: an image juxtaposed with text, usually humorous in nature. Memes are designed for rapid sharing via social media, and as they circulated among the community they worked to build a shared common understanding of events, as well as a collective sentiment. The humour in memes also provided some relief from the continuing trauma the community was experiencing.

The airport protest on 26 July saw the latest manifestation of the Lennon Walls: a number of protesters, dressed in black, with their faces masked and yellow hard hats on their heads, offered themselves as human Lennon Walls. They stood motionless as supporters affixed multicoloured Post-it Notes to their clothing, hard hats, and outstretched limbs. As one Human Lennon Wall reached capacity, others would volunteer themselves to join the line-up. Some wandered around the arrivals hall as mobile Human Lennon Walls.

In the course of the 2019 protests, the Lennon Wall was transformed from a *site* to an *idea*, an instrument and expression of protest, and became as a result significantly more powerful and enduring — and, ultimately, indestructible. One protester slogan read: 'You can tear down Lennon Walls. You cannot tear down ideas.'

Whether it was an online graphic printed out and pasted onto a Lennon Wall, or a meme printed on a T-shirt, many of Hong Kong's protest texts and artworks engaged in an interchange between the online and offline worlds, often to the surprise and delight of the artists who created the works. In June 2019, Kokdamon, a Hong Kong artist based in Switzerland, created a cartoon depicting the famous Tank Man of Tiananmen to commemorate the thirtieth anniversary of the Tiananmen Square Massacre. Some activist friends asked him if they could borrow the image for a rally in Hong Kong to mark the occasion, and from there the image took on a life of its own. Later in the year, it appeared on signs carried by protesters and on Lennon Walls. 'I never expected my image to spread in this way,' Kokdamon told me. Reflecting on the role that visual expression has played in Hong Kong protests, Kokdamon said, 'This has in some ways shaken the whole position and role of artists. It's not just artists responding, it's ordinary citizens — the people are the ones who are standing up and expressing themselves. It's beautiful.'

The narrow backstreets of Melbourne, Australia, famed for their lively street art, are a long way from the bustling streets of Hong Kong. It was here, in a quiet café on Flinders Lane, that I met dissident Chinese artist Badiucao. Originally from Shanghai, but resident in Australia for over ten years, Badiucao may at first blush have seemed an unlikely figure to be playing a key role in a Hong Kong protest movement.

But for Badiucao, Hong Kong was personal. In 2018, a major exhibition of his work set to be held in Hong Kong was abruptly cancelled following threats made to his family in the mainland. At the time, his situation was seen as yet another example of the broader erosion of freedom of expression and civil liberties in Hong Kong. It also, paradoxically, helped to forge a bond between the artist and the city. 'I have always received so much help and support from the Hong Kong community, both before and after my show was cancelled,' Badiucao explained. After the cancellation, supporters printed out posters of his work and pasted them across the facade of a state-owned bookstore. As he watched the events of 2019, Badiucao said, 'It's sad for me to witness these good people and this great community being destroyed. I can't stay silent in the face of that.'

Badiucao became extremely active during the 2019 protests, creating his satirical artworks for distribution online. His artwork often responded directly to events on the ground. On 1 July, within hours of Carrie Lam toasting the anniversary of the handover, Badiucao's version of the official photograph of Lam's toast, with symbols of the protests — yellow hard hat, umbrella, and raincoat — floating in a red sea of blood, was circulating online. Following the 21 July attacks in Yuen Long, he adapted the images of police standing and chatting to the white-shirted thugs to show them in a warm embrace, his take on the cosy relationship between police and the organised-crime gangs.

His art posed as much of a challenge to Beijing's authority in the city as did the black-clad youth in the streets: 'My artwork dissolves their authority. Satire, humour, and absurdity are extremely powerful in deconstructing the arrogance of power.' Badiucao's images moved fluidly between the online and offline worlds, often being printed out and pasted onto Lennon Walls across the city, or carried as posters in protest marches. Badiucao thrilled at the phenomenon: 'When my show in Hong Kong was cancelled, my gallery was stripped away from me. But now, with my work in the hands of the protesters out on the streets, the whole city is my gallery! I don't think any artist could ask for more than that.'

As the protesters inscribed the city, the authorities and their supporters became increasingly concerned with erasure. Graffiti was scrubbed by government cleaning contractors — never entirely cleanly, but instead leaving blooming, swirling clouds of smeared paint across the cities' surfaces, looking something like an abstract Chinese ink landscape.

Junius Ho and his fellow pro-Beijing politicians announced cleaning drives, and encouraged patriotic citizens to help clean up the city by tearing down Lennon Walls. On one occasion, several coachloads of mainland tourists were bussed in at the dead of night to destroy one of the largest Lennon Walls, at Tai Po. They tore down posters and festooned the walls with the national flags of the eight foreign nations that invaded China during the Boxer Rebellion era, an accusation of 'foreign interference' being behind the protests. They also left large funeral wreaths bearing the photographs of Hong Kong pro-democracy politicians and Taiwan's independence-leaning president, Tsai Ing-wen.

Word quickly spread among protesters online, and the next morning volunteers were hard at work scrubbing the walls to clean up the mess left by the pro-Beijing mob. By lunchtime, a new Lennon Wall was blooming again. The protesters retained the funeral wreaths, and replaced the photos with images of Carrie Lam and her cabinet. They did, however, make one addition: a sign reading, 'Thank you, mainland compatriots, for donating the flowers!'

10

THE BATTLE OF SHEUNG WAN

Another protest rally was organised for the afternoon of Sunday 28 July, a rally that began in an atmosphere of simmering anger. The wounds of the previous Sunday night's attacks in Yuen Long were still raw. The day before, tens of thousands had converged in that district to 'Reclaim Yuen Long' in a march that had been banned by police due to safety concerns. The atmosphere was tense, and many people felt nervous, given the attacks that had occurred the previous week. When a police car became trapped in the crowd and was set upon by protesters, the police moved in with tear gas, and pitched battles ensued.

Police had again objected to a march on the Sunday, but had permitted a rally to be held in Chater Garden, a paved public square in Central about the size of a football pitch. However, as the crowd swelled they spilled out of the garden, and began a march eastwards through Admiralty in the direction of Causeway Bay, overwhelming the roads and blocking traffic. This was not organised, and not permitted — no one seemed to know where they were marching to, or why. This was a spontaneous expression of defiance by the people, a message to those in power: *We own the streets. And we are not going away.*

The crowd arrived in Causeway Bay and began erecting barricades, but soon another idea emerged among the crowd and online, and — again, 'being water' — thousands descended into the MTR station, the trains filling with black-shirted protesters as they caught trains to Sheung Wan. There, they advanced towards the Central Government Liaison Office, the site of the previous week's vandalism. This time, the police were ready and waiting for them, with rows of riot police tens deep, backed up by squads of 'Raptors', elite police from the Police Tactical Unit who were trained to charge at high speed into crowds and to make arrests. As the crowds gathered, they began to chant at the police: 'Police–triad collusion! The evidence is clear!' ('*Ging hak hap-zok! Zinggeoi kokzok!*')

More barricades were built as the protesters faced off against police a block away from the Central Government Liaison Office. Police made several warning announcements over loudspeakers. And then, at seven o'clock sharp, the police charged. This unleashed a night of mayhem. Police launched tear gas, rubber bullets, and sponge grenades at the retreating crowd, and Raptors carried out lightning baton charges.

As the tightly packed crowd of protesters tried to flee down the narrow, winding Sheung Wan streets, the risk of the crowd panicking — and a stampede occurring — was acute. In response, the protesters seemingly instinctively developed a protocol to prevent that occurring: as the tear gas shells popped and smoked around them, the retreating crowd began to chant in unison, 'One, two, one, two!' ('*Jat, ji, jat, ji!*') and to march in time to the count. It was a brilliant use of the herd mentality — that natural tendency to act as one with a crowd — to positive effect and to avoid what could otherwise have become a deadly crush.

In response to the onslaught — and in a distinct escalation from the previous week — protesters showed a willingness to fight back.

From behind the protection of their makeshift shields — fashioned from planks of wood, the lids of hard-shell suitcases, even in one instance the roof of a telephone booth — the protesters hurled bricks at the police lines. Lengths of bamboo were ripped off the ubiquitous bamboo scaffolding on Hong Kong's construction sites and launched as javelins; again, a small number of petrol bombs were thrown.

Umbrellas were deployed as a universal tool: deflecting tear gas canisters and rubber bullets, shielding protesters from surveillance cameras as they tore up brick pavers or deconstructed metal traffic barriers to construct barricades, and deployed as an offensive weapon against police.

On this night, the crowd also appeared truly unified in an attire that protesters called 'full gear': yellow hard hats, eye goggles, and 3M gas masks with their distinctive bright-pink filters. In combination with their black-bloc attire, the protesters' visual identity was complete.

Police drenched the Sheung Wan district in tear gas, firing from the roof of a parking garage down onto the road, where sparks flew as the shells ricocheted off the bitumen. Countless ordinary civilians, going about their business on a Sunday evening in the district, could be seen suffering from the effects of tear gas. Indeed, given that most of the protesters were equipped with protective gear, civilians uninvolved in the protests were the main victims of the gas. Through the window of an adjacent McDonald's, I could see a table of foreign diners, handkerchiefs clutched over their noses and mouths. Out on the street, a couple struggling with luggage and a small child were trying to reach their hotel in the midst of the mayhem, their child crying in pain. A volunteer first-aider tended to the child while a protester helped the family reach their destination. Nearby, a group of nervous citizens asked gathered journalists whether it was safe to return with their children through the protest area to their home. From this point on, dodging tear gas would become an essential skill in navigating daily life in Hong Kong.

The protesters had developed their own means of dealing with the tear gas, and on this night those skills were on full display. While the frontlines gathered at the barricades facing police, firefighting crews were crouched about twenty metres behind them, holding orange traffic cones and bottles of water. As the tear gas shells dropped in and began to smoke, the firefighter crew leapt into action. They raced in to cover the smoking shell with the traffic cone, creating a 'chimney' that contained and funnelled the smoke away. Another team member then moved in to pour water into the cone and douse the shell, putting it out. Those without a traffic cone poured water directly onto the shells, or smothered them in wet towels.

As protesters became more experienced, other techniques evolved. One popular method involved a pair of barbecue tongs and a waterproof bag — the kind you might take on a diving trip, or an afternoon on a yacht — half-filled with water. The firefighter teams would pick up the tear gas shell with the barbecue tongs, drop it into the waterproof bag, seal the bag, and shake vigorously. The water would extinguish the burning shell, and any residual smoke would be trapped inside the airtight bag, to be safely released later on the sidelines.

Other nimble protesters, equipped with heat-proof gloves — the shells were burning hot — snatched up the shells and hurled them back towards the police lines, or to the side of the crowd, out of harm's way. Some used tennis racquets, badminton racquets, or even lacrosse nets to launch the tear gas canisters back at police. Viewed from the side, the scene was one of smoking shells being traded back and forth across the barricades. As the street slowly filled with growing clouds of smoke, the protesters continued to hold their ground, undaunted, moving through the smoke to dispose of the shells, reforming their lines, and gathering again at the barricades. And with their protective gear and their experience dealing with the gas and other police projectiles came an increasing insouciance. That night in Sheung Wan, amid a heavy barrage of tear gas and with police about to charge, a dedicated delivery man pushed a trolley piled high with loaves of bread through the crowd. As he struggled to make his way among the rubble of battle, a protester called out to those in his path: 'Hey! Look out for the bread!'

The battle raged for several hours. Finally, with word coming in that police were preparing to advance from both east and west in a kettling manoeuvre, the protesters retreated up the hill behind them into the Soho nightlife district. Civilian supporters gave directions to the protesters, pointing out a safe exit route that avoided the police lines. Safely up the hill out of the battle zone, the protesters changed out of their black bloc and packed their gear. A short while later, hundreds of young Hong Kongers dressed in ordinary civilian clothes — not a black T-shirt in sight — were streaming down the hill, like water, out of Soho and towards the Central MTR station or into a convoy of cars waiting to pick them up and 'take them home from school' — protester slang for the drivers who volunteered to shuttle protesters home.

As the youths passed, an old auntie emerged from one of the stores and called out to them, '*Siu sam aa!*' ('Take care!')

The events of the Battle of Sheung Wan that night set the template for the continuing skirmishes between protesters and police that would unfold in the months that followed, as the initially peaceful protest movement became mired in an escalating cycle of violence.

During almost every weekend from the beginning of August through to the end of November, protests took place that culminated in violent clashes between protesters and police. The protest actions were organised in different districts throughout Hong Kong. This was partly a necessity, as shutdowns of the MTR stations made it increasingly difficult for protesters to travel around town, making protests increasingly localised to the communities in their respective districts. But it was also a deliberate strategy to 'let flowers bloom everywhere' and to spread the message of the protests throughout the community.

These weekly protests would also refine the relationship between the frontline 'braves' and the 'peaceful, rational, nonviolent' protesters, not as factions but as parts of a unified and mutually supportive whole. Distinct and defined roles emerged, which could be inhabited by anyone wishing to take part in the protest movement, according to their ability and their desire.

The frontliners who geared up to clash with police were supported by the firefighter crews, who neutralised tear gas, and the engineers, who built barricades and deconstructed the urban hardware, refashioning it to support the protesters' efforts. Teams of volunteer first-aiders positioned themselves close to the frontlines, helping any protester or passing civilian affected by tear gas or pepper spray, as well as tending to more serious injuries. Scouts, equipped with binoculars, walkie-talkies, and whistles, kept lookout and reported police movements to the frontlines, blowing their whistles to warn of incoming police charges or water-cannon attacks. Further back, the logistics teams stocked up supply depots and formed the serpentine human chains that passed equipment to the frontlines.

Those with more formal roles were also regarded as supporters of the movement: pro-democracy legislators who would often attend protests to monitor police behaviour and mediate with police on behalf of protesters, and social workers who provided psychological support as stresses increased. Pro bono lawyers counselled arrested protesters, and even the media were co-opted by protesters who considered journalists (supposedly neutral and objective) as being within the ranks of their supporters.

Meanwhile, away from the streets, but no less vital to the cause were those referred to as the Keyboard Frontline: members of the publicity teams who produced the graphics and flyers publicising the movement and doing its propaganda work, and those whose IT skills formed the connective network that kept the whole movement together.

The weekly protests inevitably followed a number of set-piece acts, adhering to the classic three-act structure. They would begin with Act One, a peaceful rally or march. At a certain point, the rally would reach the point close to where police lines were established, which would usher in the climax of Act One: building barricades.

The barricades were built from dismantled and reassembled traffic barriers, construction-work dividers, rubbish bins, or whatever hardware was available, all bound together with zip ties. At one point in the protest, an architect circulated online a schematic for a 'better barricade'. The next weekend, it materialised in physical form on the street.

These barricades were ostensibly built to protect the protesters from police attack; but, while they did work to slow the police advance somewhat, they were rarely effective. Once a police charge began, they would tear through the barricades in a matter of minutes, and later the police equipped themselves with a barricade-crushing armoured car, the Unimog, which could plough directly through the barricades.

But the barricades were also an end in themselves. By defining the protest space, they were another way for the protesters to assert their right to the city. And the social practice of barricading, of building and manning barricades, acted to create what social scientists have called barricade sociality. Barricades produce 'an affective and visceral togetherness', academics Dace Dzenovska and Iván Arenas argued in their analysis of protest movements in Latvia in 1991 and Mexico in 2006. 'The pragmatic practices of building barriers, guarding streets, procuring food, or huddling together generated social relations that turned strangers into comrades and conjured up the revolutionary people.'[1]

After the barricade lines were established, and police faced off against them, the frontliners would move up to the barricades, and Act Two would begin: the clashes with police.

With every week that passed, the protesters refined and developed their tactics, improving their ability to resist police. In response, the police felt justified in using correspondingly increased levels of force to clear the protesters. The result was an ever-escalating cycle of violence. The weekly images of riot police battling crowds of youths throwing stones through clouds of tear gas were disturbingly reminiscent of other, less stable parts of the world — a far cry from the glittering international financial hub that Hong Kong had always thought itself to be.

Yet, watching the violence more closely, something else became apparent. The violence seemed almost choreographed: each side seemed to know exactly what moves the other would make, and reacted in time and in turn. This was a performative kind of violence: violence as theatre, or ballet. It also demonstrated that the protesters had become every bit as choreographed and disciplined as one of the world's most advanced police forces. The barricade sociality had given the protesters an identity, and forged them into a cohesive unit that could match the police play for play. And if the protesters' full-gear outfits were a uniform, they were also in this sense a costume. Some became increasingly elaborate in their theatricality, revelling in a dystopian post-apocalyptic sci-fi chic: this was a protest of cosplay.

That this was a kind of theatre was apparent from the euphemistic term that protesters gave to Molotov cocktails. They called the petrol bombs 'fire magic' ('*fo mofaat*'), and those who wielded them 'fire magicians' ('*fo mofaatsi*'). It was as if this was fire deployed as a special effect, as part of some kind of circus act, not as an act of violence against police, but as a performance. A fire magician explained the role of his petrol bombs as follows: 'If a bomb explodes near [the police], they'll step aside, and slow down. This won't really do them much harm, but ... at least it makes us feel better, that way we stand a chance.'[2]

The violent conflicts were also extremely discrete: on one street, protesters would be engaging in hand-to-hand battles with police, projectiles flying in both directions, barricades burning, tear gas billowing. And yet, just a few blocks away, ordinary life would be carrying on as normal, as elderly ladies shopped for vegetables in a street market, or people sat around an outdoor restaurant table sipping tea. It was another uncanny parallel between Hong Kong and the Paris of Victor Hugo's *Les Misérables*:

> Outside its rebellious districts nothing ... is more strangely untroubled than the face of Paris during an uprising. She quickly adapts herself — 'After all, it's only a riot' — and Paris has too much else to do to let herself be disturbed by trifles. Only the largest of cities can offer this strange contrast between a state of civil war and a kind of unnatural tranquillity ... barricades are besieged, captured and recaptured ... and two streets away one may hear the click of billiard-balls in a café.[3]

As our three-act play of Hong Kong protest reached its climax, the police would break through the barricades and charge towards the protesters, leading to the final act, Act Three. In this act, police would chase protesters through the streets, firing tear gas to clear the crowds and attempting to make arrests as the protesters fled down alleys and side streets. This final act would end with the protesters 'being water', and disappearing from the scene when they realised that the police had overwhelmed them and they could no longer resist without incurring the risk of arrest. The curtain would invariably fall on police lines facing an empty street, sometimes vainly firing a final few rounds of tear gas at a few lingering reporters and passers-by.

The morning after the Battle of Sheung Wan, on Monday 29 July, Beijing announced that a spokesman for the State Council's Hong Kong and Macau Affairs Office — the cabinet-level office with responsibility for Hong Kong policy — would give a press conference that afternoon. This would be the first time that a senior Chinese leader addressed the protests directly, and all of Hong Kong held its collective breath for the press conference set for three o'clock. The moment was awaited with a sense of trepidation, but also some sense of relief: for weeks, the Hong Kong government had essentially disappeared, with Carrie Lam appearing once a week to give a formulaic press conference condemning violence and calling for calm, while her other ministers stood glumly and silently by her side. Finally, we would have an authoritative statement on the fate of Hong Kong, some kind of decision about how to resolve the present crisis. Hong Kongers were braced for potentially paradigm-shifting news. It seemed that almost anything was possible, from the resignation of Carrie Lam, to the imposition of a curfew, to PLA troops on the streets. More to the point, with the Hong Kong government sidelined and the city now openly looking to Beijing to call the shots, were we already witnessing the end of One Country, Two Systems?

When he spoke, the spokesman, Yang Guang, struck a surprisingly conciliatory tone. Yang acknowledged the peaceful protests that had been held in opposition to Lam's extradition bill, and further acknowledged that Lam had suspended work on the bill as a result. That Beijing would publicly recognise the fact and effectiveness of political protest in Hong Kong was in itself remarkable.

He expressed support for Lam and her administration, but this was accompanied by a thinly veiled criticism. Yang said that there had been 'deficiencies' in the way Lam's administration had handled the extradition bill, and that it should 'reflect' upon its governing style. Not only was this sort of direct criticism unusual in official Chinese government rhetoric, but it also had some historical resonance: following the Article 23 protests, China's president, Hu Jintao, famously advised then-chief executive, Tung Chee-hwa, to 'identify his deficiencies'. Three months later, Tung had resigned.

Unfortunately, however, it appeared that Beijing was framing the problems largely in economic terms: spokeswoman Xu Luying focused on problems such as employment opportunities, social mobility, and housing affordability — all issues that Beijing saw as contributing to the disillusion among Hong Kong's youth. Beijing seemed to be hoping that the economic carrot would be sufficient to get Hong Kong back on track.

It was a position that Beijing and the Hong Kong government went back to again and again: the discontent in Hong Kong was all about the economy. The protesters were just young people frustrated that they couldn't get a foothold on the housing ladder. It was a convenient, self-soothing narrative that seemed to completely miss the point.

To be sure, the social inequality in Hong Kong did stoke some of the rage. A searing line from the rap song '5am Mini Bus' by local Japanese–Hong Kong rapper Txmiyama was scrawled by protesters along a concrete road barrier: '7k for a house like a cell and you really think we out here [are] scared of jail?'

Yet in months of protests, not once did anyone on the street chant the slogan, 'We want affordable housing!' If the protests were about the economy, one would have expected to see some expression of anti-elite sentiment, but no such expressions were evident. The protests were pointedly not anti-rich, but anti-Beijing. The boycotts and vandalism targeted tycoons and business because they supported the government, not for being owned by oligopolistic tycoons. On the contrary, the tycoons were, rather, seen as folk heroes, emblematic of the kind of success of which Hong Kongers were capable. A figure such as Li Ka-shing, who had come to be known as 'Superman' as he built up his self-made business empire, was revered for his business savvy, rather than reviled for exploiting the people.

By offering economic sweeteners to protesters demanding democracy, the government was offering precisely what they had not asked for. Or, as a protester put it to me one evening in Mong Kok, neatly skewering two Beijing narratives — that foreign forces were organising and funding the protests, and that the protests were all about housing affordability — in one acerbic line: 'Are you here to pay me? I'm only protesting until I've saved up enough money to buy an apartment.'

Another voice was heard for the first time in 2019 following the events of 28 July. That night, a prison letter from Edward Leung was published on his Facebook page. In it, Leung struck a less militant tone:

> With your love for Hong Kong, you have shown boundless courage, and rewritten Hong Kong's history. Of course, real justice is yet to come, and it is only natural that this may fill your hearts with fury. But I beseech you all not to be controlled by hatred and, in the face of peril, maintain a rational reflection ...

[P]olitics isn't just maintaining the support of your supporters, but winning the support of those who don't support you, to get them to change their minds and support your direction ...

So, if we hope that society can look with tolerance upon those who have been called 'riotous thugs' ... we must reflect upon our every word and deed, and consider whether it will bring us closer to or take us further from this goal.[4]

Leung concluded, 'I wholeheartedly pray that every Hong Konger can peacefully pass through this historic moment.'

It must have been an unusual time for Leung: stuck inside prison, yet knowing that thousands were on the streets, chanting his slogan, looking to him as the spiritual leader of their movement. One piece of protester graffiti, presumably written by a besotted fan, read: 'Edward Leung, I'll wait a lifetime for you.' And, as with so many other political prisoners across history, Leung's power and influence were growing with each day that he sat in his cell.

11

STRIKE!

In order to keep pressure on the government, activists announced a day of general strike on Monday 5 August, what they called the 'Three Strikes' ('*Saam Baa*'), referring to work stoppages, class boycotts, and market boycotts. The week leading up to that day would see a series of protest actions aimed at building momentum for the general strike.

On the morning of Tuesday 30 July, protesters disrupted MTR trains, blocking train doors at key stations during the morning rush hour to prevent trains departing. (It would later emerge that this was a rehearsal for the following Monday.) Wednesday saw a flash mob protest by workers from the financial-services industry: many wryly commented that the situation must be dire to have reached a point where even investment bankers were leaving their desks to join a political protest.

On the Friday night, a rally of civil servants was held in Chater Garden. A stern warning from the government that the civil service had an obligation to remain both neutral and loyal — the latter raising some eyebrows — did nothing to diminish the turnout, with participants overflowing into the surrounding streets. It is unclear how many of them were civil servants, but some certainly were, and many others were office workers who had emerged from the towers of Central after work. Young activists were there, helping to coordinate, and as the rally broke up for the night and people headed into the MTR, they led chants of: '*Singkei jat, baa gung!*' ('Monday, strike!')

On the Saturday, a protest rally in Mong Kok veered off its approved route and spread across Kowloon all the way down to the Tsim Sha Tsui waterfront, where some protesters removed the PRC national flag from a flagpole and tossed it into the harbour. From there, the crowd moved on to the main Cross Harbour Tunnel, one of three connecting Hong Kong Island to Kowloon, where they blocked the tunnel entrance, causing traffic chaos on both sides of the harbour. Half an hour later, like water, they moved on again, stopping by Tsim Sha Tsui police station, which was attacked with bricks, before the protesters settled back in Mong Kok, building barricades and preparing to face off with police, following the well-rehearsed script again.

Not far away, in the residential district of Wong Tai Sin, local residents were engaged in their own clashes with police. Police deployed tear gas and pepper spray at a transport interchange on the ground floor of a residential complex, with local residents who had come downstairs from their apartments in their slippers fighting back with wok lids. The fact that the police seemed to have radicalised ordinary people in the community was striking. As observers noted, these were not protesters; these were '*gaaifong*', people from the local neighbourhood.

Sunday saw more protest marches: one in the leafy Kowloon district of Tsuen Kwan O, and another in the more fashionable Kennedy Town area on Hong Kong Island, both areas home to middle-class families who turned out to march with their children.

Later that night, having moved on to Causeway Bay, protesters revealed yet another creative protest strategy, this time involving their use of barricades. Protesters blockaded the main roads around the

Cross Harbour Tunnel entrance on the Hong Kong Island side. As rows of police vehicles and riot police on foot massed at the far end of the blockaded road and prepared to move in, the protesters suddenly removed the roadblocks, releasing the pent-up cars and buses directly into the path of the approaching police and snarling them in traffic, enabling the protesters to make their escape.

Meanwhile, Beijing issued its furious response to the flag-removal incident during the previous day's protest. 'The ugly flag-insulting acts by a very small number of radicals showed once again that they have gone far beyond the realm of free expression and slipped into the abyss of criminality,' fulminated *Xinhua*, adding that the protesters' conduct had 'blatantly offended the state and national dignity ... and greatly hurt the feelings of the entire Chinese people, including Hong Kong compatriots.'[1]

Throughout the weekend's protests, marchers chanted a constant refrain: 'Monday, strike!' As the city braced for a day of disruption, many were reminded of the last time Hong Kong had faced calls for a general strike in the face of a city-wide uprising, over fifty years before.

In early 1967, with the Cultural Revolution raging across the border in mainland China, Hong Kong was rocked by a series of strikes by pro-communist trade unions, led by the Hong Kong Federation of Trade Unions. The disturbances began when, in April that year, the Hong Kong Artificial Flower Company, owned by plastics magnate Duncan Tong,[2] announced onerous new conditions for workers that would reduce wages and job security. Workers protested the new conditions and sought to negotiate with management; however, the company responded by dismissing over 600 employees, prompting strikes and protests outside the factory. The dispute escalated into violent confrontations that spread to nearby neighbourhoods in

Kowloon. Police and protesters clashed, and tear gas was used to disperse the crowds. In a dynamic that would be echoed over fifty years later, the use of excessive force by police to break up the demonstrations, including the beating of protesters violently with batons, further inflamed tensions. The trade unions called the police action a 'bloody suppression', and protesters posted slogans reading: 'Blood debts must be repaid in blood.'[3] In the face of police violence in 2019, protesters would use the same slogan.

In May, loyalist groups led and coordinated by the Hong Kong branch of the Xinhua News Agency (Beijing's unofficial embassy in pre-1997 Hong Kong) turned the focus of their protests to the British colonial authorities. Pro-Beijing protesters, brandishing copies of Chairman Mao's *Little Red Book*, besieged Government House, plastering the gates with Maoist big-character posters and shouting anti-British slogans. In Central, the Bank of China building broadcast revolutionary messages over a loudspeaker system, which the British authorities countered by installing their own loudspeakers on the nearby Government Information Services building and blasting out pop songs by the Beatles. Further support from the mainland came in the form of a front-page *People's Daily* editorial on 3 June 1967, calling on 'Hong Kong and Kowloon compatriots ... to answer the call of the motherland and smash the reactionary regime of British imperialism.'[4]

The chaos continued into the summer of 1967. Protests deteriorated into confrontations with police and further violence, and unions around the territory staged strikes and work stoppages, disrupting the government shipyards, mail services, and the textile industry. The industrial action culminated in a territory-wide four-day general strike called for the end of June. Workers from vital industries, including the transport, public utilities, dockyards, and food industries, joined the strike action in an attempt to bring the

British administration to its knees. Students from leftist schools joined a class boycott. Their aim was to replicate the great Canton–Hong Kong Strike of 1925, an anti-imperialist strike lasting some sixteen months that crippled the territory.

During the 1967 strike, transport was disrupted, with the bus companies, tramways, and ferries all grinding to a halt. Water supplies were cut, and stop-work actions affected Hong Kong's two electricity companies. Food supplies from the mainland, upon which Hong Kong was reliant, stopped for the duration of the four-day strike, causing food prices in markets to spike. On 2 July 1967, the leftists ended their strike, deeming it a triumph, with the *People's Daily* declaring that the strike 'badly shook the Hong Kong authorities and demonstrated the power of the workers'.[5] However, the reality was that the strike had little effect on the British administration, and thousands of striking workers were sacked.

The worst of the turmoil was yet to come. A week later, the first of what would become a series of terrorist bomb attacks struck Hong Kong. The bomb attacks became an almost daily occurrence on the streets of Hong Kong through to the end of 1967. Reports alleged that the bombs had been made in the classrooms of left-wing schools and planted indiscriminately on the city's streets.

Two incidents in particular provoked widespread horror, and quickly turned public opinion against the insurgents and in support of the colonial administration. On 20 August, an eight-year-old girl, Wong Wee-man, and her two-year-old brother, Wong Siu-fun, were killed by a bomb while playing outside their home in Ching Wah Street, North Point. Then, on 24 August, commercial radio host Lam Bun, who had been critical of the leftists, and his cousin, Lam Kong-hei, were attacked while driving to work: their car was firebombed, and the two men set on fire. Both died as a result of their injuries.

By the time order was restored in December 1967, fifty-one

people had been killed (including ten police officers), and 832 injured. Police claimed to have found over 8,000 suspected bombs, of which over 1,000 were genuine. Almost 2,000 people were convicted of various offences, including riot, unlawful assembly, and explosive offences.

In the wake of the 1967 'disturbances', as the colonial administration referred to them, the British significantly overhauled their governance of Hong Kong, in particular under the administration of governor Murray MacLehose, who took office in 1971. The 1967 disturbances had highlighted deep social problems in Hong Kong — poverty, inequality, a lack of labour rights, and inadequate education and housing — and prompted a wide-ranging policy response. The dissatisfaction over workers' rights was immediately addressed. Maximum working hours were reduced, and a raft of labour reforms — including improved health and safety standards, workers' compensation, and employment-contract protections — were introduced. MacLehose introduced numerous progressive social reforms as well, including public-housing programs, universal compulsory free education, and the provision of medical and social-welfare services. An urban district-officer system was established to improve engagement with the community. Chinese was formally recognised as an official language of Hong Kong, jointly with English, in 1974.

Another group that did well out of the events of 1967 were the Hong Kong businesspeople who established real estate companies in the wake of 1967 and profited as the economy recovered. They would go on to become the tycoons who control so much of the Hong Kong economy today. Chief among them was Li Ka-shing, who also made his start in the plastic-flower business. Li daringly snapped up property during the 1967 property slump, the foundations of a fortune that would ultimately make him Hong Kong's richest person.

The response to the 1967 riots was also a defining moment in the formation of a distinct Hong Kong identity. In order to win public support for their actions to quell the 1967 unrest, the colonial government appealed to a sense of community and citizenship among the local populace, encouraging people to think of Hong Kong as home. For much of the population who had fled hardships in the mainland and seen Hong Kong as only a temporary refuge, this came in parallel with a growing realisation that a return to the mainland was either impossible or unattractive. At the same time, the post-war baby-boom generation born in Hong Kong were coming of age, and had only ever known Hong Kong as home. All of these forces came together at this moment in Hong Kong's history to forge what would become a distinct people: the Hong Kongers.

Posters promoting the 5 August 2019 strike appeared online, styled as tourism advertisements for the various districts across Hong Kong where protest gatherings were scheduled to be held. 'Picnic in Tamar!' 'Go bike riding in Tai Po!' 'Play football in Tsuen Wan!' 'Go dancing in Tuen Mun!' 'Worship at the Wong Tai Sin temple!' Protesters were assuming the MTR system would be paralysed by the strike action, so the rallies would have to be local.

Early in the morning, prior to the commuting rush hour, activists again descended on the MTR system, swarming the platforms, blocking train doors to prevent departures, and rapidly bringing large sections of the MTR system to a halt. Tempers flared in some locations, leading to confrontations between activists and some commuters, but most were supportive and resigned in the face of the disruptions.

At the same time, news began to filter in from the airport: air-traffic controllers were calling in sick, and other aviation workers were joining the strike. Images of the departure board filling with 'Flight Cancelled' messages spread online as over 200 flights were cancelled.

The occupation camp in Admiralty during the Umbrella Movement.

The Umbrella Movement Lennon Wall in Admiralty.

'No extradition to China.' March of one million, 9 June 2019.

March of one million, 9 June 2019.

'Faan sung Zung.' March of one million, 9 June 2019.

March of two million, 16 June 2019.

'Five demands, not one less!'

Frontline 'braves' on the move in Wan Chai.

The frontline faces police, umbrellas and shields at the ready.

Protester 'firefighter' crews await incoming tear gas.

Protesters are enveloped in tear gas outside PolyU.

A footbridge burns during the siege of PolyU.

LEFT: Lady Liberty on display during a rally in Central.

BELOW: Mobile Lennon Walls at a protest at Hong Kong airport.

ABOVE: A volunteer first-aider's helmet.

RIGHT: 'If we burn, you burn with us.' Outside LegCo, 1 July 2019.

Many private businesses joined the strike action, while those who could do so chose to work from home. Even the Disneyland cast had reportedly decided not to report to work that day.

Imprisoned Occupy Central leader Benny Tai joined the strike action from prison by refusing to participate in prison-assigned labour tasks that day, and was reportedly placed in solitary confinement as punishment.[6]

In midmorning, Carrie Lam — having disappeared from public view since her disastrous press conference following the Yuen Long attacks two weeks earlier — emerged to give yet another stony-faced performance. Lam declared of the strikes: 'Such extensive disruptions in the name of certain demands or uncooperative movement have seriously undermined Hong Kong law and order and are pushing our city, the city we all love, and many of us helped to build, to the verge of a very dangerous situation.'[7]

She also condemned protesters for their use of Edward Leung's 'Reclaim Hong Kong! Revolution of our times' slogan, saying that the nature of the protests had changed into an anti-China campaign. The fact that protesters now had an audio recording of Lam uttering the slogan was put to quick use, however, and they gleefully played recordings of her chanting the slogan on a loop at protests later that day.

Lam's response drew exasperated responses even from pro-Beijing politicians, with DAB legislator Ann Chiang complaining on her Facebook page, '[Lam] raised many questions at the news conference, but where are the solutions?' In the face of one of the most significant days of civil disobedience in decades, with the city seemingly teetering on the edge of a precipice, Hong Kong's leaders appeared to have no policies to address the unrest, and nothing new to say.

At one o'clock in the afternoon, as the sun beat down on a blazingly hot, 34-degree tropical day, strike rallies began in seven different districts. The rallies almost immediately descended into conflicts with police, ushering in what became a long, violent, and chaotic day. Districts across Hong Kong boiled and raged all through the afternoon and into the night. In Wong Tai Sin and Tin Shui Wai, police unleashed vast quantities of tear gas, cloaking entire districts in clouds of gas for most of the day. In Admiralty, a hop-on, hop-off tourist sightseeing bus was stranded at a bus stop as protesters swarmed the roads outside government headquarters, making an incongruous sight when it provided shelter for frontline protesters as they dodged rubber bullets and threw bricks and petrol bombs at the police lines. Police stations became a focus for anger and attack, as protesters hurled bricks and other missiles, and police responded with tear gas, baton rounds, and rubber bullets. Tear gas was fired in fourteen out of Hong Kong's eighteen districts during the course of the day. The frustration and anger seethed on all sides, as reports emerged of triad gangs attacking protesters and members of the media in North Point, a stronghold for Fujianese gangs.

As the night wound down, many wondered how to assess the day's events. Certainly, the strike had succeeded in bringing the city to a standstill for a day; indeed, the city had threatened to spin out of control. It was difficult to assess how many had participated in the protests, given that they took place simultaneously in multiple locations across the city, and difficult to assess how many had decided to join the strike action, as opposed to those who were simply unable to get to work amid the disruption.

One of the key reasons the 5 August strike did not have a larger impact was that, unlike in 1967, the pro-Beijing Federation of Trade Unions, still the largest labour group in Hong Kong, did not support the strike action. It was a constraint that did not escape the attention of activists. In the months following the strike, a wave of new independent unions were formed, not only with a view to protecting labour rights but specifically to facilitate future strike action. 'We want to introduce a new culture that trade unions are not just about labour rights — they could also consolidate the voices of the industries to resist the authorities,' one union organiser told the *South China Morning Post*.[8] A protester pamphlet titled 'Organise Labour Unions; Everyone Strike', explained: 'Do you want to strike, but are afraid of being the only one? Actually many other people feel the same. Join a union, and you won't have to battle alone!' At least twenty-four new trade unions were established in 2019, almost double the number established the previous year, according to the Hong Kong Labour Department. New unions were established for hotel employees, information-technology workers, and hospital-authority employees, as well as a white-collar office workers' union. Dozens of others were planned as activists embarked on a campaign actively to encourage the establishment of new unions. If their campaign is successful, the next general strike organised in Hong Kong may look very different from that on 5 August 2019.

At the end of the day, the strike revealed nothing so much as the impotence of Carrie Lam, who angered the community all over again a few days later when she stated, in a press conference in reaction to the strike, 'A small minority of people ... did not mind destroying Hong Kong's economy, they have no stake in the society.' The protesters — many of whom were members of the younger generation, whose claim to a stake in the future of Hong Kong society was greater than anyone's — bristled at the characterisation. Just as maddening to many was Lam's refusal to offer any form of apology or justification for police behaviour that had horrified the wider community. Lam seemed to have a unique ability consistently to misread the mood of the city.

It seemed clear that Lam had long before been sidelined and was now reading from whatever script Beijing provided her. As the smoke cleared, and with Lam's impotence apparent to all, there was a sense that events in Hong Kong had reached a point where, one way or another, Beijing would have to intervene.

12

THINGS FALL APART

Speaking in Hong Kong on 1 July 2017, on the twentieth anniversary of Hong Kong's return to Chinese sovereignty, Chairman Xi Jinping issued a blunt warning:

> Any attempt to endanger China's sovereignty and security, challenge the power of the central government ... or use Hong Kong to carry out infiltration and sabotage activities against the mainland is an act that crosses the red line, and is absolutely impermissible.

Two years later, Hong Kong's protesters were getting dangerously close to — if not flagrantly stepping across — Xi's 'red line.'

The day after the 5 August strike, Beijing held another press conference, in which the tone was markedly harsher. 'Don't ever misjudge the situation and mistake our restraint for weakness,' warned State Council spokesman Yang Guang. 'Don't ever underestimate the firm resolve and immense strength of the central government.' It is unlikely that Yang was aware of the protesters' use of the *Hunger Games* slogan, 'If we burn, you burn with us,' but it was nevertheless ominous when he warned, 'Those who play with fire will perish by it.'[1]

On Wednesday of that week, Beijing's Hong Kong and Macao Affairs Office summoned fifty of Hong Kong's pro-establishment elites — lawmakers, businesspeople, and other community leaders — to attend a closed-door meeting across the border in Shenzhen. Zhang Xiaoming, the head of the office, addressing the meeting, said, 'The most pressing and overriding task at present is to stop violence, end the chaos, and restore order, so as to safeguard our homeland and prevent Hong Kong from sinking into an abyss.' He also said that there was clear evidence that the protests were a 'colour revolution', Beijing's term for any movement seeking regime change — and, therefore, an existential threat to the party.[2]

The meeting came with a none-too-subtle message: businesses and other Hong Kong leaders should ensure they publicly and unequivocally support Carrie Lam, her government, and the Hong Kong Police Force. Any public suggestions to the contrary would not be tolerated.

Protests that week culminated in another bloody day on Sunday 11 August, the most violent day yet in the 'summer of discontent', and a day that many referred to when it was over as Hong Kong's darkest day since 1967 (although there would be worse to come). As anger over police brutality boiled over yet again, protesters and police clashed in mobile protests across numerous districts, with local residents emerging to confront police, and protesters launching siege-style attacks on police stations and living quarters with bricks and Molotov cocktails. Police deployed large amounts of tear gas in return, and it seemed no place was exempt. Police fired tear gas down the main road of the Wan Chai bar district, much to the dismay of boozing expats. Across the harbour in Kowloon's busy Sham Shui Po shopping district, tear gas drifted across roadside fishball vendors, who were pictured stoically continuing to ply their trade, handkerchiefs clutched over their mouths. Most controversially, police even fired tear gas inside two MTR stations. The use of tear gas indoors or in any other poorly ventilated location contravenes manufacturers' guidelines, potentially increasing the concentration, toxicity, and, therefore, danger of the gas. In addition, given that the purpose of tear gas is to cause a crowd to disperse, it was unclear where the crowd in this instance was expected to disperse to, given that they were inside a subway station.

Elsewhere, police shot pepper pellets into a crowd at point-blank range in Tai Koo MTR station, and beat protesters with batons as they tried to flee down a steep escalator. In Tsim Sha Tsui, a first-aid volunteer helping the protesters was blinded in one eye after reportedly being hit in the face with a police beanbag round. The chilling image of the first-aider's cracked and bloodied goggles lying on the ground was circulated online, and the girl's injury became a potent symbol of police violence. The incident led to protesters adopting a covered-eye gesture to memorialise the incident, and numerous works of protest art were produced showing a girl with a bloodied, bandaged eye.

Meanwhile, in Causeway Bay, police disguised as protesters — wearing the protester uniform of black T-shirt and yellow hard hat — suddenly turned without warning on their neighbours in the crowds, leaping on them and effecting violent arrests. One particularly gruesome video captured by *Hong Kong Free Press* showed a protester crying for mercy as arresting officers ground his face onto the pavement in a pool of his own blood, his front teeth knocked out and a police knee on his head.

This controversial police tactic would have several consequences. It would, not surprisingly, stoke suspicion and paranoia among protesters, prompting attacks on civilians suspected of being undercover officers hidden among their number. (Indeed, it is likely to have been directly responsible for the events that occurred at the airport a few days later.) It would also give protesters a basis on which to disclaim any act apparently committed by a protester that turned out to be unpopular or unadvisable: it could be blamed on undercover police agents provocateurs. Finally, it would encourage the protester re-minder: 'Tuck your shirt in!' Undercover police were thought to be carrying hidden firearms in their belts, which could be obscured by an untucked shirt. The Hong Kong protesters soon appeared extremely well kempt.

On Monday 12 August, protesters announced another protest action at Hong Kong International Airport. This time, the tone was very different from the exuberant protest of a few weeks earlier. Then, the slogan had been 'Fly With You' ('*Wo Nei Fei*'). This time, the slogan was 'Suck With You' ('*Ho Nei Sak*'), the English being a pun on the word '*sak*', meaning 'jammed' in Cantonese. This time, the airport protest would be a blockade.

On Monday and Tuesday, protesters swamped Hong Kong's international airport, forcing a shutdown that left thousands of travellers stranded, with all inbound and outbound flights cancelled for the best part of two days. Protesters filled the check-in aisles and blockaded the entrance to the departure area with luggage trolleys. Some travellers tried to climb through the crowds of protesters blocking access to the security area, and were shouted at or jostled by protesters. But if the images of tearful and desperate foreign travellers begging to be allowed to board their flights was a bad look for the protesters, worse was to come.

On the Tuesday night, the airport protesters turned on two main-land Chinese men in the crowd, who, they alleged, were government agents. One of the men was carrying a mainland security-service ID card bearing a name that protesters said matched a name appearing on a database of Shenzhen police officers. They beat him senseless and dragged him, disoriented, around the stifling hot crowds in the departure hall for hours before first-aiders were able to extract him from the crowd.

The second man said he was a member of the media; but after arousing the suspicions of the crowd, he was searched and found to be carrying in his bag a blue T-shirt with an 'I Love HK Police' logo, an identical T-shirt to that worn by pro-Beijing thugs who had threatened protesters. The man was beaten and bound to a luggage trolley with zip ties, where video captured him announcing to the crowd in Mandarin: 'I support the Hong Kong Police. You can beat me now.' (*'Wo zhichi Xianggang jingcha. Ni keyi da wo le.'*) It soon emerged that the man, named Fu Guohao, was an employee of Beijing news/propaganda outlet the *Global Times*, with editor-in-chief Hu Xijin announcing on Twitter that Fu was a reporter with that paper, and demanding his release.[3]

In clashes at the airport that night, protesters threw bottles and projectiles at police, and a police officer pulled his service revolver on the crowd after being beaten with his own baton, snatched out of his hands by an angry protester.

As the situation at the airport spiralled out of control, there was a sense that things were falling apart in the protest movement, that a collapse in discipline had pushed events to a volatile and dangerous point — a point at which Beijing would have no choice but to respond forcefully. In a press conference following the airport attacks, a Beijing spokesperson said that the protesters in Hong Kong were 'showing characteristics of terrorism', a further escalation in rhetoric that indicated that Beijing was now viewing the situation in Hong Kong as a matter of national security. Beijing's tolerance was being pushed to the limit. A question was being asked ever more urgently: would Beijing send the People's Liberation Army into Hong Kong?

This was not idle speculation. Beijing and its proxies had been alluding to the availability of this option for some weeks. A few weeks earlier, a PRC Ministry of Defence spokesperson had said that PLA troops could legally be deployed in Hong Kong. This was essentially a restatement of the legal position under the Basic Law, but it was reported in the media with the tone of a threat.

The previous week, the *Global Times* released a video of People's Armed Police, or PAP, troops engaging in anti-riot drills. The officers faced protesters dressed in black and wearing yellow hard hats, and were pictured engaging in exercises in urban-battlefield settings, one prominently featuring a burned-out Hong Kong taxi. 'Disperse or face the consequences of your actions!' an officer announced over a megaphone in Cantonese. The implications of the video were not subtle.

Then, as the airport protests unfolded, official Chinese social-media accounts began to publish footage of thousands of mainland PAP forces arriving in Shenzhen in long convoys of armoured vehicles. By midweek, international media were publishing footage of the troops encamped at a Shenzhen sports stadium just across the border, a short drive across a bridge and down the highway into the heart of downtown Hong Kong.

It was into this turbulent atmosphere that the US president, Donald Trump, fired off a tweet in the early hours of Wednesday morning: 'Our Intelligence has informed us that the Chinese Government is moving troops to the Border with Hong Kong. Everyone should be calm and safe!'[4] Speculation in the international media reached fever pitch, as Hong Kong suddenly found itself contemplating the unthinkable.

There were many reasons why the unthinkable did not come to pass and, at least in the current environment, remains extremely unlikely.

Beijing is keenly aware that any deployment of Chinese troops in Hong Kong would mark the death of Hong Kong's status as an international financial hub. This would have catastrophic consequences for the Hong Kong economy, and the collapse of Hong Kong, together with the related international reaction, would most likely have a devastating economic impact on the rest of China as well.

Beijing also knows the impact that such deployment would have on China's reputation. China's leaders have been living in the shadow of the events of Tiananmen for thirty years. Accession to the World Trade Organization in 2001, a triumphant Beijing Olympic Games in 2008, and the continuing global outreach of the Belt and Road initiative were all steps in rebuilding China's global standing after being a pariah state in the bloody aftermath of Tiananmen. Now, Chairman Xi had a bold ambition of China being recognised as a global leader, on a par with — and ultimately eclipsing — the United States. All of this, and with it Xi's 'China Dream', would have been snuffed out the instant Chinese tanks crossed the Shenzhen River into Hong Kong.

That is not to say that Beijing would not be willing to bear these costs under any circumstances. As the party leadership showed in 1989, when faced with an existential crisis threatening their rule, no option was truly unthinkable. However, in the case of Hong Kong, it seems that there were only two circumstances in which Beijing would be prompted to take that step.

The first was if the Hong Kong government and police lost control of the city. Beijing has always maintained the position that it would not intervene so long as the local authorities were able to maintain order. The situation in Hong Kong, while volatile, was still a long way from the scale of the unrest in 1967, when British army troops were deployed to assist police. Indeed, the real question from Beijing's point of view would most likely be not the ability of the local authorities to maintain order, but their willingness to do so: however, there were no signs of any divergence of views between Beijing, the Hong Kong government, and the police.

Beijing's military planners may also have been aware that any such intervention would likely be extremely messy. The narrow, winding backstreets of Hong Kong would not easily accommodate tanks or armoured personnel carriers. PLA troops entering Hong Kong would be seen by most of the population not as liberators but as an occupying force, and any incursion may well have provoked the entire city into genuine revolt and sparked an urban guerrilla war of resistance.

Simply put, the situation in the Hong Kong streets in 2019 did not necessitate such a disruptive and risky intervention.

The second circumstance in which Beijing would feel obliged to intervene forcefully in Hong Kong was if there was any risk of 'contagion', of the unrest in Hong Kong spreading to the mainland and threatening the party's authority there. Again, in 2019 there were no signs that the situation in Hong Kong presented any kind of existential threat to Communist Party rule.

People in the mainland did not generally have a sympathetic view of Hong Kongers, regarding them as spoiled and ungrateful, and their protest demands as unrealistic. This impression went back at least as far as the Umbrella Movement, and continued into the 2019 protests. Among the more generous views was that Hong Kongers already enjoyed many freedoms that those on the mainland did not enjoy — such as the freedom to carry out the very protests in which they were engaged — and really had nothing to complain about. Less charitable, and notably gendered, views painted Hong Kongers as a version of a petulant child or ungrateful mistress, spoiled by their overindulgent parent or lover, but nevertheless pouting and complaining. These views, as well as the longstanding sense that Hong Kongers considered themselves superior to their mainland brethren, meant that there was little chance of a Hong Kong–inspired protest movement winning popular support on the mainland.

Even if the sentiment or inclination were there, China's internet-censorship apparatus was so highly developed, and Beijing's control over information flows into the mainland so near absolute, that Beijing could carefully manage any information mainland residents received about the situation in Hong Kong. In this regard, the events at the airport that week played right into Beijing's hands.

Following the attack on the Central Government Liaison Office in July, the full weight of the Chinese state propaganda machine had been unleashed upon the Hong Kong protesters. Official state media was blanketed with coverage critical of the protests — Beijing clearly had no fear of contagion. The *Global Times* adopted post–Cultural Revolution rhetoric in depicting four key Hong Kong pro-democracy figures as a 'Gang of Four Ruining Hong Kong'.

Beijing now released the shackles from China's heavily censored domestic internet, and images of the airport chaos — and, in partic-ular, its mainland victims — flooded Chinese social media, together with the caption: 'I support Hong Kong Police. You can beat me now.' The move further inflamed domestic Chinese sentiment against the protesters, and by extension against Hong Kong more generally. Beijing was not afraid of stirring up intra-ethnic animosity when it suited its own interests.

Eventually, this became couched in the Maoist terms of class struggle. Observers were surprised to hear Carrie Lam, in the course of a public statement in mid-November, describe the protesters as 'enemies of the people'.[5] It was classic party-speak, harking back to Mao's theory of contradictions, which held that anyone who sup-ported the party came within the category of 'the people', while all those who resisted and were hostile to the socialist revolution were 'enemies of the people'. It was a theory that had fallen out of fashion until having been recently revived by Chairman Xi. Lam's use of the phrase — surely not accidental, and occurring a week after she had visited Beijing and appeared in public with Xi — showed how Beijing was framing the Hong Kong problem. Those who were loyal to the party would be rewarded, and those who were not were 'enemies of the people' and would be the proper subject of 'struggle', setting citizen against citizen.

As if to further mark the divide between Hong Kong and the mainland, and as an indication of how seriously China was taking the security threat presented by the protests, mainland border officials began demanding that travellers entering China from Hong Kong surrender their mobile phones for inspection. Those whose phones had photographs or messages relating to the protests were detained for questioning. After travellers caught on to the practice and began carrying only 'burner' or clean phones, they found themselves being quizzed because their phones were suspiciously clean. The practice seemed to be a significant retrograde step, recalling the experience of travelling to China in the 1980s, when flight attendants scoured the aisles of incoming flights to collect all foreign newspapers before landing.

The phone searches were already sending jitters through the Hong Kong business community, many of whom had business interests that spanned the border, and travelled frequently between Hong Kong and the mainland. But it soon became apparent that Beijing's efforts to exert pressure on businesses were only just beginning.

On Friday 16 August, a few days after the airport shutdowns, Cathay Pacific abruptly announced that CEO Rupert Hogg and another key lieutenant had resigned. The reason given for their resignation was 'to take responsibility as a leader of the company in view of recent events', according to Cathay's official statement to the Hong Kong Stock Exchange, which was filed half an hour after China's CCTV broke the story.

Beijing had reportedly demanded Hogg's head for the political 'misdeeds' of Cathay's staff, in particular their visible support of the airport protests. In a sign of the ethno-nationalist aspect of the politics at play, an anonymous source told the *South China Morning Post* that the appointment of the replacement CEO, Augustus Tang, was necessary to enable Cathay's majority shareholder, Swire, to 'show Beijing they've got a Chinese face'.

The development ushered in a purge of the airline — some called it a 'white terror' — with numerous Cathay employees reportedly hauled in for meetings with management, at which they were presented with printed screenshots of their Facebook pages or even private chat groups in which they had voiced support for the protests. They were asked to confirm that the posts were theirs and, if they answered in the affirmative, were fired on the spot. Rebecca Sy, the chair of the Hong Kong Dragon Airlines Flight Attendants' Association, was among those dismissed, while pilot and pro-democracy legislator Jeremy Tam voluntarily resigned from the airline in the hope of sparing it from further politically motivated attacks. The anonymous pilot whose heartwarming in-flight announcement had gone viral during the July airport protest was also reported to have left the company.[6]

Other businesses also came under pressure. Following the publication of a crowd-funded advertisement supporting the demonstrations in the name of 'a group of Big Four accounting firms' employees', the *Global Times* called upon the Big Four to 'fire employees found to have the wrong stance on the current Hong Kong situation'. Statements such as this appeared to presage a War on Terror–style 'You're either with us or you're against us' campaign, with Beijing demanding that businesses publicly declare their position on the protests, and take action to back those words up.

———

In the meantime, the collective brow of Hong Kong was furrowed by a pair of cryptic front-page newspaper advertisements that appeared in two leading Chinese-language papers on the morning of Friday 16 August, signed in the name of 'A Hong Kong citizen: Li Ka-shing.' Li, now ninety-one years old, had been known for his close relationship with former president Jiang Zemin. Under Jiang's watch, Li had been allowed to purchase a mammoth real-estate development site on the corner of Chang'an Avenue and Beijing's main commercial street, Wangfujing. Jiang, it was commonly believed, had also come to Li's assistance when Li's son Victor was kidnapped by a notorious Hong Kong gangster, 'Big Spender' Cheung Tze-keung. Li quietly paid the HK\$1 billion ransom Big Spender demanded, and did not pursue the case with the Hong Kong police. But two years later, Big Spender was arrested on the mainland and — in spite of concerns over a Hong Kong resident being tried in the mainland for crimes committed in Hong Kong, and with attempts to have him extradited back to Hong Kong unsuccessful — he was found guilty, and executed.

Jiang's 'Shanghai clique' party faction was politically opposed to the 'princeling' Xi Jinping. As Xi assumed power, Li had steadily divested himself of his business interests in mainland China and diversified his business globally. Now Li was seen as a potential ally by protesters, who began parsing his messages, looking for coded signs of support. They soon found what they were looking for.

The first advertisement contained a quotation from a Tang Dynasty poem: 'The melon of Huangtai cannot bear to be picked any further,' meaning that something has suffered so much that any further attack would ruin it.[7] This was not the first time Li had used the quotation to respond to questions about politics, and its ambiguous nature served his purposes well. This time, readers could be forgiven for wondering, *Who does Li think is doing the ruining?*

The second advertisement carried a more straightforward

message with bold characters reading, 'No Violence.' However, the accompanying headline, 'The Best Intentions Can Lead to the Worst Outcome', was once again ambiguous. Whose intentions was Li referring to — those of Lam, or the protesters? Protesters were further cheered when picking out the final characters of each line of Li's advertisement gave them the message: 'The blame lies with the nation. Let Hong Kong rule itself.'[8]

Regardless of whether Li was deliberately sending coded messages of support or otherwise, his was a voice that commanded some moral authority in the community, and the fact that he chose to speak out at this crucial time was significant, possibly helping to restore the balance of sentiment back to equilibrium at a time when it threatened to collapse entirely.

A few weeks later, Li was captured on video urging political leaders to offer an olive branch to the young protesters. In response, Beijing's Central Political and Legal Affairs Commission published a post on social media accusing Li of 'condoning crime', and a pro-Beijing politician in Hong Kong branded Li the 'king of cockroaches'. Li quickly backpedalled, saying his comments had been misrepresented and reiterating that any actions that violated the rule of law should not be tolerated.[9]

Hong Kong's other property developer tycoons also found themselves under attack from Beijing. In September 2019, several commentaries appeared in official media blaming the protests on unaffordable housing in Hong Kong, laying the blame at the feet of the 'vested interests' of the property developers, and calling upon the government to expropriate land from the developers' huge land banks.[10] Some responded to the pressure, with developer New World announcing it would donate over 27 hectares of rural land from its land bank to the government for affordable housing.[11]

——

Businesses outside Hong Kong and China were not immune to Beijing's pressure over Hong Kong. Just one week in October saw four different companies around the globe being pulled into the Hong Kong maelstrom:

- The manager of the Houston Rockets NBA basketball team, Darrel Morey, tweeted the Hong Kong protesters' international rallying cry: 'Fight for freedom; stand with Hong Kong.' He quickly deleted the tweet, but not before it was picked up by Chinese netizens and blown into an international incident. The NBA initially rebuked Morey, but then stood behind him, caught between admonitions from members of the US Congress on the one side and, on the other, a China-wide government-led boycott of the NBA, which included cancelling all NBA pre-season match broadcasts and withdrawing merchandise from sale.
- Video-game company Blizzard (a subsidiary of American gaming giant Activision Blizzard, in which PRC internet titan Tencent owns a 5 per cent stake) penalised a Hong Kong player nicknamed 'Blitzchung' who shouted the protest slogan 'Reclaim Hong Kong! Revolution of our times!' during a video game live-stream. Blizzard withheld his prize money and suspended him from competition, prompting an outcry from gamers and international calls to boycott the company. Blizzard eventually relented, and restored Blitzchung's prize money.
- Apple withdrew from sale on its App Store the HKMaps app after complaints from China. The app revealed the locations of Hong Kong police in real time in order to help protesters

avoid police lines, but Apple said they had evidence the app was being used to target police for attack.

- Jeweller Tiffany withdrew an advertisement that showed a model covering one eye, because it was thought to resemble the covered-eye gesture adopted by Hong Kong protesters after the young first-aider had been shot in the eye by a police beanbag round.

Foreign companies and prominent individuals have long become accustomed to dealing with Chinese efforts to police their speech on a growing list of 'sensitive' topics, from the 3Ts (Tibet, Taiwan, and Tiananmen) to Xinjiang and the South China Sea. Following the events of 2019, Hong Kong has now been added to that list of sensitive topics. All of these companies were reacting to the risk of provoking the Chinese government — or the Chinese consumer — by self-censoring, fearing that if they did not do so, Beijing would make its displeasure known, with serious financial consequences.

Beijing uses tools such as market access, professional opportunities, and visas as leverage to police the speech of anyone who works for or is affiliated with a business, university, cultural or social organisation, or sports team that has business in or connections to China, no matter where in the world or online they speak. This often works to prevent them exercising their freedom of speech on foreign soil in relation to Hong Kong or on other issues relating to China, with the result that China exercises what *New Yorker* writer Evan Osnos called 'extraterritorial rights of censorship'.[12]

This was just one way in which the impact of the Hong Kong protests was felt in the wider world, and, with it, there was a growing risk that Beijing's handling of Hong Kong would drive a wedge between China and the international community.

———

As Beijing fanned sentiment in the mainland against the Hong Kong protests, it was inevitable that this would flow out to diaspora communities. It was — perhaps not surprisingly — felt first on university campuses that were home to significant communities of both Hong Kong and mainland Chinese students. With universities in the northern hemisphere still on summer vacation, the first incidents occurred in Australia, where, at the University of Queensland, mainland students clashed with protesting Hong Kong students. Campus security intervened to break up the melee. Similar clashes occurred at the University of Auckland, in New Zealand. The Chinese consulates in both Brisbane and Auckland controversially issued statements praising the mainland students for their 'spontaneous patriotic behaviour'.

Conflict on other campuses would follow, often focused on sites where Hong Kong students had sought to build their own Lennon Walls with messages in support of the Hong Kong protests. Numerous incidents were reported of pro-China students attacking the walls, with some campuses posting security on permanent guard over them to prevent vandalism.

On the streets of cities around the world, rallies in support of the Hong Kong protests were disrupted by pro-Beijing counter-protesters. Often the ensuing scenes were not flattering for Beijing and its supporters. In London, a pro-China protester standing in front of a PRC flag held up a poster reading, 'Kneel Down and Lick Your Master's Ass'. In Vancouver and Toronto, PRC flags were waved from revving Ferraris by pro-China supporters who mocked Hong Kong protesters for being poor. In Melbourne, as pro-China supporters sang the national anthem and clashed with demonstrators supporting the Hong Kong protests, one of their number attacked a television crew.

The impression was of pro-China supporters exercising the freedom of speech they enjoyed in countries outside China in order to prevent others exercising that same right. The campus clashes served to heighten awareness abroad of the impact of Chinese influence on campuses, and more generally across politics and business, undermining those very efforts. In Australia, Confucius Institutes have come under increased scrutiny as a result.

The conflicts also played out in cyberspace. After pro-China internet trolls came out in force on social-media platforms targeting Hong Kong protesters, Twitter announced in August that it had terminated hundreds of accounts that it said were part of a 'coordinated state-backed operation' that was 'deliberately and specifically attempting to sow political discord in Hong Kong'.[13] Facebook took similar action, terminating a number of accounts originating in China and focused on Hong Kong that it said 'coordinated inauthentic behaviour'. Twitter also said it would no longer accept advertising by state-controlled news media entities after PRC propaganda outlets had been advertising anti–Hong Kong messages extensively on the platform.[14]

If the 2019 protests had a global significance, it was that they served to reveal the face of Chinese power to the world. The Hong Kong protesters, in their yellow hard hats and black shirts, battling with police in clouds of tear gas on the Hong Kong streets, became a potent visual symbol of state violence. Citizens around the world saw this same violence enacted in microcosm on their own campuses and streets. In the process, the Hong Kong protesters awoke the world to the scale and impact of Chinese influence globally.

This was reflected in the results of the Pew Research Center's annual global-attitudes survey, which showed that favourable opinions of China, in particular in developed countries, had dropped markedly from 2018 to 2019. In the United States, 60 per cent had an unfavourable opinion of China in 2019, compared to 47 per cent in 2018. In Canada, unfavourability rose to 67 per cent in 2019, from 45 per cent in 2018 (likely prompted in part by China's detention of two Canadians in December 2018 in retaliation for the detention of Huawei executive Meng Wanzhou in Canada). Australia, where awareness of China's influence was already high, showed a modest rise, from a 47 per cent unfavourable opinion in 2018 to 57 per cent in 2019. And among respondents in the United Kingdom, with its close historical connection to Hong Kong, unfavourable opinions of China rose from 35 per cent in 2018 to 55 per cent in 2019.[15]

One place paying particular attention to events in Hong Kong was Taiwan. It was no secret that China aspired to apply the One Country, Two Systems formula in reuniting Taiwan with the rest of China, and it had been commonly assumed that Beijing would treat Hong Kong well in an effort to woo the people of Taiwan. Now, Taiwan watched with some degree of horror as Beijing took the gloves off with respect to Hong Kong. President Tsai Ing-wen from the independence-leaning Democratic Progressive Party was facing a presidential election in January 2020, and had been trailing in the polls. Now, she suddenly found a resurgence of support, with the slogan 'Today Hong Kong, Tomorrow Taiwan' increasingly common. In November, Tsai tweeted a prominent graphic featuring the characters '*Bu keneng*' ('Not a chance') with the accompanying message: 'In the face of attempts to push Taiwanese people to accept "one country, two systems," we have only 3 words to say in response: not a chance.'[16]

By pushing back against Beijing's rule in Hong Kong, the protesters were calling into question what China had been touting as a kind of 'Beijing Consensus', or 'China Model': that idea that people would willingly trade political rights and live under authoritarian rule in return for economic development, prosperity, and stability. In showing that this was not a deal they were willing to accept, Hong

Kongers were laying down a fundamental challenge to Beijing's view of the world.

They took that challenge global, with Hong Kong activists engaging in a campaign of international diplomacy that prefigured a kind of post–nation-state politics, where representatives of non-state actors could engage with sovereign governments as equal interlocutors. Images of Hong Kong pan-democrat politicians and activists meeting with members of Congress or ministers of European governments to lobby for Hong Kong democracy — and against Chinese interference — infuriated Beijing. Joshua Wong, notwithstanding his diminished influence on the ground in Hong Kong, played a key role in these efforts, touring global capitals to rally international support for the protesters' cause and to warn others of Beijing's influence. Speaking at a gathering in Berlin in September 2019, Wong said: 'If we are now in a new cold war, Hong Kong is the new Berlin.'[17] It was a striking statement, one that situated Hong Kong as a city on the border of the free world, and at the very frontlines of a growing global backlash against China. The Hong Kong protests represented the vanguard of the challenge to Xi Jinping's authority.

Wong consciously aligned himself with that position, arguing, '"Stand with Hong Kong" is much more than just a mere slogan, we urge the free world to stand together with us in resisting the autocratic Chinese regime.'[18] Wong seemed to be arguing that Hong Kong's young protesters were freedom fighters not only for their own city, but for the world. When the Hong Kong people took to the streets, they were protesting not just for their own rights and freedoms, but for the rights and freedoms of everyone.

13

A PROTEST OF ENCHANTMENT

There were immediate recriminations among the protesters following the debacle at the airport. Apologies circulated online, together with an attempt on LIHKG to formulate a new code of conduct for protesters that included not targeting journalists. A couple of young activists appeared at the airport again the next day with a sign reading: 'Dear Tourists, We're deeply sorry about what happened yesterday. We were desperate and we made imperfect decisions. Please accept our apology.'

The following Sunday, 18 August, the Civil Human Rights Front called for a gathering in Victoria Park. It would be a test of whether the previous week's events had undermined support for the protest movement. Many supporters of the movement were gloomy about the prospects for continued community support — not to mention enthusiasm — in light of the events of the previous week. One said to me, 'The movement is over.'

But as crowds began to gather for the protest on Sunday, it seemed that those pessimistic expectations would be proved wrong. As my taxidriver dropped me as close as he could get to the park in Causeway Bay, he looked at the crowds of people in black T-shirts flocking along the footpaths and said to me, 'See? Not just young people! All ages!'

Police had banned a march, permitting only a rally to be held in the park, but the crowds that turned out were far beyond its capacity. Thousands stood in the surrounding streets, waiting in the hope that they could join the rally. And then the rain came down — sheets of rain in a tropical downpour. As people stood under their umbrellas, the rally became a march, crowds circling into and out of the park, up the roads towards Central, and then winding back towards the park in Causeway Bay again, in what pop singer and activist Denise Ho called a 'sushi conveyor belt' protest.

Police estimated that 128,000 attended within Victoria Park alone; organisers said a total of 1.7 million marched on the day.[1]

With almost no visible police presence, the rally was entirely peaceful and incident-free. Not only did it demonstrate that enthusiasm for the movement had not waned, but it also completely undermined Beijing's attempts to portray the protesters as violent rioters unrepresentative of the wider Hong Kong community.

The protest movement had shown itself to be an almost conscious organism: it had sensed that things had spun out of control in the course of that week, and had self-corrected. In return, the turnout at the rally showed that the movement's supporters were continuing to adhere to their 'no splitting' principle, that the movement was forgiven for its excesses, and that public anger at police violence was still capable of bringing large numbers of people out onto the streets.

Following the brutality of the previous weekend, Hong Kong celebrated its first tear gas–free weekend in a month. The week of turmoil had ended in a weekend of reprieve, and a moment of transcendence. It paved the way for what would be another transcendent night the following Friday.

———

It almost felt like magic. A few people standing on the street were joined by a few more; people lining the footpath of one block connected to those on the next block. And suddenly, there they all were, hand in hand, chanting slogans and singing songs. On 23 August 2019, the thirtieth anniversary of the Baltic Way — a human chain linking the capitals of Estonia, Latvia, and Lithuania to demand the Baltic republics' independence from the Soviet Union — more than 200,000 people came out onto the streets of Hong Kong to form the Hong Kong Way. From the crowded streets of Wan Chai on Hong Kong Island, to the famous waterfront of Tsim Sha Tsui, to the suburbs of the New Territories, to the peak of Lion Rock, people linked hands in a continuous human chain that measured 60 kilometres in total.

This was another of those protest actions initiated in the online forums, and spread via Facebook, chat group, and word of mouth. Maps were circulated online, together with a schedule: gather at seven o'clock, form the Hong Kong Way at eight, end at nine. But would it work? Or, like many of these suggestions floated from the online community, would it just fizzle out?

As I left my apartment at the designated time that Friday evening and went down the hill to the spot where the Hong Kong Way was supposed to pass my neighbourhood, a number of people were already gathered along the footpath, but there was also a fair amount of disarray. Where exactly should the chain go, what route should it take, who should do what? A somewhat harried older gentleman carried a sign suggesting the chain should cross the road at this corner, but also admitted that he wasn't local to the area and didn't really know what was going on. I wandered along a block or two, but the footpaths seemed empty.

Feeling a little dispirited, I turned a corner and then, suddenly, I found it. The footpaths were lined all the way down an adjacent street and around the corner, and more people were coming, the streets slowly filling, people moving along to fill any gaps.

And then, as the clock struck eight, the people held hands, and began chanting protest slogans, waving their mobile phone lights in the air. Cars driving by tooted their support; people waved from the windows of passing trams. The mood was ecstatic, jubilant.

As a protest action, the Hong Kong Way was extremely effective: entirely peaceful, a striking visual spectacle, and a very physical manifestation of the broad support the movement enjoyed from across the community. People of all ages and from all walks of life, families with young children, the elderly — all joined the chain, putting paid to any suggestion that the protesters were just a few hot-headed young student agitators. It also covered the entire city geographically, ensuring that people could participate wherever they were without needing to travel, and spreading the message of the protests by means of a spectacle that could be witnessed in every district.

It was a sharp contrast to the scenes of recent weeks: the pandemonium at Hong Kong airport, the violent clashes between protesters and police, the threat of the PLA looming at the border. The Hong Kong Way created a moment of enchantment. The feeling of 'enchantment', according to political theorist Jane Bennett, is a 'state of wonder' characterised by a 'temporary suspension of chronological time and bodily movement' that leaves one 'transfixed, spellbound'.[2] Places or moments of enchantment can inspire a sense of wonder or awe, even fill us with overwhelming feelings of generosity and love for the world. But enchantment can also serve a political purpose.

Hong Kong in 2019 felt overwhelmed by the forces of disenchantment. The continuing protests drew upon a deep-seated malaise, with a population who felt they were stuck with a leader they hadn't chosen, running a government that didn't listen to them, in a city whose housing they could not afford, and with wages and an economy that were going nowhere. Many of those who could leave were actively planning to do so. Others were caught in a despair that had driven them out onto the streets in the increasingly desperate protests.

It is hard to love a disenchanted city. Disenchantment breeds cynicism, and creates an emotional detachment from the community. As the city continued to reel from months of protests, sites or moments of enchantment, as was experienced by tens of thousands of Hong Kongers on the night of the Hong Kong Way, provided a reprieve from the escalating cycle of violence, and with it offered a solution to Hong Kong's political and social ennui. That 'state of wonder' lifted the fog of cynicism and disenchantment, encouraging engagement in civic life, and offering rays of hope for the protest movement and for the city.

Hong Kong's activists have long had an ability to capture this sense of enchantment: from the solemn lawyers' silent marches or annual 4 June candlelit vigils held to commemorate Tiananmen Square, to the vibrant tent city of the Umbrella Movement and the blossoming Lennon Walls of 2019.

This often is the result of an engagement with culture. Indeed, looking back on the Umbrella Movement, its greatest significance today is arguably as a cultural event rather than a political one.

In 1997, cultural studies scholar Ackbar Abbas, reflecting on Hong Kong culture on the cusp of the handover, argued that Hong Kong's was a 'culture of disappearance': a culture that appeared only when faced with the threat of its imminent demise.[3] And in the post-handover years it indeed felt like Hong Kong's culture was disappearing. The regional influence of Cantopop was being eclipsed by Mandopop, J-pop, and K-pop. Hong Kong's previously vibrant cinema fell into a slump, its last sigh coming with Wong Kar-wai's *In the Mood for Love* (2000). The film was soaked in nostalgia for a lost Hong Kong — poignantly highlighted by the fact that the film was shot mostly in Bangkok, because the old 1960s Hong Kong neighbourhoods in which the story was set had long been obliterated. (Was it a similar instinct for nostalgia that drove the demand in 2019 to 'Reclaim Hong Kong'?) The perception of Hong Kong as a cultural desert had always felt unfair, but one started to wonder whether it might not be true.

But, coincident with and perhaps prompted by this slow fall from grace, Hong Kong's protest culture began to grow — a protest culture linked to questions of local identity, which in turn prompted a growing cultural identity. The 2000s saw a wave of social movements focused on post-materialist values such as heritage, community, and the environment. The pre-1997 'borrowed time, borrowed place' attitude that had enabled Hong Kong's 'culture of disappearance' began to give way to a sense of local identity; that this was 'our time, our place'. Protests over heritage sites, including the Star Ferry and Queen's Piers in Central and Li Tung Street ('Wedding Card Street') in Wan Chai, became the crucible in which concerns about Hong Kong identity and collective memory fused with protest, culture, and the arts.

This culminated in the Umbrella Movement, where the intersection of politics, identity, and culture prompted an artistic rejuvenation. With the Umbrella Movement followed by the protests of 2019, Hong Kong had become, more than ever, a contested space. And that made it an intrinsically interesting space: a space where competing ideas of identity and culture inspired exciting forms of artistic expression. Hong Kong may have begun its post-handover life under the shadow of a culture of disappearance. But twenty years after the handover, its culture was unequivocally reappearing.

The Lennon Walls — in both their 2014 and 2019 incarnations

— were themselves sites of enchantment. They transformed a plain footbridge or underpass into an art gallery, not only overwhelming in size, but also organic and ever-changing. One would be filled with a sense of delight upon entering a nondescript pedestrian underpass while going about one's business in the city, only to discover that the tunnel had been 'Lennonised', embracing one in a cacophony of colour, imagery, and text. With the Lennonisation of an urban space, the commuter's passage through that space became a journey of wonder, with constant opportunities for visual stimulation and, perhaps most importantly, for humour.

The use of humour and puns has been a common theme across protest movements in Hong Kong, and 2019 was no exception, generating a vast amount of satirical material: from online memes to comics to posters; from re-dubbed videos to fully crafted manga-style animated shorts.

It was perhaps symptomatic of this being a youth-led movement. The young generally relish in poking fun at authority, but this generation of youth in particular had grown up with the mash-up, remix, parody culture of the internet, and were fluent in employing it.

The LIHKG forums, Telegram chat groups, Facebook, and Instagram were the primary channels for distribution of this cultural content. The creative works responded to current events and images that appeared in the press, invariably with a strong dose of irreverence. After the clashes between protesters and police in Sha Tin's New Town shopping mall, online satirists created a faux advertising poster for the mall with an image adapted from a press photo of the mayhem and the slogan 'A Whole New Shopping Experience'.

Many of these materials played with the Chinese language, which lends itself to puns. Chinese characters were also used in graphic jokes. After a police officer was captured on video taunting protesters who had barricaded themselves inside a shopping mall with the phrase, '*Ceot lai a, diu nei lou mou, zijau hai!*' ('Come on out, you motherfucking freedom cunts!'), protesters quickly combined the characters '*zijau*', meaning 'freedom', and the obscene term for the female genitalia, '*hai*', to make a new compound character that they printed onto T-shirts with the English slogan 'Freedom Hi!'.

In another incident, a member of the media, confronted by a police officer, appealed: 'I'm a journalist!' only to receive the response from the police officer, '*Gei nei lou mou!*' (literally, 'Journalist, your mum!', but probably better translated as 'Journalist, my arse!'). The phrase was soon taken up by the protesters' satire machine. The Hong Kong Journalists Association logo was reworked to read 'Hong Kong Journalists Your Mum Association', and journalists were seen reporting at the frontlines with 'Journalist Your Mum' keychains hanging off their backpacks.

When protest is seen through the perspective of enchantment, the entire city becomes a canvas for expression and for protest. This was realised on the Friday night of the Hong Kong Way.

I walked along the chain for a couple of kilometres. It was unbroken, save for crossing major roads: at some intersections, I watched the chain form and then disperse with each cycle of the pedestrian lights.

In a city in which interpersonal relationships can often seem cold and distant, it was of great significance that participants were holding hands: this physical act, of reaching out and touching one's neighbour, was a powerful expresssion of solidarity.

And then, just as remarkably, as the clock struck nine, people began to say, 'That's it! Time to go!' and they dispersed, waving to each other as they went, back to their homes, back to the tea houses or bars, off into the night.

Fifteen minutes later, the footpath was completely empty.

And that, perhaps, is the one final essential characteristic of enchantment: it is a fleeting moment, by its nature transitory. And so, by its very impermanence, even more enchanting.

If the continuing protest movement was to be successful, it would need to continue to create these sites and moments to capture the imagination. This was, after all, something that the authorities appeared signally incapable of doing. Beijing and the Hong Kong government tried to exhort the population to 'Love Hong Kong' by deploying crude propaganda and economic bribes — in the midst of the protests, financial secretary Paul Chan announced a 'mini-budget' that purported to relieve the economic stress of the protests by offering residents a few thousand dollars' worth of subsidies. The government failed to understand that this was not a battle that could be won in dollars and cents, or through brute force. It needed to enchant the people if it wanted to compete with the protests.

Even when the government attempted to do just that, their efforts always seemed to fall short — government-sponsored tourist spectacles such as the Hong Kong Observation Wheel or the nightly Symphony of Lights come to mind — particularly when they also simultaneously closed other sites of genuine community engagement: the government cleaned up Lennon Walls, cracked down on performing-arts venues in warehouse spaces, and shut down a pedestrianised busking street in Mong Kok.

In August, another practice was initiated by protesters: the 'Ten O'clock Calling'. Every night at ten o'clock, people were encouraged to open their windows, stand on their balconies, and shout out the slogans of the movement, in a call-and-response style. Their voices would echo around the densely packed apartment tower-blocks of

Hong Kong's suburbs.

'*Gwong fuk Heung Gong!*' ('Reclaim Hong Kong!') one voice would call. '*Sidoi Gaakming!*' ('Revolution of our times!') would come the response.

Another group of voices, chanting together, would shout: '*Hoenggong jan …*' ('Hong Kongers …') Elsewhere, a voice would reply: '*Gaa jau!*' ('Add oil!')

A lone female voice, calling alone in the distance: '*Ng daai sou kau …*' ('Five Demands …') would find its answer with a resounding: '*Kyut jat bat ho!*' ('Not one less!')

The Ten O'clock Calling was a novelty, but also an important means of building solidarity: although residents were sitting alone in their tiny Hong Kong apartments, they were not alone — the people all around were with them, their voices supporting them. And sometimes the calling would degenerate into a series of cathartic screams, expressing nothing less than the frustration and desperation of a protest movement that was receiving no response from its government. At least, with the Ten O'clock Calling, their voices were heard; they received a response.

One Thursday night at the end of August, communities in over twenty locations across Hong Kong organised outdoor moonlight cinema screenings of the documentary *Winter on Fire: Ukraine's fight for freedom* (2015), about the Euromaidan protests of 2013–2014. In my neighbourhood, the projector screen was set up at the bottom of a sloped pedestrian street, and a large crowd gathered up the hill: some brought stools or sat on mats on the concrete; others stood around them, the crowd watching silently and rapt through the entire film. The screening built a sense of community, the audience very much local to the area, neighbours side by side, with a shared understanding that, at that same moment, other neighbourhoods across Hong Kong were engaging in the same activity.

By almost magical coincidence, the end of the screening coincided exactly with ten o'clock. Over the closing credits and applause, the crowd spontaneously began chanting the slogans of the movement, which were taken up in response by voices from the towers above, in the Ten O'clock Calling — two moments of enchantment merging into one in the summer night.

On the night of the Moon Festival, Friday 13 September, the call had gone out online for the people of Hong Kong to climb a mountain to view the moon, and, of course, to protest. I had thought to join those trying to climb Lion Rock.

Lion Rock is one of the most prominent natural landmarks in Hong Kong — a craggy, cliff-edged mountaintop, its shape said to resemble a crouching lion, looming over the Kowloon Peninsula. In the 1970s, a popular television series, *Below the Lion Rock*, told the stories of ordinary families struggling to make ends meet in the housing estates and squatter settlements of Hong Kong. The series, and Lion Rock itself, came to symbolise the values of hard work and striving for a better life in the face of adversity — something that is referred to in Hong Kong as the 'Lion Rock spirit', a kind of precursor to 'Hong Kong core values' amid the beginnings of an emerging Hong Kong identity in the post-1967 era. As a result, the site carried with it cultural resonances, and a certain nostalgia, for many Hong Kongers.

Lion Rock had been a site and symbol of protest five years earlier. During the Umbrella Movement, a group of activists hung a six-metre-wide, twenty-eight-metre-long yellow banner bearing the movement's slogan '*Ngo Jiu Zan Pousyun*' ('I Want Genuine Universal Suffrage') from the rock, visible from across Kowloon. The feat was an attention-grabbing act of political protest, all the more impressive for the athleticism and daring required to carry it out. The imagery of their action was incorporated into Umbrella Movement protest artworks, with representations of the banner on Lion Rock appearing in everything from paintings to dioramas to online memes.

A group calling themselves 'The Hong Kong Spidie' claimed responsibility for the action they called 'Occupying Lion Rock', and posted a video declaring their manifesto. In the video, an activist appears dressed as Spiderman — a hero who operates outside the official systems of law and order, fighting for justice for the ordinary people of the city, and who also subverts the physical structures of the city, unconstrained by the usual limitations of horizontal and the vertical. The activist in the video delivers a speech explaining the group's actions: 'The people fighting for real universal suffrage all over Hong Kong have shown great perseverance. This kind of fighting against injustice, strength in the face of troubles, is the true Lion Rock spirit.'[4]

Given the emotional resonances of the site and its protest history, it was not surprising that the Mid-Autumn Festival in 2019 found protesters back at Lion Rock. I did not expect many takers for a night-time hike on an evening when people would usually be at home having a family dinner to celebrate the festival. However, I emerged from Lok Fu MTR station to find queues of people filling the roads leading to the rock. It took over an hour just to cover the short distance to the foot of the rock, where the crowd came to a standstill in the car park. Lion Rock was full: all the paths leading up to the peak were packed with people out to protest, and to celebrate. There was nothing to do but join the crowd in the car park, who were chanting protest slogans, singing songs, and shining lanterns and laser beams. Standing in the park below, we could look up at Lion Rock, its ridge-line outlined with the lights of protesters who had successfully made the climb, the outline of the rock glowing bright against the star-filled night sky above.

This was just one of many outdoor events unfolding across the city that night, in what was possibly the largest ever collective public celebration of the Mid-Autumn Festival in Hong Kong. People gathered in parks; others climbed mountains. A group of protesters on Victoria Peak on Hong Kong Island shone lights and lasers at those on Lion Rock, some ten kilometres away across the harbour on Kowloon.

Back at Lion Rock, the fact that the attempt to scale the mountain was unsuccessful did not seem to daunt those who had come out. But the joyful atmosphere belied a serious intent, as one protester explained to me: 'The government still doesn't listen. We are not coming out to play. We are coming out for something.'

I could not resist seeing something of a metaphor: notwithstanding that the people would not be able to scale this mountain, they were still going to come out and try. And they were not going to give up.

14

THE END OF SUMMER

People had been calling it Hong Kong's 'summer of discontent'. And then we reached the last day of summer.

The Civil Human Rights Front announced a protest march for Saturday 31 August, but police refused to grant permission. Protesters said they would march anyway. Then, the night before the proposed march, two protest organisers were beaten by thugs, and six pro-democracy figures were arrested: Joshua Wong and his fellow Demosistō party member Agnes Chow, two pan-democrat legislators, one district councillor, and Andy Chan, convenor of the controversial pro-independence Hong Kong National Party.

The anger was palpable by the time the protesters faced off against the police the following afternoon in what was, from the moment it started, an unlawful assembly. Outside the government headquarters in Admiralty, thousands of black-clad protesters with their yellow hard hats and pink-filtered glass masks lined up across from the two-metre-high water-filled police barricades, holding umbrellas and makeshift shields fashioned from planks of plywood and road signs — some poised with orange traffic cones ready to smother the police tear gas canisters.

There were cracks and pops as the police guns fired, and a clattering as rounds of tear gas shells bounced off the umbrellas and shields of the protesters at the frontlines. The protesters began to creep their way forward under the shelter of their shields, and then launched their own assault: broken chunks of brick, and petrol bombs, flew towards the police.

As more tear gas shells dropped in behind the protesters' frontlines, the firefighter crews leapt into action: some dropped the traffic cones over the shells and poured on water; others swept in to scoop up the shells, and threw them back over the barricades towards the police. Some aimed their throws over the walls of the adjacent PLA barracks building. One throw fell short, and a tear gas shell bounced off my helmet. 'Sorry! Sorry!' came the shouted apology.

Then, from up on the bridge above us, someone cried out urgently: '*Seoi paau ce!*' ('Water cannon!')

The police had been foreshadowing their recently commissioned water cannons for months, conducting public demonstrations for legislators and the media, and road-testing them on the city's streets. The water cannons had made their first operational debut the previous week at a protest in Tsuen Wan, but were deployed then only to help clear debris from the roads. This would be the first time they were deployed against human targets.

The crowd scattered — the water cannon's reputation has preceded it. Various protester infographics circulating online gave advice on how to handle different elements of the police's offensive weaponry, from tear gas to pepper spray. The infographic on the water cannon had only one piece of advice: 'Run!'

I ran with them, climbed up onto the overpass, and looked down as some brave frontliners remained on the road and were buffeted by the water cannon. As the water cannon began to direct its stream up at the protesters and media on the bridge, I dropped further back

— the spray was not just water, but a highly irritant form of pepper spray called pelargonic acid vanillylamide, or PAVA. The police not only directed the spray in powerful jets; they fired it up high into the air, where it misted, forming a spreading cloud of PAVA droplets that drifted on the breeze. Those without gas masks coughed and choked as the pepper spray caught in their throats.

From further back, I watched as bright-blue plumes suddenly came shooting from the water cannon — police had mixed the water with an indelible dye intended to mark protesters for later arrest. The blue clouds appeared almost festive, and there was an instinct to run towards them, arms outstretched. But then those hit by the dye came running back from the frontline, their limbs and clothes soaked in blue. They smarted in pain and vainly scrubbed at their blue-tinged skin with alcohol wipes.

The crowd fell back further down Harcourt Road, and began clearing towards Admiralty, as people in the crowd screamed out that police were approaching from their headquarters in Wan Chai. A few frontline protesters built barricades facing that direction, and began beating out their 'death rattle', the clang of bricks bashed against traffic railings forming a tribal beat. From a footbridge above, I watched as the police approached from the far end of the road, and a small detachment of black-clad protesters made their way crouched along another traffic bridge that arched up and over the road from where the police were approaching. When they drew parallel to the police lines, they threw petrol bombs down onto the road in front of the police. The police retreated, letting off more volleys of tear gas back into Admiralty.

Now the crowd retreated, and I ran with them, through Admiralty and back into Wan Chai. Just past police headquarters, protesters began to build a large road barricade. From down the block, there came a roar from the crowd and a slowly growing rumbling, screeching sound. As the roar of the crowd and the screeching approached, I saw that the protesters had appropriated a huge section of steel sports-stadium seating, ripped out of the Southorn Playground several blocks down, and were pushing it down the road to reinforce their barricade. Finally, the barricade, a mess of plastic road barriers, wooden pallets, and metal sports-ground seating, was doused in petrol and lit ablaze. Smoke billowed from the burning plastic. Over the heads of the crowd, the protesters' blue and green laser pointers cut through the smoke. By now, the sun had set, and the flames of the burning barricade danced and leapt against the night sky. The city was on fire.

The fire brigade arrived on the scene and soon doused the fire, and the protesters, knowing that once the fire was out the police would be coming through to clear the area, retreated again, back towards Causeway Bay and into the MTR.

Where to next? The night was still not over; the protests were flowing like water. The train carriage was full of black-clad young protesters, and as we travelled along the MTR line, my phone pinged as messages were AirDropped by protesters on the train around me: 'Riot police on Nathan Road.' 'Police at Tsim Sha Tsui station exits A1 and B12.'

I got off the train a few stations further north in Mong Kok. Out on Nathan Road, a small group of protesters were blocking traffic again. They dispersed soon after I arrived, and the crowd lining the pavement, waiting for their buses, which had been delayed by this protest action — people who quite rightly might have been angry at this small group of protesters for disrupting their Saturday evening — cheered and applauded. They shouted out as the protesters departed: 'Reclaim Hong Kong! Revolution of our times!'

There was some confusion back inside the Mong Kok MTR station: it was unclear where the crowd was going next. I missed the next train out. And then, suddenly, the station seemed to leap into another dimension. Passing trains were not stopping, and people began shouting out and running along the platforms, first-aiders vaulting across multiple levels of escalators to jump between platform levels. The display screens in the station suddenly started flashing bright red: 'Serious incident. Please leave the station immediately.'

I climbed the stairs back up to ground level to see dozens of riot police pouring into the station. Outside on the street, hundreds had gathered and were haranguing police. It was only as I looked at my phone and saw the updates coming in on Twitter and Telegram chat groups that I understood what had happened: at Prince Edward Station, one stop to the north, a fight had erupted between protesters and their antagonists on the train that I had just missed. Riot police had stormed Prince Edward station, directing pepper spray into the carriages and beating passengers with their batons. For many, the incident would mark the final breakdown in the relationship between the city and its police force.

By the early 1970s, the Hong Kong Police Force had such a reputation for being corrupt that it had become known as 'the finest police force money could buy'. One former officer observed that 'some police divisions worked like criminal corporations', running protection rackets and standover operations.[1] It was part of the broader culture in Hong Kong at the time, an era in which corruption was rife across the government and the payment of 'tea money' was needed to get almost anything done.

That culture began to change in 1971, when the government introduced the Prevention of Bribery Ordinance. One of the most senior police officers to be investigated under the new ordinance was chief superintendent Peter Godber, a leading veteran of the 1967 riots. Godber was discovered in 1973 to have secret overseas bank accounts containing more money than he had officially earned in his entire career, an amount of cash in excess of double his annual salary in his freezer, and lists in his car of underground gambling dens and brothels. He also, however, had an airport security pass, and, while still under investigation for bribery offences, he used it to pass unhindered through airport security and onto a flight back to London. (He was eventually extradited to Hong Kong to face trial in 1975, receiving a four-year prison term.) Godber's escape prompted community outrage and student-led protests. Governor MacLehose responded by appointing a judicial inquiry, the recommendations of which resulted in the establishment of a powerful new independent corruption body, the Independent Commission Against Corruption, in 1974. Hong Kong's ICAC was a world-leading institution, and became the model for anti-corruption bodies elsewhere around the world, including Australia.

The ICAC pursued its mandate with vigour, focusing in particular on the notoriously corrupt Hong Kong Police Force. The police, in turn, felt they were being disproportionately singled out for attention by the ICAC, and treated unfairly by investigators. They resented the ICAC meddling in what they felt was the established culture of the force. By 1977, that resentment was at boiling point. On 28 October of that year, 4,000 off-duty officers gathered at police headquarters to protest against the ICAC's investigation practices, as well as to demand better working conditions for junior officers. They presented a petition to the police commissioner, who, in response, agreed to the establishment of a new Junior Police Officers Association and to consider their other demands.

Following the gathering, however, a mob of around forty off-duty and retired police officers went on to the nearby offices of the ICAC, where they vented their frustrations in a violent attack, assaulting staff and vandalising the offices. The press called it a 'Police Mutiny'.

A week later, Governor MacLehose announced that he would give police a partial amnesty: the ICAC would cease investigating any offences committed prior to 1 January 1977, other than for the most serious cases. This meant immunity for those who had broken the law in the past as the price to pay for a clean slate for the future. (Notably, this was a price that Carrie Lam declared herself unwilling to pay, in the name of Hong Kong's rule of law, in the face of demands for an amnesty for protesters in 2019.) This became the foundation on which the Hong Kong Police Force eventually built a reputation as 'Asia's Finest'. It was a reputation that the force would maintain well into the post-handover era.

However, during the Umbrella Movement protests, cracks in that reputation began to show. The deployment of tear gas on 28 September 2014 represented the first shock. As the stunned crowd that day came to terms with the reality that Hong Kong police were firing tear gas at their fellow citizens, they screamed back at the police: 'Shame on you!'; 'We are all Hong Kongers!'; and 'Take off your uniforms and go home!'

In a second incident, towards the end of the first week of the Umbrella Movement, counter-protesters — some associated with triad gangs — attacked the protesters' encampment in Mong Kok. For several hours, police took no action as protesters were violently assaulted and some female protesters were sexually assaulted. When the police finally did arrive, they were seen in some instances ushering the attackers away from the scene and sending them quietly on their way. The incident was the beginning of what would become a continuing protester narrative of police–triad collusion. It was also the beginning of the protester taunt hurled at police: 'Triads!' ('*Hak sewui!*')

The final, most serious incident in 2014 was the police beating of social worker and activist Ken Tsang Kin-chiu. In mid-October, as police were engaged in violent skirmishes with protesters blocking a road in Admiralty, Tsang was apprehended by police while allegedly pouring urine down on them from a bridge. Television news cameras recorded what happened next: Tsang, his arms bound behind his back with zip ties, was dragged by seven police officers to a 'dark corner' behind a utility station by the side of the road, and repeatedly kicked and beaten for several minutes before being dragged off, bloodied and bruised, for arrest. The footage was broadcast on the following morning's TV news, sending shockwaves through Hong Kong.

Tsang's assailants were eventually sentenced to two years' jail. The sentences prompted a protest gathering of tens of thousands of police officers, their families, and supporters at the Police Staff Recreation Club in Kowloon, the first such protest since 1977. Many saw the gathering as an open affront to Hong Kong's rule of law, while police were frustrated that protesters were receiving what they felt were overly lenient sentences while their own were being treated unfairly.

In light of these incidents, the relationship between much of the Hong Kong community and its police force was in a parlous state following 2014. However, with the events of 2019, that rupture reached a point where it may be irreparable.

The images of police pepper-spraying defenceless and terrified passengers inside the MTR carriage at Prince Edward station on 31 August were just the latest images of police violence to send a jolt through Hong Kong. The incident, together with the Yuen Long attacks, inspired the anti-police protest chant: '7.21, they don't turn up; 8.31, they beat us up.' ('*721 M gin jan, 831 Daa sei jan.*')

Week after week, protesters faced the excessive use of force by police: indiscriminate tear gassings of large sections of the city; the punitive use of pepper spray, often against peaceful or non-resisting crowds; and baton beatings. A *Washington Post* investigation subsequently revealed that the police, in their use of water cannons, chemical agents, and less lethal munitions (rubber bullets, beanbag rounds, and pepper pellets), had repeatedly breached their own use-of-force guidelines.[2]

Protesters also complained of physical and even sexual abuse by police while being arrested and while in custody. These complaints were corroborated in a damning report published by Amnesty International in September 2019.[3] Amnesty documented what it called 'an alarming pattern of the Hong Kong Police Force deploying reckless and indiscriminate tactics', as well as 'evidence of torture and other ill-treatment in detention'. Amnesty accused the Hong Kong police of engaging in 'retaliatory violence' against protesters, and cited an alarming catalogue of arbitrary arrests, brutal beatings, and other abuse meted out during arrest and in detention, and delayed access to medical care and legal counsel.

The police force's public image was also not helped by the fact that the events in the streets were so visible via live-streaming. A whole host of local and international media organisations had journalists on the frontlines throughout the protests, taking photographs and videos, and live-streaming events to such services as YouTube and Facebook. As a result, the 2019 protests were arguably the most thoroughly documented episodes of civil disobedience the world had yet witnessed. The police violence was there in plain sight online, making their denials and obfuscation in the following day's press conferences all the more infuriating. Throughout the course of 2019, no officer was suspended from duty in connection with any incident relating to the protests, nor charged or prosecuted over protest-related actions.[4]

As a result, in the course of 2019, Hong Kong's young protesters, and many of their supporters, developed a deep, visceral, and possibly permanent hatred of their police force. In October 2019, a survey conducted by academics at the Chinese University of Hong Kong found that, when asked to rate their trust in their police force, on a scale of zero (absolute distrust) to ten (absolute trust), a staggering 51.5 per cent of respondents gave police the rating of zero. In the same survey, 69 per cent agreed that Hong Kong police had used excessive force, and close to 70 per cent agreed that the Hong Kong Police Force was in need of a major restructuring.[5]

This dynamic manifested itself on the streets. Whenever police turned up, they would immediately be subject to tirades of abuse, not just from protesters, but from passing citizens of all ages and all demographics. The insults would range from the simply rude — 'Dirty cops!' ('*Sei hak ging!*'); 'Piss off!' ('*Saupei*'); 'Fuck your mum!' ('*Diu nei lou mou!*') — to the more complex — 'Hong Kong police are all rubbish' ('*Hoenggong gingcaat cyunbou laapsaap!*'); 'Hong Kong police knowingly break the law' ('*Hoenggong gingcaat zifaat faanfaat*') — to the disturbing, 'Dirty cops, may your whole family die!' ('*Hak ging sei cyun gaa!*'). On a weekly basis, I witnessed massed crowds of hundreds full-throatedly chanting at a group of police: 'Triads!' ('*Hak sewui!*')

Protesters also deployed laser pointers to irritate and distract police. Police officers on duty had laser pointers constantly shone in their eyes, and laser pointers dazzled the windows of police buildings. Police took to arresting people caught carrying laser pointers for possessing offensive weapons.

Many of the older Hong Kong police stations still retained architectural features that were a legacy of the colonial era: they were fortified, with spike-topped walls and concrete pillboxes on the corners. Even just a few months before the 2019 protests broke out, I found myself driving past one such police station, shaking my head and chuckling at the anachronism of a police station built to withstand an invasion by restless native populations.

But a few months later, the anachronism was no longer a laughing matter — nor anachronistic. Police stations became targets for attack. This began when police stations were known to be holding arrested protesters, and their families and supporters would gather outside, demanding their release. However, protesters soon began targeting police stations for their own sake, merely because they were physical representations of the hated police force.

Police stations were attacked almost nightly by protesters, who set up catapults to launch bricks and other projectiles at the windows, or hurled petrol bombs at the entrances. Ordinary citizens gathered around their local police stations to hurl insults and abuse.

The already fortified police stations were reinforced further, with water-filled barricades established around their entrances. Hong Kong's fleet of police cars were retrofitted with wire cages over their windows, to protect against the bricks that were being hurled at them from the footpaths.

It was, without question, an unacceptable level of violence and abuse to direct towards a police force, and critics were quick to point out that, had protesters behaved this way in the West, they would have been met with lethal force. Yet the 'Try that in the US and you'd be shot dead' argument overlooked some important differences between liberal democracies and the political reality faced by protesters on the streets of Hong Kong. If one-quarter of the population of a democratic country took to the streets in protest, the government would resign or, at least, mindful of its imperilled electoral mandate, respond to the protesters' demands. They could not leave the protesters ignored and unanswered for months, the problems festering in the streets until they exploded into this level of violence. Also, any police force in a liberal democracy is accountable to its democratically elected government: if people are unhappy with the behaviour of their police force, they can, by putting pressure on their elected representatives, push for a change in policy or in the leadership of the police. None of those safety valves was available in Hong Kong in 2019.

The policing tactics themselves also contributed to this breakdown. The kind of policing seen on Hong Kong streets in 2019 was excessive and inappropriate, according to international experts, with one telling *The New York Times*, 'This is basically an essay on how not to police a protest movement.'[6] When citizens began to gather on the streets, police would immediately turn up in full riot gear — their faces covered in black masks, making them appear like anonymous automatons — even when the gatherings were peaceful. This had the effect of immediately ratcheting up the tension of the crowd and, correspondingly, significantly increasing the likelihood of violent conflict erupting. Police also turned to tear gas as an initial tactic, rather than as a last resort.

The tactics reflected a fundamentally misguided approach to policing crowds, according to Clifford Stott, professor of social psychology at Keele University, who was selected by the Hong Kong government to join a panel of international experts to advise the IPCC during its investigations of the 2019 protests. Stott argued that crowds are not anarchic and mindless, as suggested by the traditional theories of mob psychology. Instead, Stott advocated a theory of crowd behaviour known as the 'Elaborated Social Identity Model'. Members of a crowd, this theory holds, not only retain their own individual identity but also develop a temporary additional social identity, shared with that of the crowd and aligned against a common enemy — frequently, the police.

As a result, Stott says, 'The authorities, and in particular the police, can often have a profound role to play in producing the very violence that they pretend to stop.'[7] Policing tactics can make a situation worse: once a crowd initially gathered to express one grievance — say, to oppose the extradition law — is angered by police, this creates a new grievance, and a new common bond.

In light of this dynamic, the traditional 'contain, disperse, and arrest' approach to policing crowds could in fact be counter-productive. In order to break the cycle, police would need to step back from confrontation and instead engage in dialogue.

Stott's advice would go unheeded. Hong Kong's police were already caught in a paradigm that characterised the protesters as violent rioters, and that required law and order to be forcefully restored. The international panel of experts of which Stott was a member collectively resigned in mid-December, citing an inability to work constructively with the IPCC.

All of this pressure inevitably took its toll, with police morale collapsing and many frontline officers reportedly seeking counselling support. Others feared that their children would be bullied and their families maligned. Deep rifts opened up in families containing members of the police force and relatives sympathetic to the protesters.

No matter how professional and how well trained a police force is, this sort of treatment will inevitably provoke a natural human response, and it did so in Hong Kong. Police were seen referring to protesters as 'cockroaches', taunting protesters, and making obscene gestures. In one video, a police officer is seen complaining to his commander, 'Let us throw petrol bombs at them!' Police also became increasingly impatient with members of the media, who regularly found themselves being pepper-sprayed or manhandled by police while trying to report from the frontline.

More disturbingly, a culture of impunity appeared to be growing in the force. Police officers began deliberately obscuring the ID numbers on their uniforms, and then simply stopped wearing them altogether (rendering it impossible to make an effective complaint about individual officer's behaviour to the authorities). The police often appeared disorderly in their behaviour on the streets, apparently failing to heed orders and sometimes having to be physically dragged into line by colleagues. This was indicative of a seeming collapse in command and control of the force. One seasoned human-rights observer described to me his encounter with a group of Hong Kong police as being like dealing with a gang of militia.

However, it is also important to understand the near-impossible position in which the Hong Kong Police Force had been placed. In its unwillingness, or inability, to deal with the issues underlying the protest movement, the Hong Kong government was treating a political problem as if it were purely one of law and order.

And in the vacuum of governance that ensued as Lam and her colleagues disappeared from public view, the police were pushed into a role as the only direct interface between the public and the state. This was a role they should never have been called upon to play, a role that they were equipped to handle in only one way: using the coercive tools of police power. Meanwhile, the protesters, in the face of an unresponsive government and with no other channels for dialogue or mechanisms through which to voice their discontent, had only the police as a target for their frustration and anger. It was a toxic and self-perpetuating dynamic entirely of the government's making.

Having put the police in this position, Lam also seemed to have no way of getting them out, and perhaps no desire to do so, as she was entirely reliant on them to maintain the government's rule over the city. Meanwhile, Lam was steadfastly resisting the one thing that might have begun to heal the rift — an independent commission of enquiry.

A commission of enquiry would not only be a forum through which grievances could be aired and some path towards reconciliation found, possibly involving amnesties for both protesters and police. It would also provide an opportunity for the government to learn important lessons — as the colonial government did in the wake of 1967 — to inform policy initiatives.

It seemed to be a missed opportunity, just like the same opportunity was missed in 2014. C.Y. Leung had failed to hold any inquiry into the Umbrella Movement protests, notwithstanding that those protests had brought the city to a standstill for almost three months. If Leung had held an inquiry, it might have found answers to some of the key questions — What is the appropriate level of force to be used by the police, in what circumstances? What is driving disaffection among Hong Kong's youth? What broader social issues should government policy be addressing? — that had recurred, with renewed force, in 2019.

It was reported that Lam had proposed just such a commission as a means of defusing the crisis, but that the police force refused to allow it. This muscular imposition by the force on the government occurred a number of times during 2019. When chief secretary Matthew Cheung apologised for the slow police response to the Yuen Long attacks in July, he was roundly rebuked by the police and forced to withdraw his apology. This trend had rather alarming implications: was the police force no longer accountable to the civilian government of Hong Kong?

It should go without saying that the position Hong Kong found itself in was not a healthy position for any society. A society needs its police force to maintain law and order, and a well-governed and functioning society needs a relationship with its police based on consensual, community-based policing — where a community agrees to give Weber's famous 'monopoly on violence' to a police force, drawn from and accountable to that community, in return for law and order being maintained in society, and on the understanding that that violence will be wielded within the bounds of the law.

However, in Hong Kong in 2019, a shift appeared to be occurring, as the contemporary notion of consensual, community-based policing was reverting to a colonial model — where the police are imposed upon society by an external power to maintain law and order over the local population — and with police accountability moving from the Hong Kong government to Beijing.

The co-option of the Hong Kong Police Force by Beijing was one of the most disturbing trends to emerge in the course of the 2019 protests, and one man was emblematic of that trend: bald-headed Officer Lau.

At the end of July, protesters gathered outside the Kwai Chung police station, where arrested protesters were being held. Police emerged from the station to try to disperse the crowds, and violent clashes ensued. As a small group of police officers found themselves cut off from the station and surrounded by protesters in a nearby bus terminal, one of the officers — a shaven-headed officer surnamed Lau — brandished a Remington shotgun, and pointed at the crowds from close range with his finger on the trigger. (Later, police clarified that it had been loaded with beanbag rounds.)

The image of the angry Lau pointing his shotgun at unarmed civilians caused outrage in Hong Kong, but the reaction on the mainland was very different. There, Lau was immediately hailed as a national hero for standing up to the 'violent rioters', and the image was circulated as a laudatory example of Hong Kong's police force. 'Bald-headed Officer Lau' (*'Guangtou Jingzhang Liu'*), as he came to be affectionately known to his mainland fans, established an account on the mainland Weibo blogging platform, where he quickly attracted millions of followers, and then used that platform to make partisan political commentary, clearly in breach of Police General Orders, which required police to maintain neutrality.

Bald-headed Lau was one of a number of Hong Kong police officers invited as special guests to Beijing for the 1 October National

Day celebrations, where he was feted as a hero and pictured watching the National Day military parade at Tiananmen and touring the Great Wall — images that were disquieting, to say the least.

The implications for the Hong Kong police were clear: on one side of the border, there were thousands reviling, cursing, and physically attacking them; on the other side of the border, there were millions treating them like heroes. In such circumstances, it seemed, one would figure out very quickly where one's loyalties lay.

The risk is that the Hong Kong police will come to be perceived as a partisan political force, as Beijing's enforcers in Hong Kong: a new colonial police force. This perception has been actively encouraged by the pro-Beijing parties for their own political purposes: their support base is pro-government and pro-police. These parties have effectively sought to give the Hong Kong police their own brand, organising 'Support the Police' rallies and rendering any statement of support for the police as a political slogan.

But the reality is that every citizen in a society, regardless of their politics, should 'support the police'. And, on the flip side, such support should not be unquestioning. No citizen should support illegal behaviour by police. Supporting the police does not mean police should not be accountable for their actions. The fundamental principle of the rule of law is that everyone, including the government and its police force, is subject to the law.

The confusion of these notions was part of a broader institutional collapse in Hong Kong that resulted from the incidents of 2019, one that would manifest itself beyond the police force.

In the weeks to come, conspiracy theories would flourish around the 31 August Prince Edward incident, with rumours that as many as ten people had been killed by the police at Prince Edward Station.

The station entrances were turned into makeshift shrines, with people leaving flowers, burning incense, and praying for the 'lives lost'. None of the allegations was ever proved, and it seems unlikely that any deaths did indeed occur. But the city had reached a stage where distrust of the government and police was absolute.

It was an environment that made fertile ground not only for conspiracy theories, but also for the spread of hyperbolic protester propaganda, some of which approached the level of mass hysteria. Images of protesters being loaded onto an MTR train in order to transport them from the scene of arrest at a station were mischaracterised as protesters being put onto trains to be transported across the border to the mainland. Rumours circulated that various cases of suicide were actually arrested people who had been murdered by police while in detention and their bodies dumped in the harbour. One notable example was the case of Chan Yin-lam, a fifteen-year-old student whose body was found in the harbour in September. Authorities concluded that her death was a case of suicide, and her mother made public statements confirming that her daughter had been troubled, and appealing for her family to be left in peace. However, that did not stop conspiracy theories that Chan had been a victim of police murder, and even that the woman making media appearances as her mother was in fact an imposter. Chan was commemorated by protesters as a martyr, her image posted with messages of condolence on Lennon Walls.

Protester propaganda materials at times elevated the troubles in Hong Kong to exaggerated levels, referring to the continuing policing situation as a 'humanitarian crisis', or making inappropriate comparisons to historical events such as the Tiananmen Square massacre or even the Holocaust. When police were pictured writing numbers on arrestees' arms to aid in identification, images circulated online placing those images alongside images of the tattooed arms of concentration-camp detainees.

Indeed, some of the protester propaganda in 2019 was uncannily reminiscent of that circulated by leftists during the 1967 riots, both in terms of sentiment and even specific content. One book from 1967, titled *We Shall Win! British imperialism in Hong Kong will be defeated!*, published by pro-Beijing newspaper *Ta Kung Pao*, is typical.[8] It tells of 'political persecution, economic exploitation, and cultural corrosion' at the hands of the colonial authorities, 'bloody suppression' and 'atrocities' by police, 'trumped-up charges' against protesters, and (British) military manoeuvres as a 'show of force'. All of these phrases were unconsciously recycled in 2019. In the book, black-and-white photographs show protesters in clouds of tear gas alongside the caption, 'Riot police released large numbers of tear gas shells and made wholesale arrests.' Another photograph shows rows of spent shell casings from munitions used by police against protesters. Near-identical photos would circulate in 2019, only this time in colour, and online.

Looking back at them now, the 1967 materials appear to be laughably crude propaganda, couched in the Cultural Revolution language of the era. However, it should give protesters pause to consider how some of the materials produced in 2019 might be viewed in hindsight. Some of the more extreme discourse in 2019 ultimately served to undermined the protesters' credibility and was not constructive to their cause, yet conspiracy theories remained firmly held by many supporters of the movement. It did not help that, in many cases, the authorities did little to dispel the rumours, often releasing only partial evidence or explanations that did just as much to fuel the conspiracy theories as it did to dispel them. This was the case with the Prince Edward incident, with the MTR Corporation releasing screenshots, but not complete CCTV footage, of the incident in an unsuccessful attempt to alleviate concerns.

The Prince Edward incident also signalled the final breakdown in trust of the MTR Corporation. The MTR, while partly privatised and listed on the Hong Kong Stock Exchange, is still 75 per cent owned by the Hong Kong government. In the early weeks of the protests, the MTR did its best to keep doing its job: to facilitate the transport of citizens around the city. The MTR arranged extra train services to cope with the surge of crowds during large protests. When police trapped protesters inside MTR stations, the MTR arranged for trains to shuttle the protesters away. The MTR had always been the pride of Hong Kong, and continued to be a friend of the people.

However, all that changed at the end of August when, after protesters marking one month since the 21 July attacks clashed with police in Yuen Long, the MTR put on extra train services and allowed protesters to travel for free to leave the scene. In response, the official party newspaper, the *People's Daily*, launched a blistering public criticism of the MTR with the headline, 'Special Train Convoy for "Black Shirts". Has MTR weighed up the consequences?'. The *People's Daily* editorialised, 'These "Black Shirts" are breaking the law and violating discipline, and yet enjoy this kind of "VIP treatment". What are MTR thinking?' It accused the MTR of 'betraying its duty'.[9]

The change in tone at the MTR in response to the criticism was immediate. The following weekend, the MTR shut down stations for several stops around planned protest sites in two remote districts of Hong Kong in order to prevent people joining the protests, notwithstanding the significant inconvenience this caused to residents of those districts. This trend would continue, culminating in early October when the MTR cooperated with the government to shut down its entire system in a *de facto* curfew on the city. The MTR was also seen providing dedicated trains to transport police officers while they were policing protests, and allowing police to rest inside closed stations, further angering protesters: the MTR would no longer help 'us', but it would help 'them'.

In the protesters' eyes, the MTR had betrayed them, and had become a collaborator with the government, the police, and Beijing. It was given the nickname 'the Party's Railway' (*'Dong tit'*, a pun on *'Gong tit'* for 'MTR' in Cantonese), and MTR stations and facilities became a target for protester vandalism. Week after week, stations were graffitied, ticket machines and turnstiles destroyed, and station windows and glass panels smashed. Protesters turned on fire hoses and flooded stations with water, or set fires at barricaded station entrances. For some members of the wider community, this was unacceptable: notwithstanding their political position, attacking the city's beloved MTR and inconveniencing thousands of commuters was going too far. Yet such actions did not undermine broader support for the movement.

It was one of the great tragedies of the 2019 protests: a collapse of public trust in those previously trusted institutions upon which citizens relied in their day-to-day lives. From the police and the MTR, to the Airport Authority and Hong Kong's flag-carrier airline, Cathay Pacific, to, later, the city's largest bank, HSBC, all were institutions whose identity had hitherto been closely tied to that of the city and its people. And all were now being pressed into service by Beijing to oppose the protesters.

Late on the night of 31 August, I stood behind a burning barricade across Nathan Road in Mong Kok as the crowd taunted and abused the police. Eventually, the fire brigade came to extinguish the fire, and the police departed the scene, to the continued jeers of the crowd.

It was the last day of the summer, but far from the end of Hong Kong's discontent.

15

ONE STATE, TWO NATIONS

On the afternoon of Wednesday 4 September 2019, almost three months after the first one-million-person march against the extradition bill, Carrie Lam announced that the bill would be formally withdrawn from the legislative agenda. It had come after Lam had insisted for weeks that such a move was unnecessary. At the same time, Lam reiterated her previous position on the protesters' other demands, but said that she would establish an 'investigative platform' to look at the causes of the unrest and suggest solutions.

The response from the protesters online was instantaneous: 'Five demands, not one less!'

Lam's move was seen as an attempt to calm down sentiment ahead of China's National Day on 1 October. China would be celebrating the seventieth anniversary of the founding of the People's Republic, and Chairman Xi Jinping had planned a grand military parade in Beijing, determined to project an image of national power, and unity, to the world. Hong Kong's protesters were just as determined to show the world that they wanted no part of it.

The last weekend of September saw more protests, and more clashes with police, culminating in a global 'anti-totalitarian' march on Sunday 29 September. This was something of a landmark: Hong Kong's online activists had conceived of and promoted this global event, which resulted in people marching on the streets of dozens of cities across the world on a global day of action, notionally against 'totalitarianism', but, in reality, a thinly disguised anti–Communist Party of China (CPP) march.

National Day presented exactly the kind of split-screen moment for global television that Xi had no doubt been hoping to avoid. While rigid rows of PLA soldiers marched in front of flag-waving crowds at Tiananmen in Beijing, black-clad protesters skirmished with police on the tear gas–filled streets of Hong Kong.

The National Day protest, from the moment it began, had an aggressive anti-China, and anti–Communist Party, mood. The placards carried by protesters and graffiti on tram stops and bus shelters along the route bore messages such as '*Tinmit Zunggung*' ('Heaven destroy the CCP') and '*10.1 Ho nei lou mou*' ('10.1 celebrate my arse'). Placards and banners bearing National Day celebratory messages were torn from buildings and trampled upon or set alight, and PRC national flags burnt. A giant poster of Xi Jinping's face was pasted to a wall, and a supply of dozens of eggs placed alongside — the crowd gleefully lined up to pelt Xi's face with eggs in a kind of subversive carnival game. Beijing-affiliated businesses, in particular the premises of the PRC state-owned banks, were vandalised and graffitied with slogans such as 'Communist Bandits' or 'Die Chee-na'.

Notwithstanding the march having been banned by police, tens of thousands, of all ages, joined. At the official National Day flag-raising ceremony that morning, the Chinese national anthem had been played. But as they marched that afternoon, they sang another anthem: 'Glory to Hong Kong'.

———

In May 2019, before the protests had even begun, Dr Brian C.H. Fong, a comparative political scientist at the Education University of Hong Kong, published an academic paper that now seems startlingly prescient. In it, Fong positioned Hong Kongers alongside the Catalans, Scots, Quebecois, and Kurds as members of 'stateless nations' — political communities that, while not having a state of their own, self-identify as a distinct people with aspirations of self-government.[1]

Fong argued that the foundation of the Hong Kong nation had been laid with the imposition of formal border-controls between China and Hong Kong after 1949, was reinforced by the increasing devolution of powers from London to Hong Kong from the 1950s through to the 1970s, and then was de jure recognised by the Sino-British Joint Declaration of 1984 and Hong Kong's Basic Law in 1990.

As a result, with the handover of 1997, Fong explained when we met in a café in the bustling Tsim Sha Tsui tourist district — a stone's throw from where protesters had tossed the PRC national flag into the harbour several weeks earlier — 'Britain not only handed over Hong Kong sovereignty to China. Actually, at that time, they also handed over a young Hong Konger nation to China.' When China resumed sovereignty over Hong Kong, said Fong, 'they actually were dealing with a new, young nation, or at least with a group of people who considered themselves different from their sovereign. That is the basic dilemma.'

It was a dilemma that manifested most sharply in Hong Kong's younger generation, who were making up the vast majority of those protesting on the city's streets every weekend.[2] They had a strong and recurring slogan: 'Hong Kong Is Not China!' Beijing had clearly lost the hearts and minds of an entire generation.

Or perhaps they never had them to begin with. Hong Kong's

younger generation had grown up under One Country, Two Systems, when the distinctive Hong Kong system and lifestyle had been formally institutionalised. This led to a generation gap between them and the older generation, who had grown up in earlier decades when the distinction was less clear. Unlike this older generation, who had extensive dealings with China through business or family connections, the post-1997 generation had few interactions with the mainland.

To understand the 2019 protests through this prism casts light on many aspects of the movement: from the perceived threat posed by the extradition bill through to the attack on LegCo and the strong anti-China sentiment, and even the vast cultural output of the movement. All of those memes, posters, and artworks functioned on multiple levels. At the most immediate level, they were communications media, ways of transmitting information, propaganda tools. The artwork also functioned as an enchanting method of capturing the attention of the public. But, in addition, this artwork did the important work of identity-building. The resulting cultural products and icons carried the DNA of a national identity.

The idea of a nation can be difficult to grasp in the abstract, and is best communicated in embodied form. 'Identity must be lived in day-to-day life,' Fong explained to me, 'and in day-to-day life you need these cultural icons.' The cultural icons created by the movement, according to Fong, 'help[ed] mainstream the Hong Kong identity'.

Two cultural icons in particular were emblematic of this phenomenon. The first was an iconic monumental sculpture. The Statue of Liberty had served as a direct inspiration for the emblems of two previous Chinese protest movements: in 1989, when the Goddess of Democracy towered over Tiananmen Square, and again in 2014 with Umbrella Man. The 2019 movement had its own version: Lady Liberty. Lady Liberty was a white statue of a female frontliner in full gear: hard hat, goggles, gas mask, backpack, an umbrella clasped in one hand and, raised defiantly in the other, a black flag emblazoned with the slogan: 'Restore Hong Kong! Revolution of our times!'

In Lady Liberty, the distinctive visual look of the protesters inspired a cultural artefact that also acted as a powerful symbol of identity. True to the methods of the movement, the statue was designed by a team of volunteers convened online, the designs voted upon in LIHKG, and the production costs crowdfunded.

Lady Liberty was displayed on university campuses and at various protest rallies, before finally being carried by a team of volunteers up to the peak of Lion Rock, which they declared her final resting place, gazing down on the city. But the very next day, the statue had been vandalised, smashed apart and splashed with red paint. Lady Liberty, however, would not be so easily destroyed. The 3D printing files remain freely available online, enabling anyone to create their own replica statues.[3] Mini Lady Liberties have since been appearing all over Hong Kong, and the power of the statue as a cultural icon lives on.

The second cultural icon was the anthem 'Glory to Hong Kong'. Beijing had long been infuriated by Hong Kongers openly booing the Chinese national anthem at football games, a trend that gathered pace around the time of the Umbrella Movement. Indeed, such was Beijing's fury that it specifically formulated a National Anthem Law that criminalised disrespecting or parodying the national anthem, and decreed that the law should apply to Hong Kong as well as the rest of China.

In 'Glory to Hong Kong', Hong Kongers had an anthem that they genuinely embraced as their own. The composer, Thomas, explained his purpose in composing the song: 'Music is a tool for unity. I really felt like we needed a song to unite us and boost our morale.'[4]

Within weeks of the song being released, people had memorised the words, and it was being sung in massed gatherings at shopping malls, on protest marches, and with particular gusto at the same football matches at which the official national anthem was booed.

The experience of watching a crowd of Hong Kongers singing 'Glory to Hong Kong' was powerful and moving: in the midst of a noisy protest gathering at a shopping mall in Yuen Long, for example, the shouting of slogans and commotion in the crowd fell away to silence as the opening bars of the song boomed out over a loudspeaker. The crowd stood to attention — solemn, heads raised and eyes ahead, some with their hands placed on their hearts — and sang. Nationalism scholar Benedict Anderson described singing an anthem as an 'experience of simultaneity. At precisely such moments, people wholly unknown to each other utter the same verses to the same melody.' Anthem singing, wrote Anderson, creates 'the echoed physical realisation of the imagined community' of a nation.[5] This very physical manifestation of the shared, imagined Hong Kong nationhood was clearly evident when 'Glory to Hong Kong' rang out. And how much more that sonority echoed, how much more physically it was felt, in the glass and marble atrium of a shopping mall.

Yet Hong Kongers' aspirations for increased autonomy meet their limits when coming up against Chinese sovereignty and Chairman Xi's ambition. The Hong Kong nation is situated within a strong, centralised authoritarian state with a policy of controlling and assimilating its peripheries, from Xinjiang to Tibet, and from Hong Kong to Taiwan — a policy that seems only to have intensified under Xi. Within this context, the hopes for continued — not to mention increased — autonomy are much dimmer than they would be in a more decentralised federal system such as that of Canada, in which Quebec enjoys a relatively high degree of autonomy.

In the final analysis, Hong Kong's future will be decided in Zhongnanhai in Beijing, where the headquarters of the party and the central govenrment are located, and not on the streets of Hong Kong.

But on the streets of Hong Kong, the struggle continued. On the afternoon of National Day, police confronted the protesters with tear gas and water cannons, pushing them back from the barricades in Admiralty. A group of frontliners made an abortive attempt to storm up an escalator to a police position on the footbridge above, but were forced back by rubber bullets and sponge grenades. The police came storming down the escalator, firing tear gas as Molotov cocktails flew towards them.

As the crowd dropped back and paused, news broke that, at one of the other protest rallies in the remote Tsuen Wan district, a protester had been shot in the chest by a live police round. The crowd fell quiet as everyone looked at their phones, absorbing the news. And yet the response seemed muted: it was almost as if people were expecting that this moment — the use of lethal force by Hong Kong police — would arrive. Could it have been experienced almost as a relief? (The protester survived his injuries, and was subsequently arrested and charged.)

The crowd moved again, falling back into Wan Chai; but this time the police changed the script. Act Three would be scrapped. Police closed in on the protesters from several directions, kettling them in the backstreets of Wan Chai, and Raptor snatch squads ran in and began making violent arrests. The protesters scattered — some up the hill behind them, some into shops and restaurants, but most down alleys and into buildings where friendly locals had opened the doors to provide them with refuge from the police, in a clear show of support.

In the now-deserted backstreets, I came across a small park, the benches strewn with materiel: helmets, face masks, black T-shirts, shields, and other equipment, all dumped hastily by the fleeing protesters wanting to leave behind evidence of their participation in the protest.

I walked back through Wan Chai in the early evening, passing a trail of vandalised mainland-owned shops. Outside one office building, workers were already hard at work scrubbing away the graffiti.

I waited by the side of the debris-strewn roads, my yellow highvis Press vest hanging off me in the heat, wondering if there was any chance a taxi might pass by (the MTR had, again, been shut down), when a van pulled up alongside me. A woman leaned out the passenger window and asked, 'Where are you going?' I told her, and she conferred with her partner in the driver's seat, and then turned back, opening the rear door and saying, 'Get in!'

It was then I realised that this was a school bus.

The school bus phenomenon — fleets of volunteer drivers ferrying protesters to and from protests — was just one of the many examples of the way that broader support across the community sustained the protest movement. The refuge offered by the backstreets apartments in Wan Chai was another.

Stepping into the vacuum of vanished institutional trust, there seemed to be a new interpersonal trust developing. Hong Kong people now trusted those they met alongside them on the streets more readily than they trusted the authorities. This newfound solidarity made the imagined community of the Hong Kong nation a lived experience.

Along march routes, friendly shop-owners would place bottled water outside their stores, with a sign 'Free for protesters. Hong Kongers, add oil!' During street skirmishes in late November in Tsim

Sha Tsui, along a backstreet of shuttered shops close to the frontlines, one grocery store had its door open a crack with a hastily handwritten sign posted out the front: 'Come in and take whatever you need.'

Teams of volunteer first-aiders would assist injured protesters, civilians, and media at the frontlines. Some doctors privately treated protesters with more serious injuries who feared going to public hospitals — there were reports that hospitals had provided police with access to patient information and facilitated them making arrests.

As was the case in the Umbrella Movement–occupied zones, a kind of protest gift economy developed. Regular donation drives would result in equipment and supplies being dropped off at pre-arranged points, and then distributed to protesters. Frontline protesters who were from underprivileged backgrounds were offered food or places to stay. Supermarket coupons and restaurant vouchers were collected and distributed to protesters in need. Collectively, these community-based initiatives worked to build new institutions to replace the official institutions that had been, in some sense, lost to that community.

Many of these community efforts revolved around the idea of providing mutual support against a common enemy. Before protests began in remote suburbs, the door codes of housing estates in the area would be circulated on chat groups to facilitate protesters' escape. After a protest, the ticket-vending machines at the MTR stations were piled high with coins to enable people to purchase single-use tickets rather than use their stored-value Octopus cards, which protesters feared would enable their movements to be tracked. Bags of coloured clothing, often neatly marked by size, would be left at station entrances to enable protesters to change out of their telltale black outfits and travel home safely. And down in the streets, as the police raised their black warning flags, protesters would shout up to the residents in the apartment buildings above: '*Saan coeng!*' ('Close your windows!')

As tear gas filled the streets of Causeway Bay one weekend evening, protesters tried to press one of their gas masks into the hands of a middle-aged woman who had been inadvertently caught up in the gas. She tearfully refused it, saying to the protesters, 'You need it! I'm okay!' But the protesters insisted, pushing it back into her hands: 'Just put it on! Put it on!'

The driver of my school bus told me that he worked in film editing, producing promotional videos for a Hong Kong government agency. He and his girlfriend said that they had been doing school bus runs almost every weekend, sometimes transporting protesters' equipment in the back of their van, notwithstanding the risk of being stopped and searched by the police.

They told me they dreamed of getting out of Hong Kong, travelling the world and finding a new place to settle down. I wondered how many other young Hong Kongers shared their dream — and how many would realise it.

They dropped me off downstairs from my apartment, firmly refused my offers of payment for the journey, and drove off back towards the protest site to see if they could find anyone else to help.

16

RESIST!

On the afternoon of Friday 4 October 2019, a few days after returning from National Day celebrations in Beijing, Carrie Lam held a press conference to announce her latest plan to stem the protests.

Looking ashen-faced, Lam announced that she would use powers under the colonial-era Emergency Regulations Ordinance (not utilised since the 1973 oil crisis) to introduce an anti-masking law. The new law prohibited the wearing of face coverings during any public protest — authorised or not — with those violating the ban facing a fine of HK$25,000 and one year's imprisonment. Exemptions were available for people wearing masks for religious, health, or work-related reasons. This latter exemption appeared to exempt journalists covering protests and seeking to protect themselves from police tear gas, but that would not stop police forcibly ripping the face masks from reporters' faces in the days to come.

The anti-masking law was notable not only for its restriction of civil liberties, but because, in enacting the ban using the Emergency Regulations Ordinance, or ERO, the executive branch of government had unilaterally decreed an entirely new criminal offence, bypassing legislative scrutiny.

The ERO dated back almost a century, to a previous episode of civil strife in Hong Kong, the seamen's strike of 1922. That strike stemmed from a dispute over pay for local Chinese seamen, who were paid significantly less than foreign seamen under a racist system imposed by the British. The strike brought Hong Kong's usually bustling harbour to a standstill, and the colony became a ghost town as striking workers and their supporters abandoned Hong Kong for Canton, even leaving on foot after the authorities stopped train services to try to stem the exodus. In the midst of the crisis, the colonial LegCo rushed through the ERO, a sweeping piece of legislation empowering the governor to make whatever regulations 'he may consider desirable in the public interest' in times of 'emergency or public danger'.

The colonial government made extensive use of the ERO during the 1967 riots. Regulations were promulgated that banned the possession of corrosive substances and acids, granted police powers to carry out searches without warrants, banned public or even private meetings, and empowered courts to close criminal trials to the public. Another emergency regulation deemed any object that might arouse reasonable fears as a bomb, with those in possession of it subject to arrest for possessing bombs, while the sale and possession of fireworks was banned. Most controversial was Regulation 31, which empowered the colonial secretary to detain any person for up to one year without trial and without giving reasons, and permitted the detention to be renewed at the expiry of the one-year period. It was effectively a licence for the colonial authorities to imprison whomever they wanted, without trial, indefinitely. Henry Litton, then secretary of the Hong Kong Bar Association and later a judge of Hong Kong's post-handover Court of Final Appeal, complained at the time that Regulation 31 was 'contrary to all ordinary standards of international behaviour as laid down by international courts'.[1]

After the handover in 1997, the ERO remained on Hong Kong's

statute books. The Hong Kong government was now turning to this tool of colonial oppression to seek to impose order on a twenty-first-century city. It was the latest example of the Hong Kong government's campaign of lawfare, a campaign that had been ongoing since the Umbrella Movement.

Lawfare is the use of Hong Kong's legal system by the government as a tool to achieve political objectives. Lawfare is politically astute in that, by relying on the legal system, it enables the authorities to appeal to the need to uphold Hong Kong's rule of law, universally recognised as a core value of Hong Kong, while using that same legal system to target the actions of dissenting politicians and activists.

The use of the legal system for political purposes first became apparent when the government relied upon civil court injunctions as the legal basis for clearing the Umbrella Movement–occupied sites in 2014. Those injunctions were legally unnecessary — the protests could have been cleared by police at any time under a variety of existing laws — but they provided political cover to C.Y. Leung and his government. The injunctions meant that Leung could duck political responsibility for clearing the protesters and instead justify the action on the basis of needing to uphold Hong Kong's rule of law. It was an approach that appeared to have the endorsement of Beijing, a senior leader at the time being caught on camera saying approvingly that Hong Kong's leaders should 'deal with things in accordance with the law' ('*Yifa banshi*').

The lawfare campaign was pursued aggressively in the prosecutions of the Umbrella Movement leaders and other dissidents. These prosecutions were made primarily under the Public Order Ordinance, one of the main weapons in lawfare, a blunt-force tool wielded heavily by the state. Introduced in the dying days of the 1967 riots and still largely unchanged today since the time of its enactment, the ordinance provides that any public gathering or march to which police have objected under a 'notice of no objection' mechanism is an unauthorised assembly. Any assembly of three or more persons conducting themselves in a 'disorderly, intimidating, insulting or provocative manner' is an unlawful assembly. Taking part in an unauthorised assembly or unlawful assembly is punishable by up to five years' jail. Where an unlawful assembly results in a 'breach of the peace', it is deemed a riot, and subject to a jail term of up to ten years.

The Public Order Ordinance was not uncontroversial even at the time of its enactment. In his speech presenting the law to the Legislative Council in November 1967, the attorney-general, Denys Roberts, acknowledged criticisms that the law was over-reaching and 'a backward piece of colonialism', but argued:

> It is a problem as old as the law itself, to find the proper point of balance between citizen and state. This point, as the history of any country will show, changes from time to time. It is to be hoped that this Bill has found the right balance, taking into account, as must be done, our circumstances at the present time. If these change ... then the Government will be ready and willing to consider suitable amendment.[2]

In the last days of British Hong Kong, in recognition of the fact that the circumstances had indeed changed, the departing governor, Chris Patten, amended the Public Order Ordinance, making it significantly less draconian. It was one of many measures that Patten took to bolster civil rights and to improve democracy in the territory prior to the handover. Beijing bristled at Patten's interference, and on 1 July 1997 the Provisional Legislature — a temporary LegCo put in place by Beijing to manage the handover transition prior to fresh elections being held — unwound Patten's changes, and the Public Order Ordinance reverted to its pre-amendment form.

Week after week, in the course of the 2019 protests, the police used their powers under the ordinance to ban rallies and marches, effectively criminalising protest and foreclosing legitimate avenues for peaceful dissent. And as the protests became more violent, police would declare that they had descended into a riot and that anyone arrested would be charged with rioting, thus dangling the prospect of a ten-year jail sentence over the heads of protesters. With Edward Leung, along with many others, sitting in jail for that very offence at the time, people knew this was not a mere theoretical risk.

It was not just the use of the Public Order Ordinance, but the manner in which the Umbrella Movement prosecutions were conducted that made the lawfare campaign particularly insidious. The prosecution and sentencing of the Umbrella Movement leaders was dragged out across more than four years following the events in question. For their occupation of Civic Square, Joshua Wong and HKFS leaders Alex Chow and Nathan Law were convicted of unlawful assembly, with the judge at trial giving the trio non-custodial sentences: community service for Wong and Law, and a three-week suspended jail sentence for Chow.

However, the secretary for justice — reportedly against internal advice from his department — appealed the sentences, complaining that they were too lenient. The Court of Appeal, in the face of significant political pressure, obligingly increased the sentences: Wong received six months' jail, Chow seven months', and Law eight months'. The fact that the sentences exceeded three months conveniently meant that the trio would be excluded from running as candidates for LegCo for a five-year period. The Court of Final Appeal eventually overturned those sentences on a technicality, but endorsed the Court of Appeal's amendment to the sentencing guidelines, which provided that future public-order offences of this nature would, as a matter of course, receive a custodial sentence.

Prosecutions continued against protesters, including for breach of the Mong Kok injunctions during the clearance of the Umbrella Movement occupation, for which Joshua Wong received a further three-month jail sentence.

Finally, the Occupy Trio — Benny Tai and his associates, Chan Kin-man and Reverend Chu Yiu-ming — along with a number of other Umbrella Movement leaders, went on trial in late 2018. The Department of Justice trawled the common-law history books in formulating their charges, ultimately charging the trio with conspiracy to commit public nuisance, incitement to commit public nuisance, and — mind-bendingly — incitement to incite public nuisance. They were convicted of the former two charges, and Tai and Chan were eventually sentenced in 2019, almost five years after the events, each to sixteen months' jail. Chu, aged seventy-five and in poor health, was given a suspended sentence.

Other prosecutions in the government's lawfare campaign have targeted pro-democrat politicians. In the course of the oath-swearing fiasco when, in chaotic scenes in November 2016, Yau Wai-ching and Baggio Leung, along with three of their assistants, tried to force their way into the LegCo chamber to retake their oaths, they were arrested and subsequently charged and found guilty of unlawful assembly. They were sentenced to four weeks' jail. In April 2018, Democratic Party legislator Ted Hui snatched a civil servant's mobile phone after he alleged she was violating the privacy of legislators by monitoring their whereabouts while trying to corral them for a vote. Hui was charged and convicted in May 2019 of common assault, obstructing a public officer, and having had access to a computer with criminal or dishonest intent. He was sentenced to 240 hours' community service and is facing impeachment proceedings in LegCo as a result.

Prosecutors also made novel use of the criminal laws when targeting dissent. Online activists were regularly charged with the crime of access to a computer with criminal or dishonest intent — an offence originally intended to target computer hacking — for posting material online promoting protest actions, until the Court of Final Appeal, in a sharp rebuke to the government, ruled in early 2019 that the law should be construed narrowly and consistent with its intended purpose.

In late 2019, the government arrested four people associated with the Spark Alliance group on suspected money-laundering charges. The group had acted as a fundraising platform for the protests, collecting donations from the public and using those funds to provide financial support to protesters, including paying the legal fees and bail bonds of those arrested. Many protesters had memorised the number of Spark Alliance's legal-support hotline. The alliance remained a somewhat mysterious organisation, but was regarded as reliable by pan-democrat politicians, lawyers, and other respected civil-society groups. Following the arrests, police froze HK$70 million in funds belonging to the group. It also emerged that HSBC had ordered a corporate banking account used by Spark Alliance to be closed on the basis that it was not being used for its stated purpose. This use of money-laundering laws to target the protesters' sources of funding was another example of the lawfare campaign.

Throughout these prosecutions, a pattern emerged. Prosecutorial discretion — the decision of whether to charge someone, what charges would be pursued, and what sentences would be sought — is usually pragmatic, made on the basis of policy, and in the face of the realities of limited budgets and court resources. This was a point that the chairman of the Hong Kong Bar Association, Philip Dykes, SC, would emphasise in his speech at the opening of the legal year in January 2020 as Hong Kong was looking ahead to the inevitable criminal process for those arrested during the 2019 protests. Dykes reminded his audience, which included senior members of Hong Kong's judiciary, representatives of the legal profession, and the secretary for justice, that 'a decision to prosecute is not made just because the police have enough evidence to go to court and secure a conviction. Public interest plays a part in the decision-making process too so that individuals or some classes of cases will not end up in court, even though there is a strong case against them.'[3]

Yet in the wake of the Umbrella Movement, prosecutorial discretion was exercised almost uniformly against dissenters. The long, drawn-out nature of the prosecution process and timetables also appeared calculated to maintain pressure on the activist community. Jail, bankruptcy, ruined career prospects — the Hong Kong government through its Department of Justice was trying to make the cost of dissent intolerably high. It wanted Hong Kong's politically active youth, in particular, to think twice about the cost of standing up for their beliefs.

The post–Umbrella Movement manipulation of the electoral system formed another plank of the government's lawfare campaign. The oath-swearing controversy and the ensuing Basic Law interpretation and legislator disqualifications all could be said to have been conducted strictly 'in accordance with the law'. The political screening of candidates, begun in the LegCo election of 2016, continued in subsequent by-elections: Demosistō's Agnes Chow and independent localist Ventus Lau were both barred from running in the by-elections to replace their disqualified colleagues on the basis of their alleged pro-independence views. The practice continued in the 2019 district council election, with Joshua Wong told he could not run.

In mid-2018, the Hong Kong government prepared to take

the latest step in its lawfare campaign when it gave notice to the pro-independence Hong Kong National Party that it was minded to ban the party. With the controversy still raging, the Foreign Correspondents' Club of Hong Kong invited Andy Chan, the head of the party, to speak at a lunchtime event. The response from Beijing was furious. The club leadership were hauled into meetings with Beijing representatives, who demanded that the event be cancelled. The club's response was that, given that the Hong Kong National Party was not (yet) an illegal organisation, and consistent with the club's commitment to freedom of expression, which was protected under Hong Kong law, the event would go ahead. Senior *Financial Times* journalist Victor Mallet, the acting president of the club, was the public face of the club at the time, and hosted Chan's event.

A month later, the Hong Kong National Party was banned, with the government relying on powers under the Societies Ordinance ordinarily used to ban triad criminal organisations. But more was to come: in October 2018, news emerged that Mallet's application to extend his work visa in Hong Kong had been rejected, and he was subsequently refused permission to enter Hong Kong as a tourist. The Hong Kong government appeared to have expelled a journalist on purely political grounds.

The Mallet ban rattled the international business community in Hong Kong. If even the most senior journalist at one of the world's most respected news organisations was not safe, was anyone? Questions that had not previously been asked in Hong Kong began to be asked. Reporters wondered whether it was safe to report on independence activists. Academics wondered whether it would be wise to discuss issues such as the right to self-determination in classes.

In pursuing its lawfare campaign, the government appeared to be ignorant of, or indifferent to, the risk that, by appealing to the values espoused by Hong Kong's rule of law while simultaneously undermining those same values, the campaign was having a corrosive effect on Hong Kong's legal system. This had implications not just for political dissenters but for business confidence in a city that sought to distinguish itself from the rest of China almost solely on the basis of its independent, transparent, and predictable justice system. Many of the actions taken in the name of lawfare also stoked fears that Beijing was chipping away at Hong Kong's autonomy — the same fears that had driven Hong Kong's nation-building sentiments.

The gradual crackdown on dissent under the lawfare campaign seemed to succeed without drawing any significant public outcry, permitting the authorities a false sense of reassurance. What it was in fact doing was compressing an ever more tightly wound spring, stoking the resentment that would eventually burst forth violently in the protests of 2019. As the pro-establishment political figure and former LegCo president Jasper Tsang would observe in an interview in late 2019, 'In the last five years, the Hong Kong government and many of my colleagues in the pro-government camp thought that we were winning victory after victory; but every time, people became angrier.'[4]

This weaponisation of the judicial system was also, ironically, precisely the fear stoked by the extradition bill. It was therefore surprising that Lam seemed to be choosing to double down.

In addition to Lam's anti-masking law, the government obtained an array of civil court injunctions during the 2019 protests, continuing the trend begun in the Umbrella Movement of using injunctions to regulate political behaviour. Injunctions were obtained to prohibit the public from inspecting the registry of voters, and from damaging or obstructing police residences. The Airport Authority obtained injunctions prohibiting protesters from gathering at the airport, and the MTR Corporation obtained injunctions to prevent disruption to their services and damage to their facilities.

Two such injunctions, in particular, had a far-reaching impact on civil liberties. In late October, a few weeks after Lam's anti-masking law, the Department of Justice obtained an injunction that prevented anyone 'unlawfully and intentionally':

- 'using, publishing, communicating or disclosing' the personal data — including the photograph — of any police officer; or
- 'intimidating, molesting, harassing, threatening, pestering or interfering with any Police Officer' or their families.

Breaching the injunction would result in criminal-contempt charges, the same charges used to jail Joshua Wong in relation to the Mong Kok injunction.

The order was ostensibly obtained to prevent the doxxing of police and their families. The practice of doxxing — revealing the personal details of people online, thus exposing them and their families to potential harassment — had unfortunately been carried out by the more extremist elements on all sides of politics in Hong Kong: some sites maliciously targeted police officers and their families, while a pro-Beijing site hosted in Russia doxxed protesters, journalists, and pro-democracy politicians. But the means adopted to prevent it in this case not only went far beyond what was necessary, but also singled out for protection only one side — police and their families — from a practice that had also adversely affected many others.

The order could be read to prohibit anyone taking a photograph of a police officer — including those on duty policing protests — and posting that photograph online. It could also be read to criminalise any action that 'harassed' or 'pestered' police, a description that could be applied to a wide range of behaviour that had become common during the protests. The restrictions were a concern in an environment in which legitimate questions were being asked about police conduct. It was clearly in the public interest, and in the interests of the administration of justice, for citizens to have the right to document police (mis)behaviour as well as to identify the police involved, in order to have evidence for any complaints lodged with the much-touted IPCC, to facilitate future disciplinary action or even criminal charges. This injunction seemed to frustrate attempts to do just that.

In theory, the injunction would only apply to behaviour that was in itself already both unlawful and intentional, thus constraining its scope. However, that would be cold comfort to anyone tackled to the ground by police who thought the injunction gave them the licence to arrest anyone who was annoying them or taking their photo. And anyone who was arrested would then suffer the lost time, costs, and stress of defending themselves in court. The greatest impact of the injunction was therefore in its chilling effect. Given the risk of being arrested, many would conclude it was safer to stay silent.

A second injunction, obtained a few weeks later, prevented the dissemination online of any information that 'promotes, encourages or incites the use or threat of violence' to a person or property. Again, the terms were wide, including 'circulating, publishing or republishing' any such information, as well as 'assisting, causing, counselling, procuring, instigating, inciting, aiding, abetting or authorising'. The injunction would potentially catch not just the people posting the information, but also the operators of platforms such as the LIHKG forum site and administrators of Telegram chat groups (both services were specifically mentioned in the injunction), as well as internet service providers and server hosts.

The injunction effectively gave the Hong Kong police a licence to censor the internet, and was a serious incursion on freedom of expression. Views will vary about the desirability of, say, trashing a Chinese bank branch or MTR station; in any case, such action would — as it should — attract legal consequences. But with this injunction, the government sought to prevent people even talking about the idea of doing so.

Both of these injunctions, like the anti-masking law, appeared to be examples of bad law: law that was vague, difficult to interpret, and of questionable enforceability, and that gave excessive discretion to those enforcing it. It also appeared that these laws were enacted with the full knowledge that they would not be consistently and properly enforced. People would continue to wear face masks; people would continue to join illegal protests to which the police had objected under the Public Order Ordinance; and people would continue to take photographs of police and sing 'Ah! Dirty cops!' (*'Ah! Sei hak ging!'*).

Using the legal system in this manner wasn't about upholding the rule of law. Rather, it undermined the rule of law, introducing elements of uncertainty, discretion, unpredictability, and non-transparency into Hong Kong's legal system. But perhaps the Hong Kong government's intention was that none of these laws were intended to be properly enforced anyway — they were there precisely for their chilling effect.

It is difficult to see what Lam's ham-fisted anti-masking law was intended to achieve. Hong Kong's protesters were already facing prison terms of up to ten years for rioting and unlawful assembly, and were not going to be been deterred by the prospect of an additional charge for being masked.

In the meantime, for the peaceful protesters, masks were a form of protection — not so much against being identified for arrest, but to prevent reprisals from employers or pro-Beijing supporters. At peaceful rallies of office workers in Central in the weeks prior to the face-mask ban, volunteers stood with boxes of surgical face masks at the entrance to the rally, handing them out to those who did not come already prepared. A climate of fear prevailed, and face masks were the enabler for the peaceful exercise of people's right of freedom of association.

The anti-masking law was also a rankling act of hypocrisy. Since the SARS epidemic of 2003, the government had been encouraging the Hong Kong populace to wear face masks to prevent the spread of infectious diseases. Now that same government was telling everyone to remove their masks, and in the face of a government-created health and safety risk against which even ordinary citizens needed protection: police tear gas.

After Lam announced the face-mask ban, a clip of Edward Leung speaking in an election debate during his 2016 by-election campaign began circulating online. In the clip, Lam says in response to a pro-establishment candidate's suggestion of a face-mask ban, 'A few years ago, Ukraine passed an anti-mask law. Do you know what happened in Ukraine? A revolution started in Ukraine. You want to do it? Do it, we will fight till the end.'[5]

As Leung had predicted, Lam's face-mask ban provoked a furious response. Almost immediately that Friday afternoon on 4 October 2019, people began massing on the streets of Central, and crowds swelled as workers finished the working day and left their offices to join the protest. Many were still dressed in their office attire: men in suits, and women in high-heeled shoes carrying designer handbags. Schoolchildren joined the gathering as well, some turning their school shirts inside out so the emblems were not visible. All were defiantly wearing masks. The ban was due to come into effect at midnight.

The crowd chanted two new slogans. The first was a perhaps obvious augmentation to their demands. What had previously been five demands were now six: withdrawal of the masking ban had been added to the list. But another striking slogan echoed around the office blocks and footbridges of Central as they marched. Previously, the protesters' rallying cry had been *'Heung gong yan, gaa jau!'* 'Hong Kongers, add oil!' This evening, they would chant: *'Heung gong yan, faankong!'* 'Hong Kongers, resist!'

The crowd marched from Central through to Causeway Bay, beginning a night of rage that would continue in protests throughout the weekend. Following the vandalism that first became prominent during the National Day marches, businesses along the protest route and in the surrounding streets that were either mainland Chinese-owned or regarded as pro-government were trashed.

This was a development that would gain even greater intensity in subsequent weeks, and marked a profound change of tone from the entirely peaceful marches of the summer, when — even during the most violent clashes with police — there was no damage to property whatsoever. On the surface, it would appear that the protesters had lost control and descended into violence. But, as with the protesters' vandalism of LegCo and the Central Government Liaison Office, their vandalism was specific, targeted, and — if destruction of private property might be called this — disciplined.

Only two specific categories of business were targeted. The first category was mainland–Chinese-owned companies such as the state-owned banks; the state-owned mobile phone companies, China Telecom and China Unicom; and, later, other Chinese-owned companies such as technology company Xiaomi, traditional Chinese medicine company Tongren Tang, and state-owned bookstore Sino United Press.

The second category was Hong Kong businesses that had taken an explicitly pro-government stance or were otherwise seen to have collaborated in government oppression. The numerous food and beverage stores owned by restaurant giant Maxim's were targeted for vandalism because Annie Wu, the daughter of its founder, had criticised the protesters in the media and spoken in support of the government while testifying before the United Nations Human Rights Council. (Starbucks stores became a target because the franchise in Hong Kong is owned by Maxim's.) Convenience stores owned by the Bestmart 360 chain were trashed because they were understood to be owned by interests associated with the Fujianese triads who had attacked protesters in North Point. Japanese fast-food chain Yoshinoya found its stores targeted after its management allegedly fired an employee and its public relations agency for a satirical Facebook post that could have been interpreted as insulting police. The chain's boarded-up storefronts became sites for Lennon Walls along protest routes. HSBC was targeted, with branches vandalised and even the storied lion statues outside the bank's headquarters in Central splashed in bloody red paint in retaliation after reports emerged of the closure of Spark Alliance's bank account.

Protesters pasted posters on the storefronts of the businesses they had trashed, explaining their rationale for why the particular business had been selected for what they called 'refurbishment'. Any businesses outside these categories were left untouched. Indeed, when protesters mistakenly vandalised stores they believed were Chinese-owned but later realised were not, they would post signs apologising, or spray-paint a rough 'Sorry' on the storefront.

The government and police had been referring to the protesters as rioters since June. In those initial months, when protesters were scrupulously careful to ensure that no property was damaged, and were assiduously collecting their litter and separating it for recycling, the characterisation seemed faintly ridiculous. But as the protests became increasingly violent, and property damage became widespread, had they finally earned the title: were these protests now riots? Arguably, they were not, due to the absence of one key element: looting.

Rioting arises in the vacuum left in an urban space when the police — representing the authorities — withdraw from that space, or are excluded from it by the crowd. The unrestrained violence against persons or property that then takes place within the space constitutes the riot. This is often expressed in the form of looting, the point at which the crowd, having excluded the authorities, subverts the usual social order imposed by those authorities to claim ownership over everything within that space.[6]

Yet even when protests took place in the midst of Hong Kong's poorest neighbourhoods, no shops were looted by protesters. I saw inside vandalised Starbucks stores where the storefront and all the interior fittings of the shop had been smashed, yet snacks and bottled beverages were still sitting untouched on the counter and in refrigerators.

Every action taken had a purpose, and protesters at no stage claimed ownership over property within the urban space. This was less a riot than causing property damage as a form of punishment, a kind of vigilante justice against enemies of the movement. It was also a way of reclaiming power in an environment where the legitimate means of political expression had been systematically foreclosed, whether through the ballot box or through peaceful political protest. This was a means to exert pressure — against Beijing, through its state-owned business proxies, and against the Hong Kong government, through the MTR, and the tycoons who supported it.

The disciplined nature of this vandalism, the lack of looting — and the fact that it was violence against property, not violence against persons — may have been the reason why it attracted little criticism from supporters of the protesters. After all, referring to property damage as violence may ultimately say more about how we view property than how we view violence.[7] So it was that even those law-abiding citizens who supported the protests tended to express a view along the lines of: 'I don't agree with it, I wouldn't do it myself, but I understand why they are doing it, and forgive them for it.' It would take more than smashed Starbucks stores and graffitied Chinese banks for these radical protesters to lose their support base.

With plans for further rallies throughout the weekend, the government took an unusual step on the night of Friday 4 October: it implemented a curfew. This was done not explicitly using the powers under the ERO, but rather covertly, and with cooperation from the power of private capital.

First, the government closed down the entire MTR system throughout the weekend following the face-mask ban. The MTR said this was necessary to carry out repair work on stations and facilities vandalised by protesters.[8] To understand the impact of the MTR shutdown on transport around Hong Kong, consider that in a city of just over seven million people, the MTR system carries around five million passengers per day. With the MTR closed down, people's movement around the city was severely circumscribed. Hong Kong's unique geography also played a role: with no easy way to cross Victoria Harbour from Kowloon to Hong Kong Island, or to travel between Hong Kong's suburban satellite towns, people were effectively confined to their local districts.

Second, the government enlisted the support — whether explicitly or tacitly it was unclear — of private capital to shut down the city over the weekend.

Hong Kong is famously oligopolistic, with the vast majority of economic power in the city concentrated in the hands of a few tycoons and the two former British *hongs*, Swire and Jardine Matheson. Most of these companies made their fortunes through property development, and as a result own many of the city's shopping malls, but their economic power goes far beyond property. There is a duopoly of supermarkets in Hong Kong, with the Park & Shop chain owned by tycoon Li Ka-shing's CK Hutchison group, and the Wellcome chain owned by Jardines, which also owns the city's 7-Eleven stores. The two largest pharmacy chains, Watsons and Mannings, are controlled by the same duopoly. Many of the city's food and beverage outlets are owned by Maxim's, jointly controlled again by Jardines. Tycoon-controlled groups own the buses and ferry lines, the electricity and gas suppliers, and the mobile-phone operators, among other key businesses. The MTR Corporation also has an extensive shopping-mall portfolio of its own, as a result of its property-development rights over stations.

As the next stage of the curfew, the MTR and the tycoons announced that the city's shopping malls would be closed. Given the unique and central role of shopping malls in Hong Kong life, their closure meant that Hong Kongers were instantly deprived of their usual weekend leisure destinations. The oligopoly power of the tycoons was then leveraged further. Li Ka-shing's Park & Shop chain, around half the city's supermarkets, did not open at all on Saturday, citing travel and safety concerns for employees. Jardine's Wellcome supermarkets announced that they would be closing early, along with the city's 7-Eleven stores. Most other retailers followed suit.

These shutdowns, combined with the fear that the masking ban would provoke a violent reaction from protesters, prompted a widespread panic. On an otherwise clear-skied and mild autumn day, Hong Kong felt like it was preparing for one of the periodic typhoons that descend upon the city: queues wended their way out of supermarkets as shelves were emptied of food, and ATM machines were emptied of cash.

So, with nowhere to go and no way to get there, people closeted themselves indoors.

The partial curfew continued all week, with the MTR system closing early each evening, again ostensibly for repairs. This ensured that most of the city rushed home from work and avoided coming out onto the streets in the evenings, reducing the number of midweek skirmishes between the populace and police that had been a feature of previous weeks. Protests reduced in number and intensity. There was a sense that perhaps Lam was finally beginning to bring the city back under control.

However, the calm would not last. A month later, the city would be burning.

17

CITY ON FIRE

As October moved into November, tension remained high. Weekly protests continued, with increasing levels of destruction and violence on all sides. After five months of unrest, and with district council elections scheduled for 24 November, there was a sense that the city was being pushed to breaking point.

On 23 October, Chan Tong-kai, whose legal case had prompted the extradition-bill controversy, was released from prison, having served his jail term for money laundering. Chan announced that he was willing to surrender himself to Taiwan to face trial, but the Hong Kong and Taiwan governments soon became mired in squabbles over the procedural details, complicated by the fact that China does not recognise Taiwan as a sovereign state, and by Taiwanese domestic politics in the run-up to the January 2020 election.

Events gathered pace in the first week of November. Carrie Lam, on an official visit to Shanghai, made an unexpected public appearance alongside Chairman Xi Jinping. It was surprising that China's most senior leader would publicly endorse Lam, whose mismanagement of Hong Kong had almost single-handedly brought such irritations for China, from tarnishing its international image to pushing Taiwan further away from the mainland. It was a clear sign that Beijing intended to stand by her — for now.

Also that week, controversial pro-Beijing politician Junius Ho was attacked and stabbed while out campaigning for re-election to his district council seat. The stabbing was captured on video, and his assailant was quickly apprehended, while Ho escaped with only minor wounds. It was unclear whether the attack was politically motivated.

Then on Friday came the news of the death of Alex Chow Tsz-lok. Chow, a twenty-two-year-old university student, was believed to have been fleeing police in a housing estate carpark during protests earlier that week when he tried to escape over a wall, not realising there was a full one-storey drop onto concrete on the other side. Controversy arose over whether police delayed medical treatment or hindered ambulance access after his fall. Chow remained in a coma for several days before succumbing to his injuries. His was the first death to have arisen in connection with a policing action during the protests.

The Ten O'clock Calling, which had faded out in recent weeks, was back that night. In the past, this had been a nightly moment of enchantment. But tonight, as the calls echoed out again, there was an increasingly desperate edge to the voices. I wondered why the calling that night felt so desolate, and then it struck me: with the Ten O'clock Calling you could always hear the voices, coming from near and far, echoing among the buildings around you, but you could never see the people who were doing the calling. The callers were invisible. These disembodied voices were the voices of ghosts.

The following week, protesters called for another general strike and week of action that they named 'Operation Daybreak'.

Early in the morning of Monday 11 November 2019, as the morning commute was getting underway, protesters again began blocking roads and disrupting traffic and MTR services. Police quickly responded, leading to multiple flashpoints across the city. Then, as Hong Kongers watched their phones while queuing for their buses to get to work, or while having their breakfast milk tea and congee, a shocking scene emerged. In Sai Wan Ho, a police officer attempting to clear protester roadblocks became embroiled in a scuffle with three protesters. The officer gripped one protester around the neck with one hand and began to drag him away, while with the other hand he drew his gun and pointed it at another protester. As the second, unarmed protester approached and appeared to make an attempt to swat away the gun, the police officer fired, shooting the protester in the stomach from a metre away. He then turned and fired two shots at another approaching protester, as the first protester lay stricken, his face drained white, blood pouring from his abdomen onto the road. The whole incident was live-streamed by a local media organisation, and videos circulated quickly online, to widespread outrage.

It was the beginning of what became a week of chaos that engulfed the city.

Later that day, in Central, smartly dressed but furious white-collar office workers emerged from their offices at lunchtime, wearing face masks and joining black-shirted protesters in blockading the streets. With Chow's death and the morning's shooting, the crowd again had a new slogan. Previously, 'Hong Kongers, add oil!' had given way to 'Hong Kongers, resist!'; today their new slogan was: *'Heunggong yan bousau!'* ('Hong Kongers, revenge!')

While the office workers marched and chanted, radical protesters among the crowd vandalised nearby Chinese bank branches, graffitied walls, and blockaded the roads. Riot police soon arrived on the scene, and before long were firing tear gas and rubber bullets at the crowd in the busiest intersection in Central. (To get a sense of how unsettling this was, imagine riot police firing tear gas in the middle of Sydney's Martin Place, or Finsbury Circus in London's financial district, during the average weekday lunch hour.)

The lunchtime protests continued every day that week, with white-collar workers flooding the streets and riot police descending on Central to disperse the protesters. Tear gas was fired on multiple occasions, drifting into the adjacent shopping malls and office lobbies.

Elsewhere in the city that Monday, a police motorbike was filmed careening wildly into a crowd of protesters, who scattered across the road as the police appeared to be trying to run them over deliberately.

The protesters were not entirely blameless. In another horrific, live-streamed incident on Monday afternoon, a man arguing with protesters after an altercation in an MTR station was doused in flammable liquid and set alight; he suffered serious burns. Later in the week, during a melee between protesters and pro-Beijing gangs, a seventy-year-old bystander was hit in the head with a thrown brick, and later died of his injury. While both sides were throwing bricks during the fight, videos of the incident suggested that the offending brick was likely thrown by a protester.

The city was roiled with disruptions throughout the week, the streets lit with burning barricades, and petrol bombs hurled at police lines. The roads became moonscapes as protesters dug up brick pavers from the footpaths, and either tossed them onto the asphalt or constructed them into miniature trilithons to block traffic and impede the progress of police. Roads along block after block were rendered impassable. As a result of the transport disruptions, and with the sense that the city's streets were no longer safe, all school classes were cancelled for the week, and many people simply stopped going to work. The city ground to a standstill.

The focus then shifted to the university campuses. On Monday night, students and other protesters waged a twenty-four-hour pitched battle with police for control of a bridge leading over a major expressway and railway lines to the Chinese University of Hong Kong's hilltop campus. Police said that protesters had thrown objects from the bridge to block traffic and the rail lines below — the entire East Rail line was out of commission as a result, and traffic flows to the north-east of Hong Kong were seriously disrupted. Protesters said they wanted to prevent the police from entering the campus, which, as a matter of convention, they could do only at the invitation of the university administration. Protesters — some Chinese University students, but many others joining from outside to help defend the campus, much to the consternation of the faculty and some student groups — launched petrol bombs, threw rocks, and were even pictured firing flaming arrows that they had sequestered from the university sports department's archery facilities. In return, police subjected them to an hours-long barrage of tear gas and rubber bullets. The battle for Bridge Number 2 continued all night, with people around Hong Kong watching a live-stream broadcast that resembled a war movie rather than present-day Hong Kong. Police eventually withdrew from the university after blocking off the contested bridge, and protesters abandoned their positions on the campus.

However, clashes continued on other campuses, with tear gas fired at all four of the city's largest universities. Students at the University of Hong Kong tore apart and barricaded the campus in anticipation of a police incursion there, vandalised the university's MTR station and Starbucks store, and sprayed the campus with graffiti. One notable piece of graffiti reworked the university motto from 'Virtue and Wisdom' to 'Virtue and Revolution', while another directed at police read: 'You have to test into HKU, not break into it!' Students at City University and Baptist University also blockaded roads outside their campuses. In the wake of these incidents, university administrators declared that the semester would be finishing two weeks early.

———

At this point, it is worth considering what to make of the increasing violence in which the protests became embroiled. The protests began as entirely peaceful, with no damage to property or person, consistent with previous protest movements in Hong Kong. Yet as the violence escalated over subsequent months in a cycle of action and reaction, this did not result in a significant loss of support for the protesters. Actions such setting an antagonist on fire, or the beatings meted out during the airport protest, were deplorable. Why weren't they more widely denounced? There seemed to be several factors at play.

First, the absolute level of violence was, in the scheme of things, not high, and primarily directed at property. Whether the targets were the buildings of LegCo and the Central Government Liaison Office, or the businesses singled out for what the protesters called 'refurbishment', many supporters of the movement did not necessarily see the attacks on these inanimate objects as violence. This violence, such as it was, was selective and rational, at least according to its own internal logic.

Violence against persons remained rare, notwithstanding those attacks that had occurred. Even when protesters were throwing Molotov cocktails, they rarely directed them *at* police; rather, they were directed at the roads between protesters and police, with the aim of slowing the police advance and giving protesters sufficient time to escape. Protesters did not engage in acts of violence against persons at levels anywhere near those of, say, the 1967 deaths of the Wong children or the assassination of Lam Bun.

Second, the protester violence could be philosophically justified as a reaction against state violence, whether in the form of police brutality or the systemic violence of the political system. When peaceful protest marches were banned and violently dispersed by police, and

when the public-transport system was weaponised against the protesters to prevent freedom of assembly, violence in some form seemed
to be the only option that protesters felt they were left with. This was
violence as a cry for attention, an escalation of violence in response to
a government that did not listen to the people or acknowledge their
demands. It was also something that the government itself encouraged
when it acknowledged and responded to protester demands following
notable escalations of violence, as reflected in the protester slogan, 'It
Was You Who Taught Me that Peaceful Marches Are Useless.'

The violence was in turn used by the authorities as an excuse to
criminalise the entire movement, to describe protesters as rioters and
thereby to delegitimise them and their demands.

There was also a risk that committing acts of politically motivated
violence was coming increasingly closer to falling within one of the
various definitions of terrorism. While there is no single agreed definition under international law, Hong Kong had adopted a definition
under its terrorist-financing laws that covered, among other matters,
the use or threat of serious violence against a person or serious damage
to property for the purpose of advancing a political cause.[1]

Yet one person's terrorist is often another's freedom fighter. For the
Hong Kong protesters, fighting back was an act of self-empowerment.
You could see this in the way they equipped and armed themselves,
and the way they carried themselves when dressed in full gear. They
were transformed from ordinary youths into braves. This was an
act of taking power, of claiming agency over their destiny. In their
weekly clashes with the police, protesters knew they were hopelessly
outgunned and that they could never defeat a modern police force in
head-to-head clashes. But they said that they wanted to make the cost
higher for the government, and to draw attention to the state violence
to which they were being subjected.

John Tsang, the former financial secretary and runner-up to

Carrie Lam in the chief executive election, recognised this inequity when he told local radio station RTHK: 'Given the imbalance of power between the protesters and the government, I think the government must take the initiative to start some action to de-escalate the force they are exerting in the community.'[2]

Finally, supporters of the protesters were reluctant to surrender their hard-won solidarity. It would take an extreme act to break the bonds of the 'no splittling' principle.

By contrast, protesters and their supporters could point to numerous examples of much worse violence on the pro-government side: the Yuen Long attacks; gang attacks in North Point; attacks on various pro-democracy activists and politicians; as well as police violence. Indeed, by an unfortunate coincidence of timing, every time the protesters carried out an act that might have been seen as outrageous and deserving of public condemnation, the police inevitably carried out a more outrageous act the very same weekend, diverting public and media attention, and keeping outrage focused on the police.

There was thus a sense among all sides that, even if 'we' may have behaved badly on occasion, 'they' were even worse and far more deserving of condemnation. This was a mindset that risked a dangerous descent into tribalism, and indeed many in Hong Kong began talking in hushed tones about the Northern Ireland Troubles and whether Hong Kong might end up becoming a new Belfast.

There was one group in the Hong Kong community in particular who were becoming increasingly fearful of the risks that tribalism posed: the mainland Chinese community.

In recent years, as Hong Kong's economy had become more integrated with that of mainland China's, the services industry that made up a significant proportion of the economy had a growing need for workers with fluent Chinese language and cultural skills. The foreign expats of yore had come to be replaced by a new class of expats: mainland-born, overseas-educated professionals who now populated the banks, accounting firms, and law firms of Central, as well as staffing the Hong Kong branches of numerous state-owned companies and financial institutions. Many more visited Hong Kong from the mainland, whether for business or pleasure.

As the protests turned violent, and took on an increasingly anti-China bent, this community began to feel nervous. At a protest in Central, a mainland employee of JP Morgan became embroiled in a confrontation with protesters outside his office, and when he said in Mandarin to the agitated throng around him, 'We are all Chinese!' (*'Women dou shi Zhongguoren!'*), one black-clad protester leapt in and punched him.

It is interesting to pause on this statement: it may well have been intended as an attempt to voice solidarity, as an expression of fraternity. However, carrying as it did the political baggage of not just ethnicity but citizenship, nationhood, and therefore rule from Beijing, it was not an uncontroversial statement, especially when spoken in that context — and in Mandarin. It could have been understood by some in the crowd as an assertion of colonial rule, spoken in the language of the coloniser. But such were the complexities that mainland residents in Hong Kong increasingly found themselves having to navigate.

My mainland friends spoke of no longer feeling welcome in Hong Kong, of being fearful to go out at weekends, fearful of speaking Mandarin in public. Even if the streets appeared quiet, one told me, they never knew when they might find themselves in an uncomfortable situation. Another friend on the mainland, having originally made plans for a holiday in Hong Kong to take her daughter to Disneyland, abruptly cancelled her trip, telling me, 'I think Hong Kong is finished.'

Yet this intra-ethnic division seemed, perversely, to be precisely Beijing's strategy. On 14 November, Chairman Xi made his first public comments on the topic of Hong Kong, offering support for its government and police, and emphasising the need to restore order 'in accordance with the law'. He also said, 'Our commitment to fully implement "one country, two systems" has not changed, and we resolutely oppose any foreign forces seeking to interfere in the internal affairs of Hong Kong,' adding that the continuing violence was 'a blatant challenge to the bottom line of one country, two systems'. However, beyond this, Xi proposed no new measures to bring Hong Kong to heel.

Beijing seemed to be thinking: *Let Hong Kong burn.* As long as there was no risk of contagion, or impairment of the city's ability to act as a source of capital for China's businesses, Beijing appeared content to leave Hong Kong to consume itself in violence and rage. Their expectation was that the growing disruption and violence would ultimately undermine support for the protest movement, deepen the divisions in Hong Kong society, and create fertile conditions for Beijing to step in and impose order. In the meantime, Hong Kong would serve as an object lesson for domestic propaganda purposes in the rest of China. *Look at the mess,* Beijing could say, *that ensues from popular movements demanding so-called democracy and freedom.*

The week of traffic disruptions tested the limits of patience for many. As ordinary citizens joined efforts organised by pro-Beijing politicians across the city that weekend to clear the roads, Beijing made a tentative but significant incursion: the PLA garrison sent troops out of one of its barracks in Kowloon onto the streets, on what they said was a purely spontaneous, voluntary exercise to assist with clearing the roads. Dressed in their sports-training uniforms, they jogged out in formation and joined civilian volunteers, picking up bricks and clearing roadblocks. In response to media questioning, their commanding officer said the troops were there to spread 'positive energy' (one of Chairman Xi's catchphrases).

The incident raised eyebrows, given the sensitivity of the PLA's presence in Hong Kong, as well as the legal restrictions that permitted the PLA to operate in Hong Kong only at the request of the Hong Kong government. The government admitted that no such request had been made in this case, but said that the restriction did not apply to this act of voluntary 'charitable' work. However, clearing protester roadblocks had political significance: this was policing, not merely charitable work. Many on the pan-democrat side saw it not only as an illegal deployment of PLA troops, but as the thin end of the wedge — an attempt to socialise and normalise the presence of PLA soldiers on the Hong Kong streets. The idea that the event was voluntary was laughable: soldiers don't do anything voluntarily; they follow orders. It was hard to see the incident as anything other than a carefully managed public-relations exercise.

Over at the University of Hong Kong on Saturday afternoon, local residents joined the road-clearing efforts with gusto. The crowd was an odd mix of pro-Beijing supporters, ordinary local residents, and a handful of indignant expats, all united in their outrage and chipping away with steel bars at the brick roadblocks that had been cemented into place by protesters. Some jeered up at the students who stood looking down on them from the still-barricaded campus.

A small group of nervous academics and university administrators stood between the two groups, hoping to forestall any confrontations and prevent any non-university personnel from entering the campus. One academic frowned as we watched the near-frenzied crowds down on the road and the angry protesters on the bridge above. 'We're worried that all the protesters who were at Chinese University will come here next,' he said.

I thought about the geography for a moment — Chinese University was in the far north of Kowloon, while the University of Hong Kong was across the harbour on Hong Kong Island, with several other universities lying in between — and then joked, 'Don't worry, they'll get to PolyU first.'

18

THE SIEGE

The Polytechnic University of Hong Kong, affectionately referred to as PolyU, sits close to the Kowloon waterfront, adjacent to the Hung Hom railway station and the entrance to the Cross Harbour Tunnel. The campus is something of an island, surrounded by expressways on three sides, with footbridges stretching over the toll booths at the tunnel entrance and connecting the campus to the Hung Hom transport hub.

On the weekend commencing Saturday 16 November 2019, several thousand students and protesters took up positions inside the PolyU campus and, using the campus as a base, blockaded the Cross Harbour Tunnel entrance, bringing transport along that vital road-traffic route to a standstill. Their 'Be water!' strategy had frozen into ice. Fortified inside the castle-like campus, the protesters demanded that, in order for them to reopen the tunnel, the government promise that the following weekend's district council elections would proceed. On Sunday morning, 17 November, police began an assault on PolyU to try to break the siege and reopen the tunnel.

Arriving at PolyU on Sunday morning, shortly after the police assault on the campus began, I scrambled across a brick-strewn intersection through clouds of tear gas, and along the destroyed footpath to the university entrance. I climbed the long flight of steps, partially blocked by the twisted wreckage of classroom furniture, until I arrived at a checkpoint manned by protesters who were frisking people and conducting bag checks, looking for undercover police officers who had been infiltrating protester groups. They checked my bag semi-apologetically, and then let me inside.

The campus was barely recognisable as such. Supplies and equipment were strewn everywhere, the walls covered in protest graffiti. The main courtyard was a hive of activity as protesters shifted barricades and prepared equipment. One protester had rigged up a ride-on floor-cleaning machine with a few trolleys to form a goods train, spray-painted 'Supplies' on the side, and drove it trundling across the courtyard.

I poked my head into the American Diner Cafe, now sequestered by protesters. A few people were working behind the counter, and the remnants of foodstuffs were scattered around. 'Sorry,' announced a girl as I walked in, 'today we have only drinks, fruit, or you can make yourself some toast.' She pointed at a toaster, a loaf of bread, and a catering-sized jar of peanut butter on a table to the side. I politely declined.

Nearby, the students had designated a large classroom as the Media Centre for members of the press. The aircon was functioning, some yoga mats were set out on the floor for those who wanted to rest, and a giant screen showed four different live-streams of the scenes unfolding on the streets outside.

I moved on to another building, where I discovered the gymnasium had been turned into an enormous dormitory, with the floor covered in yoga mats on which some protesters were sleeping. A large sign at the entrance read, 'NO PHOTOS'; protesters were vulnerable, their identities exposed after having removed their face masks and other gear to sleep.

Another room had become a clinic, with first-aid supplies piled high on tables and around the walls: everything from bandages to asthma medication, from painkillers to burns cream.

Out the back of the building, five students sat chatting cheerfully at a picnic table in the sunshine as they assembled Molotov cocktails. The nearby swimming pool was empty, and had been used for Molotov cocktail practice: the pool floor was scarred with black burn marks and covered in shattered glass bottles.

Entering the campus cafeteria, perhaps what was at first most striking was that it felt just like a normal university day: protesters formed a long, orderly queue to receive meals, the tables were full, and the place buzzing. There was nothing to indicate that the people working behind the counters were all volunteers and that everything was being provided free of charge. The protesters working the kitchens were serving full hot meals: fare such as pork chops, sausages, rice, vegetables, spring rolls, and toasted sandwiches. A pile of cold McDonald's cheeseburgers sat on a tray. Plastic tumblers of tea were proffered across the counter.

The only aspect of the scene that made one realise this was unlike any other day was the attire: everyone was uniformly dressed in black, their yellow hard hats and gas masks sitting by their sides as they ate. The protesters on the site were overwhelmingly young people, many of them PolyU students or students from other universities who had come to help. Many had been at the Chinese University siege earlier in the week. But there were also outsiders there, including some as young as high school age.

In the middle of the cafeteria hall, long tables had been pushed together and piled high with a mind-boggling array of food supplies. A quick survey revealed there were boxes of apples and oranges, muesli bars, protein bars, Mars Bars, Snickers, Lindt chocolate, Pacific crackers, Ritz crackers, Digestive biscuits, Oreo cookies, Orion chocolate

pies, Quaker oatmeal, a variety of brands and flavours of instant noo-
dles to suit every taste, crisps, nuts, loaves of bread, sanitary supplies,
mineral water, fruit juice, cans of soft drink ... It was the equivalent
of a small, well-stocked supermarket. All of the food and supplies
had been donated, gradually delivered to the campus over the course
of the previous day and that morning, a clear demonstration of the
public support these protesters were enjoying.

The whole cafeteria was remarkably clean, given the number of
people there and the fact that no cleaning staff were on duty. Everyone
carefully cleared their rubbish and deposited their dishes for washing
by other volunteers. The cash register — now redundant — had been
turned into a mobile-phone charging station and 'lost and found'
department. One protester had lost his ID card and was asking the
protesters behind the counter if anyone had handed it in.

As I surveyed the scene, word began to spread among the crowd
that the police water cannons were approaching the frontlines. People
immediately stood, clearing their places and hastily swallowing down
the last of their food, and the cafeteria emptied as they pulled on their
gear and scrambled out of the building and back down to rejoin the
frontline.

The police assault was focused on the only accessible entrance:
the road on the southern side of the campus. From two sides of the
intersection, police lines were formed, from which they were firing
a constant stream of tear gas and rubber bullets. Two water cannons,
one from each direction, sprayed streams of pepper water and blue
dye towards the protester frontlines.

The protesters, sheltering behind a protective line of umbrellas
and makeshift shields, responded with petrol bombs and broken
chunks of brick. Every now and then, a police long-range audio device, or LRAD, would emit a piercing wail, and the protesters would
respond by playing 'Für Elise' over a loudhailer.

Looking up, I could see that protesters had manned the balconies high above the street — the main PolyU building is made up of a series of terraced balconies — and I decided to make my way up there. Someone pointed the way through a nearby building entrance, and I found myself walking along debris-strewn hallways past empty offices and through the entrance to a library. The books appeared unharmed. Through torn ceiling tiles, broken fire sprinklers were dripping water onto the floor, soaking the carpet, and a heavy scent of tear gas hung in the air. For some unknown reason, there was a small pile of set concrete in the middle of the floor.

As I emerged through a door onto one of the outdoor roof terraces, I found a group of protesters operating an improvised catapult to launch petrol bombs and rocks at the police lines. One clasped a yellow hard hat that had been rigged on lengths of rubber between two metal poles, and hauled it back with all his weight until he was lying almost prone on the ground. Another carefully lit a petrol bomb, placed it into the hard hat, and then — release! The catapult snapped back, and the petrol bomb soared over the parapet and across the sky towards the police. The team raced to the edge of the terrace to see if their missile had hit its target.

On another balcony, more catapults had been rigged up, firing chunks of brick towards police. Scouts peered out through binoculars across at the police lines. Occasionally, there would be a pop or a bang as a rubber bullet or sponge grenade was fired up and ricocheted off a shield. Everything — the equipment, the ground, the warriors — was dyed an eerie pale blue, where it had been doused by the water cannon. Tear gas canisters landed up on the terrace, sending clouds of tear smoke drifting across. Through the smoke, a protester emerged wearing an old World War II–style gas mask and wielding a bow and arrow, and fired over the parapet down at the police lines. This was no longer a protest, or even a riot. It was medieval siege warfare.

The battle on the street continued all day. As afternoon wore into evening and the police net tightened, the mood gradually turned from the cheerful determination of earlier in the day — a kind of school-camp atmosphere — to unease, and then, a growing panic. The police taunted the protesters over their loudspeakers: 'It's common sense that you have to face the penalty if you break the law, just like you have to pay the bill after having a meal in a restaurant. No worries, if you are stubborn, we can stay here and wait for you till Christmas Day, New Year, Easter.'[1]

As police began to gather in large numbers on a second front at the Hung Hom station, the protesters were forced to defend several footbridges connecting the station to the campus. They set barricades on the footbridges, throwing petrol bombs towards police at the far end of the bridges, who responded by firing rubber bullets back towards the protesters cowering behind their barricades and shields. As I crouched down among the protesters, many of them with petrol bombs at the ready, a girl suddenly stood up, waving an iPhone above her head: 'Hey, did anyone drop their phone?' she called out cheerfully.

Back on the PolyU campus, a message began circulating by AirDrop among phones: 'Immediately call people in the 18 districts to take action, PolyU is surrounded and even those without gear cannot leave. We need the 18 districts to distract police attention. Everyone save PolyU!'

With the police closing in, the protesters decided to set fire to the barricades on the bridges in a desperate attempt to stop police entering. On one footbridge, stockpiles of petrol bombs caught alight, and with a boom the footbridge was ablaze.

Meanwhile, on the road bridge above, a phalanx of protesters, umbrellas interlocked, faced police from behind a large barricade. One of the police Unimog armoured vehicles approached and attempted to smash its way through the barricade, but became stuck. The vehicle was immediately attacked with a shower of petrol bombs and was engulfed in flames. For a few moments, it seemed as if the vehicle and its occupants were trapped. However, the wheels somehow managed to find traction, and the vehicle pulled back away from the frontline, with the flames extinguished but the vehicle out of action.

Things had clearly reached a dangerous new level. Police made a public announcement that if protesters continued to attack police, they would be forced to respond with lethal ammunition.

At almost the same moment, news began to come through on protesters' mobile phones that police were closing their cordon around the site and had declared that anyone remaining would be arrested and charged with rioting. Police had apparently already refused first-aiders and non-accredited journalists permission to leave. Images circulated of first-aiders, volunteer doctors, and nurses arrested, lined up on the ground in their high-vis jackets, their hands zip-tied behind their backs like suspects caught in a terrorist raid. Hong Kong medical practitioner Darren Mann subsequently wrote in a letter published in *The Lancet* that the police actions in arresting medical personnel fell 'far below accepted international norms ... The arrest of these personnel is almost unheard of in civilised countries and is incompatible with the compact of humanitarianism.'[2]

The remaining protesters were left with a dilemma: surrender and leave the campus, knowing they would face immediate arrest and up to ten years in jail or, possibly, worse — many genuinely feared they would be beaten, sexually assaulted, or even killed if they ended up in a police holding cell — or, knowing their position was untenable, nevertheless stay and fight? Most stayed, announcing that they were prepared to die for the cause. The protesters dug in.

With both sides refusing to step down, the entire city was on edge, many openly wondering whether Hong Kong was about to witness a repeat of 1989's Tiananmen Square massacre. Police officers were pictured standing outside the campus with serious weaponry, including AR-15 semiautomatic rifles. There were reports of snipers being stationed on the roofs of surrounding buildings. It seemed incredible that police would actually storm the campus with guns blazing — but that seemed to be precisely what they were threatening to do. Part of the reason for police continuing the siege seems to have been their impression that hundreds of so-called radical frontline protesters were holed up inside the campus, and that they could in one action arrest this core group, emasculating the protest movement. Their impression would ultimately prove to be mistaken.

Throughout these traumatic events, the Hong Kong government was once again absent. In any other city undergoing the events Hong Kong endured that day, political leaders would have been front and centre, explaining, justifying, reassuring the public, visiting the sites of conflict, and speaking to all sides involved. Instead, Hong Kong had to console itself with deafening silence. The PolyU siege had been underway for over two days before Carrie Lam finally emerged to give a press conference on Tuesday morning, at which she announced that protesters under the age of eighteen (of which there were over 100) would be permitted to leave the site without being arrested, while asking that the other protesters surrender themselves to avoid further violence.

Pastoral visits to the besieged campus were made by other members of the community: establishment politician Jasper Tsang visited, as did University of Hong Kong law professor Eric Cheung, who reassured protesters that police would unlikely have sufficient evidence to establish rioting cases against all of them. A number of high school principals visited, trying to convince their students to leave. Many protesters chose to leave with these groups or with medical crews — assured that, at least if they left in the company of others, their chances of mistreatment by police were reduced.

———

As the siege continued at PolyU, riots broke out in the streets of Kowloon on Sunday night and throughout Monday as thousands rallied, trying to breach the police lines to rescue the trapped protesters.

Chanting, '*Gau Poly!*' ('Save Poly!') crowds charged police lines again and again in the streets leading to the campus. Protesters and police skirmished from Tsim Sha Tsui to Jordan to Yau Ma Tei. Supply lines stretching over a kilometre passed materiel down Nathan Road from Mong Kok to the frontlines in Jordan. Barricades were built with everything from bamboo scaffolding to outdoor furniture, from roadside planters to entire phone boxes, ripped from the ground and dragged into the middle of the road. The barricades burned, and tear gas drenched much of the district. Streams of disturbing images emerged: police cars driving at high speed down streets crowded with protesters; a scrambling, writhing mass of piled bodies caught in an apparent stampede in Yau Ma Tei, as protesters tried to flee an incoming charge of riot police; and young protesters lined up along walls by the score, being zip-tied for arrest.

In the backstreets of Tsim Sha Tsui, as police pursued protesters through the streets, and tear gas drifted across the neighbourhood, I saw some protesters stop to help a street-side food vendor who had been affected by tear gas. One protester tenderly washed out the vendor's eyes with saline solution, while another walked up and slapped a pair of goggles down on the counter.

On Monday evening, many had come directly from work and joined the effort. As I watched human chains comprising scores of young middle-class professionals passing chunks of brick from hand to hand up to a footbridge to be thrown at police, it was clear to me that something in Hong Kong society had broken.

Down on Salisbury Road, close to the approach to PolyU, hundreds of volunteer school bus drivers' cars had filled the road, and were tooting their horns to express their outrage and to distract police. At the frontline, where police were trying to hold off protesters from approaching the campus, a car caught fire. The fire quickly spread to the adjacent parked cars, and soon several cars were alight in a blazing ball of fire, an occasional boom emerging from the inferno as a petrol tank exploded. The crowd stood back, smoke filling the air, the flames glowing orange on their faces.

At the end of the night, I walked through a devastated Kowloon, trying to find a way to get home. The pavement was destroyed, the roads covered in brick pavers — sometimes built into trilithons, sometimes piled into half-metre-high ridges across the width of the road. This tactic had proved effective: after trying to cross the barricaded roads, one police water cannon had suffered a burst tire and broken axle. The network of blockaded roads spread across swathes of Kowloon. As I picked my way down one road covered in three-brick trilithons, a protester on the footpath called out: 'Could you please be careful? It took a long time to build all that!'

Along Nathan Road, normally a bustling commercial thoroughfare, all was dark and quiet. The road was scattered with broken umbrellas and spent tear gas shell casings. Rubber bullets bounced along the road as I accidentally kicked them while I walked. At the side of the road, the carcass of a burnt-out bus hulked in the dull glow of the streetlights.

I stopped to chat to a roadside fruit vendor. 'I have to go to work. I had to walk all the way here, but what can I do?' he sighed, resigned. He gazed helplessly out at the street, littered with bricks and debris. 'Look at what's happened to our beautiful Hong Kong.'

———

Stories soon emerged of daring escapes from PolyU through the police cordon. Some escaped by running across the rooftop of a footbridge while coming under heavy fire from police tear gas canisters and rubber bullets. Another group rappelled down a rope from a footbridge some six metres off the ground, and escaped on the back of waiting motorcycles below. Scores more escaped, miraculously and in the face of terrible risks to their safety, through the sewer system. At times neck-deep in water in the darkness, following directions given by engineers on the outside who had studied the sewer maps, they navigated their way several kilometres to an exit, where supporters were waiting to open the drain covers and retrieve them.[3]

I spoke to one young escapee, a seventeen-year-old high school student I'll call Eve. Eve had entered PolyU on Sunday afternoon to lend her help to one of the volunteer first-aid teams. By the time she found out about the police deadline, it was too late to leave. After a tense day stuck inside the campus, as the situation — and the mental state of her fellow captives — deteriorated around her, Eve was able to make contact with a former PolyU student who, using Google Maps and Google Streetview images sent over WhatsApp, was able to guide her to a little-known gap in the PolyU perimeter through which she made her escape. 'When I look back at those messages now ...' Eve's voice trailed off, and she shuddered. She was picked up by a school bus and taken to a nearby safe house.

Eve was one of many school-aged children caught up in the protests. In December, the government announced that students from over 300 high schools had been arrested in the previous six months. Numerous high schools formed 'concern groups' during the protests, and 'human chains' of high school students protesting outside their schools before class — holding hands and chanting protest slogans — became a common sight. For these high school students, and for their fellow college-aged protesters, the 2019 protests will be the defining experience of their generation.

It was anthropologist Arnold van Gennep, writing in 1909, who first described rite-of-passage rituals in tribal societies. In Van Gennep's classic formulation, a rite of passage, whether for an individual (such as the initiation rituals marking progress from childhood to adulthood) or for a social group (such as harvest or new year rituals), followed three distinct phases. There was the rite of separation, when the child is separated from family and society; the rite of transition (in a period that Van Gennep called 'liminal', from the Latin word for 'threshold'), when the child undergoes various challenges and trials beyond the normal boundaries and limits of society; and the rite of incorporation, where, having passed through the rite of passage, the individual is welcomed back into the group. Subsequent theorists, including British anthropologist Victor Turner in the 1960s, applied the theory of liminality more broadly to transformative events in the lives of communities and societies (such as wars, revolutions, and economic or political crises).

Many of the protesters in the 2019 protest movement were Hong Kong's youth, and their experience of participating in the protests could be read very much as a traditional rite of passage, after which the protest movement ended and the youths returned to their homes and families. The 2019 protest movement was also a transitional period for Hong Kong society as a whole, a time when the rules normally governing society were temporarily suspended and the city went through a crisis period of identity-searching. That crisis period peaked that week in November, when the whole city seemed to float in a state of suspension.

When the liminal experience of a significant group of individuals overlaps with a liminal experience for society as a whole, this can result in the development of a generational consciousness, the identity-forming process of a generation with particular sociopolitical characteristics.[4] Hong Kong's 2019 generation was formed by their shared experiences of these protests. Eve and her peers are a generation who, when the fifty-year guarantee of rights and freedoms under the Basic Law expires in 2047, will be in their middle-aged years, at the height of their careers, with children of their own. The 2019 generation will be the leaders of Hong Kong when it comes to face the moment that will be decisive to its future.

There is a spatial, as well as a temporal, aspect to liminality: rites of passage take place in liminal spaces. In tribal societies, rights of transition often involved a casting out into the wilderness, and the rites were enacted by way of spatial progression from this separate space back to society. Modern societies have similar physical spaces of transition, threshold, or in-between spaces.

Hong Kong has long existed in a temporal liminality: first, that of the period between the Sino-British Joint Declaration of 1984 and the handover of 1997, and now in the period between the handover and the moment in 2047 when the guarantee of the rights and free-doms and the Hong Kong way of life under the Basic Law expires. But its spatiality is also liminal. Hong Kong is a transitional zone between mainland China and the rest of the world.

And the city's spaces can seem constructed from an assemblage of transitional spaces — escalators and elevated walkways, tunnels and bridges, the podiums of multi-tower apartment developments. The protesters gathered on roads and footpaths, built Lennon Walls on walkways and in tunnels, smashed the MTR stations — all quintessen-tial transitory spaces. In these spaces, the protesters created their ritual space, the unpoliced zones behind the barricades, in which their rite of passage was enacted. They chanted slogans and sang songs, and they engaged in ritualised acts of violence. And, at the peak of that burning week in November, the PolyU campus, a luminous vessel carrying the young protesters under siege, floated above the surface of the city.

The police did not ultimately storm PolyU, as they had been threatening to do, but maintained their cordon around the campus. The siege dragged on through the week, with police reporting that over 1,100 people were arrested at the site. The numbers of protesters still inside the campus reportedly dwindled, and the protesters become increasingly desperate, paranoid, and afraid. The government refused to compromise, and the Cross Harbour Tunnel was not reopened. But the elections would go ahead.

19

THE SILENT MAJORITY

As the protests raged on, with increasing vandalism, violence, and disruption to daily life, Carrie Lam and the pro-Beijing politicians in Hong Kong spoke frequently of a silent majority in Hong Kong, those patriotic Hong Kongers who opposed the protests but were afraid to speak out. The district council elections, held every four years, with the next due to be held on 24 November 2019, would give that silent majority a chance to speak.

In the days leading up to the elections, with the PolyU siege continuing, a number of events occurred that made the week the culmination of the previous six months.

On Monday 18 November, Hong Kong's High Court overturned Carrie Lam's face-masking ban, ruling that her use of the ERO was inconsistent with the Basic Law and the Bill of Rights Ordinance. More than that, the court said that any use of the ERO in cases of mere public danger was unconstitutional. While the government would still be permitted to utilise the ERO in cases of emergency (presumably, following the declaration of a state of emergency), Lam had conspicuously refused to do that, going out of her way to declare that Hong Kong was not in a state of emergency, perhaps cognisant of the adverse public-relations impact.

The decision was estament to the strength of Hong Kong's independent judiciary and a reassuring boost to the image of Hong Kong's rule of law. And it immediately met with a furious response from Beijing. A spokesperson for the National People's Congress condemned the court's decision, and declared that the Hong Kong courts had no power to rule on the constitutionality of Hong Kong laws and acts of government. The statement not only ignored the fact that the Hong Kong courts had been doing exactly this for the twenty-two years since the handover, but also contained an implicit threat that, if acted upon, would destroy Hong Kong's rule of law.

The essential underlying principle of the rule of law is that everyone, including the government itself, is subject to it. The government's lawmaking must itself be lawful (consistent with the constitution, which in Hong Kong's case is the Basic Law). Under the three-way separation-of-powers doctrine — adopted in common-law jurisdictions, including Hong Kong (but which Beijing explicitly rejects for the rest of China) — the courts, through an independent judiciary, act as a check and balance on government power.

The threat implicit in Beijing's criticism was that the National People's Congress could make another interpretation of the Basic Law to strip the Hong Kong courts of their power. If they did that, it would fundamentally alter the landscape of the Hong Kong legal system, and could quite legitimately be said to mean the end of the rule of law as we know it in Hong Kong.

It remains unclear whether or not the statement was merely bluster, an angry response to an unwelcome ruling. At the time of writing, the Department of Justice is pursuing the appeal process, over which Beijing's shadow looms large.

——

On Wednesday 20 November, Simon Cheng, a Hong Kong citizen and British consulate employee who had been detained while visiting the mainland in August, went public with his account of the experience. Cheng had disappeared while on a business trip to Shenzhen, and re-emerged from detention two weeks later. At the time, the PRC authorities said that Cheng had been detained for soliciting prostitution. But Cheng's account was very different.

In a Facebook post as well as several media interviews, Cheng told of being detained and interrogated for his role in the Hong Kong protests.[1] He gave a harrowing account of torture and abuse at the hands of Chinese secret police, and said he was forced to film a false confession to the prostitution charges. Cheng said he had his phone searched, and was asked to provide evidence supporting the narrative that the UK had organised and funded the Hong Kong protests, as well as to identify photographs of other protesters.

Perhaps most notably, Cheng had been detained in Hong Kong, inside the West Kowloon high-speed rail station, on the mainland side of the border: something that was only possible as a result of the Hong Kong government's controversial co-location border-control arrangements. His account only served to resurrect the anxiety over the extradition bill that had been the spark for the whole unrest almost six months earlier.

On Thursday 21 November, the US Congress passed the *Hong Kong Human Rights and Democracy Act*. In a rare display of bipartisanship, the bill was passed unanimously by the Senate and with only one dissenting vote in the House, and President Trump signed the bill into law a week later.

The act provided for sanctions against individuals suppressing human rights and freedoms in Hong Kong, and importantly created a mechanism whereby the US secretary of state was henceforth required to issue an annual certification of Hong Kong's autonomy, thereby ensuring that the issue of Hong Kong would be raised annually in Congress.

The news was welcomed by protesters as an unambiguous and powerful expression of support from the world's superpower, the fruits of months of lobbying by Hong Kong activists and politicians such as Joshua Wong, Denise Ho, and Democratic Party senior statesman Martin Lee.

It was also a vindication for the small but dogged groups of protesters who had been waving American flags at protests for months. They had been looked upon with disdain by some other protesters, and in particular by foreign observers, who saw their American flag-waving as naive and unfortunate at best, or, at worst, active promotion of US imperialism. Yet they persisted, and as the act was being considered by Congress, and as Marco Rubio — one of the bill's key sponsors — was being interviewed on *Fox & Friends*, footage of Hong Kong protesters waving the Stars & Stripes was beamed across America and, most likely, into the presidential bedroom, while the host asked Rubio, 'We see these protesters in Hong Kong out there, waving our flag, what is America's responsibility here?' It was as good as a direct line into the White House.

The act was yet another example of how the Hong Kong issue had emerged globally. But it also showed how Hong Kong risked becoming a pawn in the larger global game: a conflict between two superpowers, at that moment embroiled in a bitter trade war. China was predictably incensed at the act, which, it said, was an interference in its internal affairs, and retaliated with sanctions on a number of US-based NGOs it said were fomenting the Hong Kong protests.

———

Finally, on Saturday morning, the day before the election, news broke in Australia of a man named Wang Liqiang, who said he was a PRC spy and was attempting to defect.[2] He offered information about espionage activities he had undertaken while working in Hong Kong for a Chinese company listed on the Hong Kong Stock Exchange that, he said, operated as a front for state-security apparatus. Wang claimed to have had a role in the bookseller kidnappings, and been involved in actively infiltrating and undermining the Hong Kong pro-democracy movement. Together with Cheng's account, this painted a frightening picture of PRC state surveillance and control inside Hong Kong.

With all of these events hovering in the collective unconscious, Hong Kong headed to the polls.

It is unusual for local council elections to generate much excitement even in the city in which they are being held, let alone to make headlines across the globe. Yet the 2019 district council elections in Hong Kong did just that, with the global media descending upon the city, and the world watching to see who would have the power to decide where to put an extra rubbish bin, remove a tree, or build a park bench in each of Hong Kong's eighteen districts. The elections were seen as important for two reasons.

First, they were effectively a referendum, with the pan-democrat parties acting as a proxy for the protesters, and the pro-Beijing parties representing the government, the police, and, ultimately, Beijing. The results would be the best objective measure of exactly how the people of Hong Kong were feeling after the months of protests, and where their sympathies lay.

Second, and even more important, was the influence that the

outcome would have on the election for the next chief executive in 2022. The 208 Hong Kong/Kowloon district councillors and 223 New Territories district councillors each vote as a bloc to decide which fifty-seven, and sixty, respectively of their number will sit on the Chief Executive Election Committee. This is a winner-takes-all voting process: in the past, the pro-Beijing parties had controlled a majority of district council seats and so decided who took all of those election committee seats. If the pan-democrats were able to win a majority of the district council seats in this election, it would put them in the position to decide who would fill those 117 seats, an almost-10 per cent bloc. If this were to be combined with another strong showing in the LegCo elections to be held in 2020 (all LegCo members have a seat on the election committee), it would give the pan-democrats hitherto undreamed-of influence over the chief executive election process. While they would be unlikely to command an absolute majority, it would at least put them in the position of being kingmakers if the pro-establishment side produced two rival candidates.

But, with escalating violence in recent months, and the chaos of the previous week, the pan-democrat candidates were not taking the election for granted. In the days leading up to election day, one pan-democrat candidate told me, 'If this election had happened two months ago, we would have won in a landslide. Now, after the past few weeks? A lot of people are annoyed with us, or aren't going to bother voting at all.'

Volunteers working for another candidate said, 'Support has been up and down. Last week, people were blaming us and yelling at us. It seems better this week. We are cautiously optimistic.'

There were many voters who traditionally voted pro-government but hated the extradition bill, were frustrated by Carrie Lam and the establishment parties who blindly supported her, and maybe had even joined the early protests and might have been inclined to vote pan-democrat. However, the risk was that they would have been so turned off by the violence and disruptions that they would be firmly back in the pro-government camp. Meanwhile, those voters who had always supported the pan-democrats were unlikely to have been perturbed by the violence, and would still support the pan-democrat cause. After all these months of turmoil, Hong Kong might well find itself right back where it started.

From the earliest hours of election morning, the day felt different. Queues were forming even before polling stations opened at half-past seven. By nine o'clock, there were queues stretching around the block at polling stations across Hong Kong. It was an appropriate parallel to the Hong Kong Way: the people of Hong Kong were forming lines on the streets once again, although this time protests were suspended and the prospect of an opportunity to cast a vote provided the moment of enchantment.

As the government announced hourly turnout figures during the course of the day, it became clear that Hong Kongers were voting as they had never voted before. High turnout had traditionally favoured the pan-democrats, and as the turnout figures soared, so did optimism on the pan-democrat side.

The government had said it would station riot police at every polling booth to ensure the safety of the voters. This raised fears of a heavy-handed, intimidating police presence at the polling booths; but, on the day, police maintained a relatively low-key posture, and, despite the spectre of violence looming on both sides, the day was peaceful and incident-free, the election conducted with the orderly efficiency for which Hong Kong is known.

Campaigning continued vigorously throughout the day, with

candidates and their volunteers rallying support at the borders of the no-canvass zones near the polling stations. In densely populated Hong Kong, election campaigning is very personal, and it happens — like the protests — on the streets. Candidates wearing sashes like beauty-pageant contestants stood under banners bearing larger-than-life images of their own beaming faces, and waved at passers-by. Supporters held illuminated signs and chanted slogans. At some intersections, rival candidates stood on opposite sides of the road, waving placards at each other, their supporters taking turns to chant.

After the polls closed at 10.30pm, the polling stations became counting stations, open to any members of the public who wished to watch the count. It was an impressive level of transparency — democracy happening before one's very eyes — and an experience that, after months of people fighting in the streets over this very abstract notion, was somehow deeply moving.

At the count I attended in my district, inside the primary school assembly hall where I had voted earlier that afternoon, a crowd of around twenty observers watched as counters sorted ballot papers and put them into boxes labelled for Candidate Number 1 (the pro-Beijing incumbent) and Candidate Number 2 (the pan-democrat challenger). An intense hush hung over the room, the atmosphere solemn. Most of the observers seemed to be young — some were live-streaming the count to Facebook — and as the ballots for Candidate Number 2 piled up at a rapid rate, a thrill went through the crowd. Someone among the supporters uttered, sotto voce, '*Gwong fuk Heung Gong!*' ('Restore Hong Kong!') And another replied slowly, a tremble in their voice, '*Sidoi Gaakming!*' ('Revolution of our times!')

The scrutineer announced the initial count: the pan-democrat candidate had around 3,000 votes to the pro-Beijing candidate's 2,000, with only a small handful of questionable/disputed ballots to be considered. The pan-democrat candidate was going to win. He pumped his fist, came out into the crowd to shake hands with some of his supporters, and exchanged a few hushed words while they waited for the official result to be declared.

I decided to leave and move on to another nearby counting station. As a middle-aged woman in a security guard's uniform, her hair tied back in a bun, opened the door of the primary school to let me out, she asked tensely, 'Is it finished?'

'Not yet,' I said, 'But Number 2 will win.'

'Which one was that?' she said, her brow furrowed.

'The pan-democrat,' I said.

She relaxed and grinned. 'Thank you,' she said.

That day saw the highest-ever turnout for a Hong Kong election, with 2.9 million voters (out of 4.1 million eligible voters) casting a vote, representing a turnout of 71 per cent. (Recall that the previous turnout record, for the post–Umbrella Movement LegCo elections in 2016, was 58 per cent.)

In the final result, pan-democrat candidates won 385 seats; pro-Beijing candidates won only fifty-nine seats; and eight seats went to independents. (In the previous 2015 district council election, the split was pan-democrat, 126 seats; pro-Beijing, 298 seats; and independent, seven seats.) Several prominent pro-Beijing figures, including Junius Ho, lost their district council seats. Having secured a majority of district council seats, pan-democrats had won the power to appoint 117 district council representatives to the 1,200-member Chief Executive Election Committee in 2022.

Pan-democrats won control of seventeen out of the eighteen district councils. They had previously controlled none. On two of the eighteen councils — Wong Tai Sin and Tai Po — pan-democrats won every single seat. (For one remaining council, Outer Islands, pan-democrats won a majority of the seats open to popular vote, but pro-Beijing parties retained control due to ex-officio positions given to rural chiefs.)

Pan-democrats won around 57 per cent of the popular vote, while the pro-Beijing candidates secured around 41 per cent.

Critics were quick to point out that pro-Beijing candidates had actually slightly increased their overall share of the popular vote compared to the 2016 LegCo election, and that the first-past-the-post system adopted in the district councils gave the pan-democrats an advantage that they would not enjoy under the proportional-voting system adopted for LegCo. But there was no getting past the fact that a 16 percentage point margin was a thrashing under any electoral system.

The results were unequivocal: a clear majority of Hong Kongers — despite the violence, vandalism, and disruptions of recent months — had supported the protest movement and laid the blame for the continuing chaos at the feet of chief executive Carrie Lam, her government, and the pro-Beijing politicians who supported her.

The real silent majority had spoken.

When talking to protesters on the streets in recent months, as the government withdrew the extradition bill but granted no further concessions, as protesters wearied and their spirits waned in the face of increasing violence, one would hear a common refrain: 'We have struggled so hard, we have paid such a high price, we can't walk away with nothing.'

With these district council election results, all of those efforts on the streets had been converted into a very tangible outcome, into real political power. It seemed to present an opportunity for the protesters to declare at least a partial victory, perhaps even to pause and regroup, to consider the next steps for their ambitious but messy movement.

The day after the election, one of the first actions taken by the successfully elected pan-democrat candidates was to rally at the site of the PolyU siege, to express their support for the small number of protesters still holed up inside the police cordon.

At dawn on the Wednesday morning after the election, the Cross Harbour Tunnel reopened.

Life — at least in some way — was back to normal.

20

A WAY TO LIVE

With the district council elections, Hong Kong was approaching the end of its year of turmoil with, finally, a period of relative calm.

At the end of the week, with protester numbers at PolyU dwindling, police entered the campus to conduct searches for any stragglers, as well as to clear any hazardous materials. They found large caches of Molotov cocktails, but few protesters, and officially lifted the cordon on 29 November.

On Sunday 8 December, the Civil Human Rights Front staged a large, and largely peaceful, march from Victoria Park to Central, with a turnout of over 100,000. It would be the last large-scale protest of the year.

But it is unlikely that the protests have ended entirely. Indeed, there were more protests — and more vandalism and clashes with police — on Christmas Eve and on New Year's Day as 2019 moved into 2020. It is difficult not to wonder whether this represents a new normal for Hong Kong: a constant background-noise level of discontent and civil unrest occasionally bursting out into violent confrontation. Part of the reason for that is structural, built into the very design of Hong Kong: in the face of the unrepresentative political system, protest has proven to be an effective means of forcing political change in Hong Kong, whether blocking the extradition bill, Article 23 laws, or the national education curriculum.

However, with the government remaining intransigent in the face of the massive protests in 2019, that mechanism broke down, and protest was no longer a means to a political outcome. As a result, protest became the end in itself: the point of protest was to protest. This was protest as practice; protest as method.

So, to the question 'How does it end?', the answer is: 'It doesn't end.'

The Umbrella Movement of 2014 didn't end. The protests of 2019 were its continuation. And, similarly, the Hong Kong government and Beijing would be gravely mistaken to think, just because there may be a break in the weekly cycle of protests or because there is no public outcry in response to their next squeeze on dissent, that the protests have ended or that the Hong Kong people have stopped caring. It is that same tightly coiled spring, being compressed once more, until it bursts out once again.

A survey conducted by the respected Hong Kong Public Opinion Research Institute for *Reuters* at the end of December summarised where community sentiment stood at year's end, and served to underline the district council election results.[1] The survey found that the protest movement was supported by 59 per cent of those polled, with 37 per cent saying they had personally taken part in the protests. The proposal for an independent enquiry into police brutality was supported by 74 per cent of respondents, while 57 per cent said they wanted Carrie Lam to resign.

Meanwhile, official figures confirmed that Hong Kong sank into recession in 2019, with the economy shrinking by 1.2 per cent. The retail and hospitality industries were particularly hard hit: the jewellery, watches, and valuable-gifts sector fell by 22.4 per cent.[2] Total retail sales fell by 11.1 per cent for the year. Between August and December 2019, passenger-arrival numbers at Hong Kong International Airport fell 20 per cent year-on-year.[3]

There is another link between the protests and Hong Kong's economic future that has been largely overlooked but may be pivotal, which lies in the demographic profile of the section of the population supporting the protests. This was starkly revealed by a survey conducted by the Hong Kong Public Opinion Research Institute in mid-August.[4] The survey showed that those sympathetic to the protesters generally came from segments of the population that were young (aged eighteen to twenty-nine) or who had received a tertiary education. Supporters of the government and police, on the other hand, were mainly the elderly (aged sixty-five or above), or those who had received only a primary-level education.

A few examples are illustrative of this demographic divide. In response to the question 'Who is to blame for the conflicts, protesters or government?', 51 per cent of elderly respondents and 53 per cent of primary-educated respondents said the protesters were to blame, compared to only 14 per cent of young and 24 per cent of tertiary-educated respondents. The government was to blame, according to 92 per cent of young and 85 per cent of tertiary-educated respondents, compared to just 49 per cent of the elderly and 44 per cent of the primary-educated. Satisfaction levels with police were at 17 per cent among the young and 28 per cent among the tertiary-educated, compared to 60 per cent among the elderly and 59 per cent among the primary-educated.

This social division was apparent from a cursory glance at the crowds attending the respective anti-government and pro-government protests. Anti-government protesters were generally youths, alongside urban professionals and their families. Rallies in support of the government had strong representation from the elderly and groups bussed in from the rural New Territories. (This trend was also curiously reminiscent of political dynamics elsewhere in the world, where electorates appeared to be increasingly polarised along generational and urban/rural divides.)

It was a trend that should have been alarming to anyone in government — not only from the point of view of politics, but also of economics. In the course of the 2019 protests, Beijing and the Hong Kong government had systematically alienated Hong Kong's best and brightest: its youth and the educated middle class, precisely the people upon whom the future of Hong Kong's service-led economy relies. What would it mean for the future of Hong Kong — economic and otherwise — that the government had effectively treated this entire segment of its population as the enemy? Perhaps the government felt comfortable that, if these dissenters chose to opt out or emigrate, there was a near-limitless supply of talent across the border waiting to replace them. However, at the same time, Beijing had encouraged an enmity between Hong Kong and the mainland that made mainlanders unwilling to be in Hong Kong.

This government mismanagement did not go unnoticed. In January 2020, Moody's downgraded Hong Kong's credit rating, stating, 'The downgrade principally reflects Moody's view that Hong Kong's institutions and governance strength is lower than previously estimated.'[5] Moody's called the Hong Kong government's policy response, 'notably slow, tentative and inconclusive', reflecting 'weaker inherent institutional capacity'. Fitch had already downgraded Hong Kong in September, saying that the continuing events had 'inflicted long-lasting damage to international perceptions of the quality and effectiveness of Hong Kong's governance system and rule of law'.[6] These were damning assessments of Lam's administration by respected international institutions. The damage to Hong Kong's reputation for good governance may prove to be permanent.

It is difficult not to conclude that the city has been changed permanently as a result of 2019.

In the course of the 2019 protests, social division in Hong Kong became even more entrenched along 'yellow' (pro-democracy) and 'blue' (pro-government/police) lines. Individuals, schools, and businesses became identified by reference to their affiliation, or tendency, to yellow or blue. With that, families, workplaces, and friendships found themselves split along political lines. This went beyond the largely generational divide of the Umbrella Movement, and extended beyond the family dinner table. Chat groups among alumni, or parents, were broken into separate yellow and blue groups. Initial conversations with new acquaintances would invariably begin with careful tiptoeing around the issue of the protests as one sounded out the political position of one's interlocutor.

The division also moved into the business landscape, as activists began promoting the idea of a 'yellow economy', with pro-democracy sympathisers encouraged to patronise shops that supported the movement — and to boycott blue businesses.[7] Social media and online maps were used to spread the word, with lists of yellow and blue business in various districts circulating online. Many yellow shops featured their own mini Lennon Walls, displayed political posters or slogans, offered special deals to protesters, or had strike-friendly policies for employees.

The yellow economy movement emerged as yet another innovative protest tactic, as Hong Kong's protesters realised the power of the consumer. The trend also had a localist angle: yellow businesses were invariably small and locally owned, as opposed to government- and Beijing-friendly tycoon-owned conglomerates. Supporting yellow businesses promoted self-sufficiency, a symbolic rejection of Hong

Kong's reliance on the mainland. Yellow businesses were rewarded with long queues of customers, people often travelling out of their way specifically to patronise them, even if in some cases, as one friend told me, 'the food wasn't particularly good'. With the benefits of a more prominent yellow public profile, however, also came increased risks: just as protesters vandalised blue businesses, stores identifying as yellow were singled out for attack by political opponents.

It remains to be seen whether the yellow-economy movement will lead to a permanent change in the Hong Kong consumer economic landscape. It may also contain the seeds of a creeping ghettoisation of the city along political lines. Certain neighbourhoods have a prevalence of locally owned yellow businesses — often older districts that have retained the small shopfronts, and modest rents, that enable a small business to be sustainable. Where these districts coincide with groups of residents who have overwhelmingly voted pro-democracy — as evidenced in the recent district council elections — it is possible to see a new identity as a yellow district emerging. Hong Kong's high population density and unaffordable housing means that any such trends are unlikely to emerge quickly: a district may contain large numbers of people of varying political stripes, and housing mobility is low, especially for those residents reliant on public housing. But the trend may develop over time, leading some openly to speculate whether Hong Kong might become a new Belfast.

In a similar vein, one of the most visible lasting impacts of the 2019 protests on the city has been the rise of Hong Kong as a security state. Building on the government's Haussmannisation in the face of the protests, the reshaping of the urban landscape around a security orientation has been visibly evident. At the beginning of 2020, pedestrian walkways outside government headquarters and at other key locations were encased in steel mesh. Riot police stood guard on street corners. The facades of Chinese-owned bank branches were hidden behind solid-steel barriers. Access to the airport was restricted to those holding valid travel documents. When the PolyU campus reopened in January, it featured new electronic security gates that required students and staff to use their university ID cards to access the campus. Other campuses, including City University, planned to follow suit. Like campuses on the mainland, they would no longer be places of knowledge exchange, open and freely accessible to their community. This marks a broader shift in Hong Kong towards a mainland approach to a city defined by walls, by the places you cannot go to: the Forbidden City. It is the polar opposite of the right to the city demanded by the protesters, and to values of an open, global hub that Hong Kong has long espoused.

The mass arrests of 2019 will take months, if not years, to work their way through the legal system, if the Umbrella Movement prosecutions are any indication. As of the beginning of 2020, some 6,943 people had been arrested in connection with the protests since the first mass march of 9 June. (This compares to 4,979 arrested in connection with the 1967 riots.[8]) As of the same date, 1,082 of those arrested were already in the course of legal proceedings and 338 had been released unconditionally.[9] For more than 5,000 people, the prospect of potential prosecution will be hanging over their heads, and there is little doubt the government will again adopt its tactics of lawfare in bringing targeted prosecutions against those seen as key protest leaders or pro-democracy figures.

Certainly, violence has been normalised in Hong Kong to an extent it wasn't before — both state violence and street violence. The experience of being subject to arbitrary state violence, a feature of the mainland, has now become commonplace in Hong Kong. It is no longer considered shocking for a police officer to shoot an unarmed civilian point-blank in the guts. It is no longer considered shocking for a gang of thugs to beat up a pro-democracy campaigner on the street. It is no longer shocking for protesters to hurl Molotov cocktails at police or smash up a bank. And it is certainly no longer shocking for the streets to be clouded in tear gas. In the course of the 2019 protests, Hong Kong's protesters became battle-hardened.

With this normalisation of violence comes the risk of extremism: of protesters, driven by anger and frustration — their final stand at PolyU a clear demonstration of the tactics they had been using in 2019 having reached a natural end point — adopting more violent tactics amid deepening social and political divisions. This is another aspect of the comparisons to Belfast. Already, 2019 saw some abortive attempts at bomb-making, although it is unclear who made them and what their intended targets were.

Hong Kong's young protesters are well educated and technically sophisticated. Their protest tactics evolved quickly, they learned from their mistakes, and they were plugged into a global network of activism to which they contributed as much as they took. The early Molotov cocktails made in the course of these protests were crude and ineffective, but within a few months the protesters had perfected their recipe. If, in the future, there emerges a radical wing who decide that they want to make a bomb, to target a police vehicle or a government building, they would quickly obtain the technical wherewithal to do so. That would take Hong Kong to a very dark place indeed — a place no one wants to see it go, but it would be naive to discount the possibility entirely. The psychology of the protesters engaged in their increasingly violent tactics was clearly somewhere along a continuum on the path to extremism. How far Hong Kong goes along that path, and how long it might take before reaching its horrifying, ultimate destination, is the question.

Meanwhile, after enduring six months of escalating violence, with a dysfunctional government and widening social divisions, Hong Kong is a city in a state of post-traumatic stress disorder (PTSD). This was confirmed in a study published in *The Lancet* in January 2020, which showed that the incidence of 'probable depression' among participants in a ten-year cohort study of depression in Hong Kong rose from 1.9 per cent during the period 2009–2014 to 6.5 per cent in 2017 (after the Umbrella Movement and before the 2019 protests), and again to 11.2 per cent in 2019. Suspected PTSD was found in 12.8 per cent of participants in 2019. The authors of the study concluded: 'We have identified a major mental health burden during the social unrest in Hong Kong,' which they estimated would translate into an additional 12 per cent requirement for mental-health services.[10]

This should hardly have come as a surprise. For over seven months, the city had been consumed in weekly incidents of escalating violence, while daily life had become entirely contingent. There was a sense that one didn't know what would happen from one day to the next. One image summarised this for me keenly. It was the moment I realised that Hong Kong was a city on the verge of a nervous breakdown.

It came during the second round of chaotic airport protests, in a video clip recorded by the *Hong Kong Free Press* of police pursuing protesters through Hong Kong airport.[11] In it, the police bail up a group of young women in a bathroom. One police officer screams with fury in the face of one of the women, who maintains her composure and responds to him bravely while her friend bawls on her shoulder, terrified. A colleague restrains the police officer and manages to calm him, patting him comfortingly on the shoulder. The officer stops, turns away from the women, panting, his shoulders heaving, his jaw slack. As he looks, dazed, at the small circle of media gathered around him, his vacant eyes gaze directly into the camera. That was when I saw it: the expression on his face is of a man utterly defeated, exhausted and demoralised, having suddenly come face-to-face with what he has become. A broken man.

At a time when so many residents of Hong Kong had come to see the police as the bad guys — deriding them with chants of 'Dirty cops' or 'Triads', wishing death upon their families — that single police officer came to symbolise for me the trauma of our city.

Because there was no doubt that the city, and everyone who resided here, was experiencing a massive collective trauma. How could our city go through the events of 2019 and not be on the verge of a nervous breakdown? We were a city in the throes of manic depression.

We had the mania, intoxicated by the power of the masses gathered on the streets, swept up in moments of enchantment: the Hong Kong Way, the blossoming of Lennon Walls, the joyful outdoor gatherings on Mid-Autumn Festival night.

But we had also seen moments of darkness. Individuals — driven by anger, frustration, and desperation — had deliberately provoked the violence of coercive state power in an unfair contest they went into knowing they would lose. Violence had been normalised to such an extent that we celebrated — we actually celebrated — our one single tear gas-free weekend. Were we not sick?

Was I not sick? Drawn week after week down into the streets, to the frontlines, rationalising it by telling myself that I needed to be on the ground, to be a witness — but secretly craving the adrenaline rush, longing for the tingle of tear gas on my skin, the smell of gunpowder and CS on the breeze.

If we shared anything at this moment — from yellow ribbon democracy supporter, to blue ribbon government supporter, to apathetic expat, from frontline protester to pro-establishment tycoon — it must have been a deep sense of hopelessness. That police officer's blank gaze was the blank gaze of all of us — searching for a way out, searching for our future.

The conceit of the 1997 handover of Hong Kong from Great Britain to China was that nothing would change. As Deng Xiaoping famously promised, 'The horses will still run, stocks will still sizzle, dancers will still dance.'[12]

It turned out that, in 2019, all three of Deng's promises were broken. At the height of the protests in September, the Hong Kong Jockey Club cancelled a race meeting at Happy Valley out of safety concerns arising from the 'social unrest in the vicinity' and a 'very real threat of a disturbance or possible violence'. Protesters had learned that a horse owned by Junius Ho was on the card, and so the horses did not run. Stocks also stopped sizzling in 2019, with the Hang Seng index falling from its record high in January 2018 (shortly before Poon's murder) some 22 per cent by mid-August 2019 as protesters rampaged at the airport and Chinese troops massed on the border. And, finally, on Halloween night in 2019, a traditional occasion for partying in the Lan Kwai Fong nightlife district, police first warned that — in light of the recent face-mask ban — Halloween costumes would be strictly policed, and then, as young revellers began to congregate, closed down public access to the district entirely by eight o'clock, firing tear gas to clear the streets. That night, dancers did not dance.

Be that as it may, in order to effect a seamless handover from British to Chinese administration, the pre-handover British colonial governance structure and legal system in toto was essentially replicated in post-handover Hong Kong, with little changed beyond replacing the governor with the chief executive, and removing the 'EIIR' royal cypher from the postboxes. As a result, it could fairly be argued that Hong Kong is, at least structurally, still a colony — only the colonial master has changed. This was laid bare by the use of the Emergency Regulations Ordinance — that vicious piece of colonial legislation — to implement the face-masking ban, and Beijing's vituperative response when the court called into question that exercise of colonial power by striking it down.

As a result, structurally, the belonging/not belonging dichotomy of colonialism has been, perhaps accidentally, perpetuated — you are either a native, and belong, or a colonist, and do not. This is at the root of much of the nativist/localist, anti-mainland sentiment motivating the Hong Kong protest movement.

And, like all colonies, the colonised people were given no say in how they were to be governed. All of Hong Kong's protests may have at their core the original sin of post-handover Hong Kong: that the Hong Kong people themselves were not given any say in the arrangements surrounding their return to Chinese sovereignty. Hong Kong has only as much autonomy as its sovereign grants it.

It is a dynamic that had led, by the end of 2019, to some 17 per cent of Hong Kongers expressing support for Hong Kong independence.[13] This could fairly be said to represent mainstream recognition of an idea that only five years earlier had barely registered even on the fringes of political discourse.

But for all the fanciful talk of autonomy or even independence, there is no escaping the political, geographic, and economic reality that Hong Kong is a part of China. Hong Kong — for its own good — needs to find a modus vivendi with the mainland.

Yet that is proving difficult, and may continue to be so as long as Beijing and Hong Kong have two precisely opposite understandings of the one key phrase: One Country, Two Systems. For Beijing, as it has repeatedly stated, the One Country is the precondition to the Two Systems: Beijing is only willing to suffer the separate Hong Kong system on the condition that Hong Kong accepts it is part of the One Country. But for Hong Kongers, the exact opposite is true: they insist upon having the Two Systems as the precondition for them accepting the One Country.

There was a largely unspoken subtext to the 2019 protest movement. The protests were really only about one thing: China. It was as if, twenty-two years after the handover, the Hong Kong people suddenly woke up and realised that they were living in China — or, rather, that the China they found themselves living in was not the one they expected it to be.

The whole underlying assumption of One Country, Two Systems and the promise of a fifty-year guarantee of rights and freedoms for Hong Kong when it was inked into the Sino-British Joint Declaration in 1984 — and we might surmise that this assumption was held on both the British and Chinese sides of the negotiating table — was that China would be a very different place by the year 2047. Recall that, in 1984, Deng's reform and opening-up program had been underway for almost six years, and had already ushered in significant changes in Chinese society after the ten dark years of the Cultural Revolution. The year 2047 at that point was more than sixty-three years away. In China itself, the 275-year reign of the Qing Dynasty had ended only seventy-three years earlier, and the intervening years had seen republican rule, the warlord era, the Sino-Japanese war, and finally the civil war followed by the establishment of the People's Republic in 1949. A period of sixty-three years in China could contain a lot of history.

However, thirty-five years on from 1984, China is looking very different — more economically powerful and technologically advanced, but also less liberal and less politically open — than many would have perhaps expected. It may not be a coincidence that the mood began to shift in Hong Kong as it became increasingly apparent, especially in the five years after the Umbrella Movement, that the underlying assumption had been flawed.

Suddenly, 'fifty years, no change' seemed less like a promise and more like a curse: a political system and a society frozen in the aspic of 1984, not permitted to develop or evolve, not allowed to change.

Then again, the question is not only 'Does Hong Kong accept China's rule?', but just as much 'Does China accept Hong Kongers as citizens of China?' There is an extent to which One Country, Two Systems is built on the premise of mutual non-interference that prevents Hong Kongers from assuming their place as full citizens of China. Historian Steve Tsang summed up the inherently contradictory position of Hong Kongers in the context of their role in advocating for democracy in China following the Tiananmen protests of 1989:

> On the one hand, as Hong Kong citizens, they wanted to preserve their own way of life under the 'one country, two systems' formula ... On the other hand, feeling that they were Chinese too, they believed they had a right to have a say in vital matters affecting the future of the nation, which in practice meant PRC politics.[14]

With the extradition bill, this demand could almost be rearticulated as an echo of eighteenth-century French women's rights activist Olympe de Gouges, who argued: 'Woman has the right to mount the scaffold; she must equally have the right to mount the rostrum.'[15] Hong Kongers are in effect making a similar argument: if we have the right to be extradited to face punishment on the scaffold of the mainland government's judicial system, also give us the rostrum from which to speak to that same government as fully entitled political actors. If we are to be part of China, then accept us as fully fledged citizens, entitled to engage in all the aspects of our nation. If we cannot have the Two Systems without the One Country, then let us be part of the One Country. Of course, Hong Kongers want to do this on terms that retain all of their current rights and freedoms, a demand that Beijing cannot accept.

The dramatic armed crackdown that many feared never came. After all, Hong Kong was not Beijing, and 2019 was not 1989. In the short term, Beijing remained happy to let Hong Kong burn. The violence in Hong Kong suited Beijing's interests, demonstrating the need for the steadying hand of the party, while justifying tightened control over Hong Kong in the longer term.

Reports suggested that Beijing was genuinely surprised by the outcome of the district council elections — another case of a totalitarian regime believing its own propaganda. But it would be a mistake to think that this would be the catalyst for a grand compromise. Seven months of street protests or an election loss will not be taken by Beijing as a sign that it needs to change its approach to Hong Kong. Rather, it would be seen as a mistaken choice on the part of the Hong Kong people — one that Beijing would need to address before the more important Legislative Council elections in September 2020.

What Hong Kong should expect in the coming months and years is a slow and steady squeeze, as Beijing first isolates Hong Kong in order to weaken it, and then, bringing to bear all the tools of state power at its disposal, reasserts control and pushes towards convergence and integration.

The party's key Fourth Plenum meeting, held in October 2019, reiterated Beijing's fundamental policies towards Hong Kong, as well as Macau and Taiwan, under the One Country, Two Systems formula. Three key statements emerged.

First, the plenum said it would 'build and improve a legal system and enforcement mechanism to defend national security' in Hong Kong and Macau. Many commentators leapt on this as a signal that Beijing would once again attempt to enact the dreaded Article 23 legislation in Hong Kong. (Obedient Macau introduced its version back in 2009.) That seems unlikely: Beijing understands that a proposal to introduce Article 23 laws would receive just as furious a response as did the extradition bill, at least in the present environment, and there may never be a time when that will not be the case. Beijing doesn't need Article 23 laws to manage Hong Kong in any event. The colonial legal system — as applied by the Hong Kong Police Force and a compliant Department of Justice — has already been proven to offer a more-than-sufficient set of tools to manage dissent, as the last five years of lawfare have demonstrated. That campaign is likely to continue, and be intensified, as the prosecutions of protesters and their pan-democrat enablers unfold in the coming years.

Second, the plenum focused on the need to 'strengthen the national education of Hong Kong and Macau people, especially civil servants and young people, including education on the constitution and the Basic Law, and Chinese history and culture, in order to boost their national consciousness and patriotic spirit'. Given that the 2019 protest movement, like the Umbrella Movement, was youth-led, this is hardly surprising. Beijing will probably give up on the current generation of youths, who may go down in Hong Kong history as a lost generation. They may find themselves toxic to employers, unable to visit the mainland, and their opportunities, if they remain in Hong Kong, may be greatly circumscribed, tainted by the events of 2019. But Beijing will hope to save the next generation and the generations to follow: 2047 still lies more than a generation into the future.

Again, many read this as an indication that Beijing would make another attempt to introduce a 'moral and national education' curriculum similar to that blocked by the protests in 2012 led by Joshua

Wong and his Scholarism group. And again, Beijing is unlikely to make another directly confrontational attempt when there are other methods available to it that are just as effective. A renewed focus on Chinese history classes will be one way in which the party's version of history can be instilled in Hong Kong's youth. Pressure is already being exerted through Hong Kong's Education Bureau on high school principals to pull their unruly student bodies — and teaching staff — into line. Public high school campuses have been required to prohibit any activities that might be remotely associated with protest, from chanting slogans to wearing face masks to forming human chains — in Hong Kong schools, even holding hands is now seen as a subversive act.

University campuses were already coming under pressure in the wake of the Umbrella Movement. C.Y. Leung installed a conservative pro-Beijing ally, Arthur Li, to chair the University of Hong Kong governing council, which then rejected the unanimous recommendation of a university search committee to install highly regarded Professor Johannes Chan — who was dean of the law school at the time that faculty member Benny Tai's Occupy Central plan was developing — to the position of pro-vice chancellor. Chan was seen by Beijing to have been overly sympathetic to Tai. Tai himself, released from prison in August 2019 on bail pending an appeal of his conviction, was in January 2020 facing a university committee of inquiry looking into his teaching position, a process that may lead to his dismissal. Baptist University similarly moved to relieve convicted Umbrella Movement master of ceremonies Shiu Ka-chun of his teaching post. Senior university appointments are likely to continue to be highly contentious, with appointees scrutinised for their patriotic credentials. As the 2019 protests wound down, some university administrators were already complaining that the government was punishing them through the budgeting process, withholding promised funding.

Finally, the plenum announced that Beijing would 'enhance the system and mechanism over the appointment of the chief executive and principal officials'. This was a further indication, if any were needed, that Beijing has no intention of granting Hong Kong the wider model of universal suffrage for electing the chief executive that protesters have been calling for since the Umbrella Movement, not to mention universal suffrage for election of the Legislative Council. Beijing wants to, and will always, retain ultimate control over the process by which the people who run Hong Kong are selected. Within the bounds of that principle, but not outside it, there is room for compromise.

The plenum's statement also made it clear that the political bona fides of other senior Hong Kong officials will be subject to scrutiny, and that government leaders, the civil service, and, of course, the uniformed services must demonstrate their patriotism and loyalty to Beijing. It was notable that, as one of his first official acts when he assumed the role in November 2019, new Hong Kong police chief Chris Tang changed the force motto from 'We Serve with Pride and Care' to 'Serving Hong Kong with Honour, Duty and Loyalty'. *Loyalty to whom?* many wondered.

With the courts playing such a central role in the government's control of Hong Kong, judicial appointments will likely also come under scrutiny — especially for lower-level courts, which attract less public attention, but the candidates for which eventually work their way up to the benches of the Court of Appeal and Court of Final Appeal.

When Beijing makes these pronouncements, as with its press conferences throughout the course of the 2019 protests, it thinks it is communicating with Hong Kong. The tragedy — and this may be both a failure of the Hong Kong education system and a failure of imagination among Hong Kongers generally — is that many Hong

Kongers do not understand party-speak. Beijing's message is rarely received in the way it is intended. Beijing's late-July press conference should have been understood as providing an opening for concessions. Instead, the protesters continued to push.

The same is true in reverse. Hong Kongers think that Beijing understands their demands, but they are received in garbled form. When Hong Kongers say, 'We want autonomy,' Beijing hears, 'We want independence.' And even when Hong Kongers are actually saying, 'We want independence,' that may not be what they mean. It may be intended merely as a provocation. This seems to be a hidden subtext to some statements by Hong Kong's more radical activists, such as Edward Leung, who told a RTHK radio program in December 2018: 'What localists want is for Hong Kong to resume its autonomy — Hong Kong independence is one of the ways to implement autonomy.'[16]

But instead of achieving greater autonomy, Hong Kong may be headed for greater integration. The Greater Bay Area is a key PRC national strategy to create an economic super-region, bringing Hong Kong and Macau together with Guangzhou, Shenzhen, and the broader Guangdong hinterland. Many think of the Greater Bay Area primarily in business and economic terms, but it is much more than that. Beijing intends to integrate Hong Kong and Macau more closely with the mainland, increasing the mobility of not just capital and business, but also people. All policy options are on the table as Beijing seeks to realise its vision for the Greater Bay Area, from unifying the tax system — higher tax rates being one of the key disincentives for Hong Kong–based executives to work across the border — to redrawing the very borders of the cities and regions. The Hong Kong of the future may not even cover the same territory as the Hong Kong of today.

There is a certain logic to Shenzhen becoming a satellite town of Hong Kong, with the lower-wage-earning workers unable to afford

Hong Kong's spiralling housing costs relocating across the border and commuting into Hong Kong. This portends a future where Hong Kong and Shenzhen converge economically and financially towards Hong Kong, but politically towards Shenzhen.

It might also mean that higher-wage-earners currently based in Shenzhen will move across the border to enjoy the benefits of life in Hong Kong. This raises fears of a kind of cultural assimilation, with Hong Kongers eventually becoming a minority in their own city. However, Hong Kong is no Tibet or Xinjiang, and any strategy to assimilate Hong Kong through migration would be based on flawed logic. Hong Kong has a long history of absorbing and assimilating immigrant populations, particularly those coming from China. When people come from the mainland to Hong Kong, it is not Hong Kong that becomes more like the mainland: those mainland people become Hong Kongers. Edward Leung himself, remember, was born in mainland China.

At the same time, it continues to serve China's strategic and economic interests to maintain Hong Kong's autonomy and its status as an international financial centre. That is why the other way in which Beijing will seek to assert its control in Hong Kong is through its financial power. Hong Kong will see an influx of mainland capital, with mainland-backed businesses playing a more prominent role in the Hong Kong economy and taking control of key enterprises. This can already be seen in the Central commercial real-estate market, with Chinese financial institutions and corporates squeezing international law firms and banks further out east along the MTR's Island Line, or across the harbour to Kowloon.

Pressure will continue on businesses to take a 'correct attitude'. As we have seen, the impact will be felt not just in Hong Kong, but overseas, and not just in relation to Hong Kong. As the United States and China appear increasingly to be embroiled in the beginnings of a new Cold War, businesses — and countries — around the world will be asked to choose a side. The Hong Kong protests of 2019 played a key role in bringing this into stark focus, and in highlighting the extent of Chinese influence across the globe.

Beijing's handling of the Hong Kong protests had the predicted effect on the Taiwan presidential elections in January 2020. Independence-leaning incumbent Tsai Ing-wen won re-election over her China-friendly Kuomintang rival Han Kuo-yu in a landslide. Tsai secured 57 per cent of the vote to Han's 37 per cent, and had the distinction of becoming the first Taiwanese presidential candidate ever to obtain over eight million votes. On election night, Tsai tweeted out a simple message: 'Thank you, Taiwan.' The accompanying photo showed Tsai and her team pictured from behind, bowing before a crowd of thousands of cheering supporters at a victory rally. Prominently displayed in the midst of the crowd was a large black banner reading: 'Reclaim Hong Kong, Revolution of our times!'[17]

The protests also had a broader global significance, with activists and civil disobedience movements around the world finding inspiration in Hong Kong's highly developed protest culture. Hong Kong protesters showed that, through a combination of a 'Be water!' strategy and careful targeting of key infrastructure and organs of government (the airport, the tax office, the legislature), a relatively small number of protesters can effectively shut down a modern global city and paralyse its government. They also showed, through their subversion of the urban infrastructure, that twenty-first-century cities are porous texts open to being rewritten, especially with creative narratives of enchanting protest that can capture the popular imagination. More ominously, the Hong Kong protests also appeared to offer an example to support the argument that targeted and disciplined violence against property (but not people) can be effective in the context of a broader peaceful mass movement.

———

But, in the end, the protests may also have offered their own answer to a question: what is Hong Kong for?

Hong Kong has long been a safe haven. In the middle of the last century, it was a refuge for those fleeing a turbulent China, including a whole generation of Southbound artists, writers, and filmmakers, such as Jin Yong (the pen name of Louis Cha), the world's most-read Sinophone writer, and Wong Kar-wai, Hong Kong's greatest director, who came to Hong Kong as a child when his family fled Shanghai.

During the years that China was closed to the outside world, Hong Kong was the closest that most foreign scholars of China could come to the place — they studied with exiles from the mainland, and joined the tourists gazing from Hong Kong across the Shenzhen River into Red China.

Hong Kong was also — and still is — a place to do business. While Hong Kong was once a foothold for international companies wanting to access the fabled market of one billion customers, it is now a stepping-stone for mainland companies to access international capital markets, engage in cross-border transactions, and do business globally. But in the post-handover era, there is more to Hong Kong than just business.

Hong Kong is the only place in the world that is a part of, and yet apart from, China; a place where researchers, analysts, commentators, writers, and artists can be sufficiently close to China to be well informed, to feel the zeitgeist, and yet work in an environment where they can express themselves freely; a place where international NGOs can base themselves; a place where publishers can publish without restriction. It is a haven status that is given very tangible expression every year on 4 June, when thousands attend candlelight vigils in Victoria Park, the only large-scale commemoration of that day on Chinese soil.

Accepting that China is one of the most important stories in the world today, it is in the world's interest to have a space where Chinese voices can speak freely and where global voices can freely address Chinese audiences. It happens to be in China's interest, too. During the Cultural Revolution era, Hong Kong was an economic escape valve for China, the only point of interchange for foreign goods and capital while the rest of China remained closed to the outside world. Today, Hong Kong plays that same role politically and culturally, giving China an escape valve for sentiments that have no other outlet in Xi's China, and enabling information to flow where it otherwise would not. In 2003, it was Hong Kong that helped to gather and disseminate information about the SARS outbreak. This saved China — and, most likely, the world — from the devastating epidemic that might have ensued if the mainland's instincts for suppression of information had not been undermined. Hong Kong keeps the entire ecosystem in balance.

The question confronting China now is whether to keep that valve open, or to close it off. The year 2019 may be remembered as the year that defined post-handover Hong Kong; China's answer to that question will determine whether 2019 will also be remembered as the last year of Hong Kong as it once was.

Meanwhile, the fight for Hong Kong continues. The 2019 protest movement was the latest episode in a long narrative of Hong Kong protest movements stretching, by way of the Umbrella Movement of 2014, the moral and national education protests of 2012, and the anti–Article 23 protests of 2003, back to the pre-handover era, echoing the social movements of the 1960s and 1970s, and the strikes of the 1920s.

It is still too early to understand fully the impact of this movement, or to catalogue its successes and failures. Pan-democrat legislator Dennis Kwok said to me in July, shortly after the march of two million had forced Carrie Lam to shelve the extradition bill, 'The Hong Kong people have extended the life of One Country, Two Systems by another ten years.' The events of the months since then may have extended One Country, Two Systems even further, or hastened its demise.

However, it is clear that what began as a fight against the extradition bill became something more than that: a fight for the very soul of the city. And what is the soul of a place, but its identity? The 2019 protests have been, at their core, an attempt to force a previously unimaginable identity into the political imaginary of Hong Kong; a challenge to think of a Hong Kong beyond the colonial, or even postcolonial, paradigm. This is not to imagine an identity beyond Chinese sovereignty, but perhaps an identity of a place that stands in a new relation to its sovereign.

To say that the protests of 2019 were a fight for the soul of the city is to understand the movement — as the slogan, 'Revolution of our times!' suggests — as a revolutionary one. And as a revolutionary movement, it built a revolutionary people. People who, in greater numbers than ever before, had been victims of state violence, and were pushed to a radical new position as a result. People who went from chanting, 'Hong Kongers, add oil!' to, 'Hong Kongers, resist!' to, 'Hong Kongers, revenge!' People who gathered together in the agora of the contemporary city to sing their anthem, 'Glory to Hong Kong'. People who, with a collective voice, declared their desire to 'Reclaim Hong Kong!'

At the barricades of the city on fire, a new Hong Kong identity was forged. Regardless of the ultimate fate of this protest movement, these are the seeds that will be carried within the Hong Kong people across the coming months, and the coming years, to the next protest movement, and the next.

EPILOGUE
MAP OF TEARS

We all build our own mental maps of the cities we live in: maps of the playgrounds we played in as children; maps of all the streets on which we have lived; maps of the places where we have been kissed. Over time, these maps build up in layers to form our personal topography of the city.

Many Hong Kongers now have a new layer on their maps: the map of places where they have been tear-gassed.

I have been tear-gassed in Admiralty, Wanchai, Causeway Bay, and North Point; in Sai Ying Pun and Sheung Wan and Central. I have been tear-gassed in Mong Kok, Yau Ma Tei, Jordan, Tsim Sha Tsui, and Hung Hom. In Tuen Mun, Tsuen Wan, Kwun Tung, and Yuen Long.

In 2019, tear gas maps of Hong Kong circulated online, showing all of the locations and districts in which tear gas had been fired. All eighteen districts, other than the outlying islands, were accounted for, from Sheung Shui in the north by the Shenzhen border to Aberdeen on the south side of Hong Kong Island.

Memories are fixed to points in space. We understand memory as being attached to specific spaces of significance. Upon these spaces the texts of the past are written as a palimpsest.

The 2019 protest movement wrote layer after layer of new meaning onto the palimpsest of Hong Kong.

Long after the graffitied slogans have faded from the streets, long after the Lennon Walls have resumed their roles as anonymous pedestrian tunnels, the spaces of this protest movement — as with past protest movements — will continue to live in the collective memory of the city as memory spaces.

The spaces in which the protests occurred — the sites of the Lennon Walls, the campus of PolyU, the roads surrounding the government headquarters, the forecourt of the LegCo building — are loaded with images, meaning, and memories. Memories of what has taken place there before, memories of imagined possible futures. Protesters talk of a shared dream: the dream of the day when they are victorious, and can embrace each other under the LegCo building, remove their masks, and see each other as if for the first time.

These spaces are in the real world, and also in the virtual world, embracing the cultural icons, the satirical humour, and the artwork of the movement.

These memories take their place as additional inhabitants, phantoms haunting the urban space. They live side by side with us, walk with us on the streets, whisper in our ears.

If you stand in the cement canyons under the freeway overpasses, between the buildings, you can hear the echoes of their voices.

'Reclaim Hong Kong! Revolution of our times!'

ACKNOWLEDGEMENTS

Portions of this book were first published, in different form, in the following publications: 'The End of Hong Kong as We Know It', *The Atlantic*, 10 September 2019; 'Singin' About a Revolution: the soundtrack of this year's Hong Kong protests marks a somber turn from the Umbrella Movement', *Quartz*, 26 September 2019; and 'What Do We Call Hong Kong's nameless "2019 Protests" in 2020?', *Quartz*, 20 December 2019.

This book would not exist without the many family, friends, colleagues, and supporters who helped me along the way. In particular, I would like to thank:

The editors who commissioned and published my writing on the 2019 protests, including Prashant Rao at *The Atlantic*; Linda Jaivin and the team at the Australia Centre for China in the World; Matthew Brooker at Bloomberg; Susan Jakes and Isaac Stone Fish at *ChinaFile*; Jenni Marsh at CNN; Burhan Wazir at *Coda*; James Palmer at *Foreign Policy*; Rhiannon Cosslett and Bonnie Malkin at *The Guardian*; Minh Bui Jones at *Mekong Review*; Gavin Jacobson,

Jasper Jackson and Hettie O'Brien at *New Statesman*; Kaiser Kuo and Jeremy Goldkorn at SupChina; and Tripti Lahiri at *Quartz*.

Henry Rosenbloom and the team at Scribe.

Shelley Gare, for encouragement and introductions.

Anthony Garnaut, for providing invaluable comments on an early draft of this book, and more importantly for a friendship that has spanned three continents and more than two decades — long may it continue.

My friends in the Department of Comparative Literature at the University of Hong Kong: Gina Marchetti, Esther Yau, Winnie Yee, Jason Coe, and Sebastian Veg.

All the members of the media I spoke to, and spent time with on the streets, for their camaraderie and great conversations; Sean Tierney for technical and safety advice; and the many other friends at the frontlines who provided solidarity and good humour.

For A. & M., from whom I was away far too much during all those days and nights on the streets, I have only this book to offer in return.

For M., D. & E., who may wonder why I am still in Hong Kong twenty years later, I hope this book is at least part of an answer to that question.

NOTES

PROLOGUE

1   It is often incorrectly reported that 28 September 2014 was the first time tear gas had been deployed in Hong Kong since 1967. In fact, Hong Kong police deployed tear gas against anti–World Trade Organization protesters during a WTO ministerial summit in December 2005. However, given the targets of that police action were primarily non–Hong Kong protesters (most were Korean farmers), this was not regarded as an attack by Hong Kong police on their own people in the same way as the 2014 or 2019 tear gas deployments were. See Jeff Wasserstrom. *Vigil: Hong Kong on the brink*, Columbia Global Reports, 2020, p. 50.

2   Feigenbaum, Anna. *Tear Gas: from the battlefields of WWI to the streets of today*. Verso, 2017, p. 56.

3   Parry, Simon. 'The Truth about Tear Gas: how Hong Kong police violated all guidelines for the "non-lethal weapon"', *South China Morning Post*, 16 August 2019, www.scmp.com/magazines/post-magazine/long-reads/article/3022942/truth-about-tear-gas-how-hong-kong-police.

4   Haar, Rohini J., et al. 'Health impacts of chemical irritants used for crowd control: a systematic review of the injuries and deaths caused by tear gas and pepper spray.' *BMC Public Health*, vol. 17, no. 831, 2017, doi.org/10.1186/s12889-017-4814-6.

5   Chan, Emily Ying Yang, et al. 'Use of tear gas for crowd control in
    Hong Kong.' *The Lancet*, vol. 394, no. 10208, 2019, pp. 1517–18, doi.
    org/10.1016/S0140-6736(19)32326-8.
6   Winchester, Simon. *In Holy Terror: reporting the Ulster Troubles*. Faber,
    1974, p. 32.

CHAPTER 1: A DEATH IN TAIPEI

1   Poon, Hiu-wing. *Facebook*, www.facebook.com/cici.kaikai.
2   A detailed account of the murder is available in: Siu, Jasmine. '"Body
    folded in suitcase": gruesome details emerge of Hong Kong man's
    killing of pregnant girlfriend in Taiwan.' *South China Morning Post*,
    13 April 2019, www.scmp.com/print/news/hong-kong/law-and-
    crime/article/3005990/body-folded-suitcase-gruesome-details-
    emerge-hong-kong.
3   Liu, Qinghou in *Liberty Times Net*, news.ltn.com.tw/news/society/
    breakingnews/2364406.
4   Cheng, Kris. 'Hong Kong's new one-off China extradition plan seeks
    to plug legal loophole, says Chief Exec. Carrie Lam.' *Hong Kong Free
    Press*, 19 February 2019, www.hongkongfp.com/2019/02/19/hong-
    kongs-new-one-off-china-extradition-plan-seeks-plug-legal-loophole-
    says-chief-exec-carrie-lam/.
5   A detailed account of the extradition bill process is available in: Jeffie
    Lam and Gary Cheung, 'Has Carrie Lam lost Hong Kong in her bid
    to push through extradition bill?' *South China Morning Post*, 29 June
    2019, www.scmp.com/week-asia/politics/article/3016577/has-carrie-
    lam-lost-hong-kong-her-bid-push-through-china.
6   Ng Kang-chung. 'Mother of Hong Kong woman killed in Taiwan
    pleads for change to law to ensure justice for her daughter.' *South
    China Morning Post*, 12 February 2019, www.scmp.com/news/hong-
    kong/law-and-crime/article/2185895/mother-hong-kong-woman-
    killed-taiwan-pleads-change-law.
7   Cheng, note 4 above.
8   Lam and Cheung, note 5 above.
9   Hong Kong Bar Association. 'Statement of the Hong Kong Bar
    Association on the decision of the NPCSC of 27 December 2017 on
    the co-operation agreement between the mainland and the HKSAR
    on the establishment of the port at the West Kowloon station of the

Guangzhou-Shenzhen-Hong Kong express rail link for implementing co-location arrangement', 28 December 2017, www.hkba.org/sites/default/files/20171228%20-%20Bar%20Co-Location%20Arrangement%20Statement%20%28English%29%20FINAL_0.pdf.

10 Mitchell, Tom and Nicolle Liu. 'Beijing's hand behind move to suspend Hong Kong bill.' *Financial Times*, 16 June 2019, www.ft.com/content/ab78b108-9015-11e9-aea1-2b1d33ac3271.

11 For further background see: Vivienne Zeng. 'The curious tale of five missing publishers in Hong Kong.' *Hong Kong Free Press*, 8 June 2016, www.hongkongfp.com/2016/01/08/the-curious-tale-of-five-missing-publishers-in-hong-kong/.

12 Griffiths, James and Kristy Lu Stout. 'Incoming Hong Kong leader says she defers to China on missing booksellers.' *CNN*, 23 June 2017, edition.cnn.com/2017/06/22/asia/hong-kong-carrie-lam-gui-booksellers/index.html.

13 For further background, see: Michael Forsythe and Paul Mozur. 'A Video, a Wheelchair, a Suitcase: mystery of vanished tycoon deepens.' *New York Times*, 10 February 2017, www.nytimes.com/2017/02/10/world/asia/xiao-jianhua-hong-kong-disappearance.html.

14 Lague, David, et al. 'How murder, kidnappings and miscalculation set off Hong Kong's revolt.' *Reuters*, 20 December 2019, www.reuters.com/investigates/special-report/hongkong-protests-extradition-narrative/.

15 Stevenson, Alexandra and Keith Bradsher. 'As Hong Kong Erupted Over Extradition Bill, City's Tycoons Waited and Worried.' *New York Times*, 20 June 2019, www.nytimes.com/2019/06/20/business/hong-kong-business-extradition.html.

16 Jerome Cohen speaking on 'Jerome Cohen on the Hong Kong protests and the law.' *Sinica Podcast*, 31 October 2019, supchina.com/podcast/jerome-cohen-on-the-hong-kong-protests-and-the-law/.

17 Wang Xiangwei. 'China's legal system has a long way to go before it can be trusted.' *South China Morning Post*, 13 July 2019, scmp.com/week-asia/opinion/article/3018421/chinas-legal-system-has-long-way-go-it-can-be-trusted.

18 Sum, Lok-kei and Alvin Lum. 'Hong Kong government to take drastic step in fast-tracking controversial fugitive bill.' *South China Morning Post*, 20 May 2019, www.scmp.com/news/hong-kong/

politics/article/3010946/hong-kongs-controversial-fugitive-bill-skip-legislative.

19 Stevenson and Bradsher, note 15 above.

20 Lum, Alvin and Sum Lok-kei. '"Record 3,000" Hong Kong lawyers in silent march against controversial extradition bill.' *South China Morning Post*, 6 June 2019, www.scmp.com/news/hong-kong/politics/article/3013461/thousands-hong-kong-lawyers-launch-silent-march-against.

CHAPTER 2: THE MARCH OF ONE MILLION

1 See Government of the Hong Kong Special Administrative Region. *Proposals to implement Article 23 of the Basic Law*. www.basiclaw23. gov.hk/english/.

2 Government of the Hong Kong Special Administrative Region. 'Government response to procession.' 9 June 2019, www.info.gov.hk/gia/general/201906/09/P2019060900587.htm.

CHAPTER 3: BLOCKING THE BILL

1 Information Office of the State Council, People's Republic of China. *The Practice of the 'One Country, Two Systems' Policy in the Hong Kong Special Administrative Region*. 10 June 2014, www.fmcoprc.gov.hk/eng/xwdt/gsxw/t1164057.htm.

2 See: *Joshua: teenager vs. superpower*. Directed by Joe Piscatella, June Pictures, 2017.

3 'Occupy Central — The Debate: Full coverage of student-government talks.' *South China Morning Post*, scmp.com/news/hong-kong/article/1621141/live-hong-kong-students-prepare-meet-government-officials-democracy.

4 Agence France-Presse. 'CY Leung: "Democracy would see poorer people dominate Hong Kong vote".' *South China Morning Post*, 21 October 2014, www.scmp.com/news/hong-kong/article/1621103/cy-leung-democracy-would-see-poor-people-dominate-hong-kong-vote.

5 Ng, Joyce. 'Hong Kong Chief Executive Carrie Lam accuses anti-extradition bill protesters of "organising a riot".' *South China Morning Post*, 12 June 2019, www.scmp.com/news/hong-kong/politics/article/3014250/hong-kong-chief-executive-carrie-lam-accuses-anti.

6 Ibid.

CHAPTER 4: THE MARCH OF TWO MILLION

1 English translation by John Minford and Geremie Barmé, available at 'An Anthem to Restore Hong Kong.' *China Heritage*, chinaheritage. net/journal/an-anthem-to-restore-hong-kong/.

CHAPTER 5: BE WATER!

1 Hong Kong Free Press. 'Hong Kong leader Carrie Lam 'sincerely apologises' for extradition row, but refuses to retract bill or resign.' *Hong Kong Free Press*, 18 August 2019, www.hongkongfp. com/2019/06/18/live-hong-kong-leader-carrie-lam-sincerely-apologises-extradition-row/.

2 Bruce Lee, video available on *YouTube*, youtu.be/cJMwBwFj5nQ.

3 Awakening Dubbing, video available on *YouTube*, youtu.be/xlE8_CPru4M.

4 A vivid example of this in relation to the August airport protests is described in Shelly Banjo, et al. 'How Hong Kong's Leaderless Protest Army Gets Things Done.' *Bloomberg*, 23 August 2019, www. bloomberg.com/graphics/2019-hong-kong-airport-protests/.

5 Telegram founder and CEO Pavel Durov: 'IP addresses coming mostly from China. Historically, all state actor-sized DDoS ... we experienced coincided in time with protests in Hong Kong (coordinated on @ telegram). This case was not an exception.' *Twitter*, 13 June 2019, twitter.com/durov/status/1138942773430804480.

CHAPTER 6: STORMING THE SYSTEM

1 Johannes Chan speaking on, 'Ep. 21: The Rule of Law in Hong Kong (Part Two) – Johannes Chan.' *CSCC Podcasts*, 24 October 2019, cscc. sas.upenn.edu/podcasts/2019/10/24/ep-21-rule-law-hong-kong-part-two-johannes-chan.

2 Government of the Hong Kong SAR. *Chief Executive Policy Address.* 2015, paragraph 10, www.policyaddress.gov.hk/2015/eng/index.html.

3 Sataline, Suzanne. 'What Hong Kong's man without a mask wants you to know.' *The Christian Science Monitor*, 18 July 2019, www.csmonitor. com/World/Asia-Pacific/2019/0718/What-Hong-Kong-s-man-without-a-mask-wants-you-to-know.

4 Leung, Brian. 'Activist Brian Leung at storming of the legislature: "Hongkongers have nothing left to lose".' *YouTube*, uploaded by Hong Kong Free Press, 6 July 2019, youtu.be/n3EsrjpgKbQ

5 Ho Kwai-lam, Gwyneth. 'Hong Kong Belongs to Everyone Who Shares Its Pain: the vision of July 1st's only unmasked protester.' *Stand News,* 17 November 2019, www.thestandnews.com/politics/hong-kong-belongs-to-everyone-who-shares-its-pain-the-vision-of-july-1st-s-only-unmasked-protester.

6 Lum, Alvin. '"It wasn't violence for violence's sake": the only unmasked protester at storming of Hong Kong's legislature gives his account of the day's drama.' *South China Morning Post,* 5 July 2019, www.scmp.com/news/hong-kong/politics/article/3017327/it-wasnt-violence-violences-sake-only-unmasked-protester.

7 Sataline, note 3 above.

8 See: Chan, Jacky Man Hei and Jun Pang. 'The untold story of Hong Kong's protests is how one simple slogan connects us.' *The Guardian,* 11 July 2019, www.theguardian.com/commentisfree/2019/jul/11/the-untold-story-of-hong-kongs-protests-is-how-one-simple-slogan-connects-us.

9 Government of the Hong Kong Special Administrative Region. 'Fugitive bill is dead: CE.' 9 July 2019, www.news.gov.hk/eng/2019/0 7/20190709/20190709_104811_661.html.

10 Sum Lok-kei and Tony Cheung. 'Hong Kong's controversial extradition bill may be "dead" but city leader Carrie Lam still unable to win over her critics.' *South China Morning Post,* 9 July 2019, www.scmp.com/news/hong-kong/politics/article/3017795/hong-kong-leader-carrie-lam-says-extradition-bill-dead.

CHAPTER 7: 'RECLAIM HONG KONG! REVOLUTION OF OUR TIMES!'

1 Edward Leung speaking in *Lost in the Fumes*. Directed by Nora Lam Tze Wing, Outfocus Productions, 2017.

2 Bland, Ben. *Generation HK: seeking identity in China's shadow.* Penguin, 2017, p. 102.

3 Fung, Owen. 'New storm: Hong Kong Indigenous candidate Edward Leung admits he was born on the mainland.' *South China Morning Post,* 7 March 2016, www.scmp.com/news/hong-kong/politics/

article/1921966/new-storm-hong-kong-indigenous-candidate-
edward-leung-admits.

4 Moss, Stephen. 'Is Hong Kong really rioting over fishball stands?'
The Guardian, 10 February 2016, www.theguardian.com/lifeandstyle/
shortcuts/2016/feb/09/hong-kong-fish-ball-revolution-china-riot.

5 Wong, Alan, 'China Labels Protesters "Radical Separatists," and
They Agree', *New York Times*, 20 February 2016, www.nytimes.
com/2016/02/21/world/asia/hong-kong-indigenous-separatism.html.

6 Bland, note 2 above, p. 109.

7 Cheung, Karen. '"A turning point": pro-democracy Civic Party's
Alvin Yeung wins NT East by-election with 37% of votes.' *Hong Kong
Free Press*, 29 February 2016, www.hongkongfp.com/2016/02/29/a-
turning-point-civic-partys-alvin-yeung-wins-new-territories-east-by-
election-with-37-of-votes/.

8 Cheng, Kris. 'Decision to bar Edward Leung from election "has legal
basis," says Secretary for Justice.' *Hong Kong Free Press*, 3 August 2016,
www.hongkongfp.com/2016/08/03/decision-bar-edward-leung-
election-legal-basis-says-secretary-justice/.

9 McLaughlin, Timothy. 'Meet the Spiritual Leader of the Hong
Kong Protests.' *The Atlantic*, 31 October 2019, www.theatlantic.
com/international/archive/2019/10/hong-kong-protests-edward-
leung/601015/.

10 Barmé, Geremie. 'Restoring Hong Kong, Revolution of Our Times.'
China Heritage, 6 August 2019, chinaheritage.net/journal/restoring-
hong-kong-revolution-of-our-times/.

11 Ibid.

12 Barmé prefers to translate the term '*guangfu*' as 'restore', which is
the more accurate translation, but the Hong Kong protesters more
commonly rendered the term into English as 'reclaim', and this
translation also better captures the aspect of the slogan that so raised
hackles in Beijing.

13 Hong Kong Public Opinion Research Institute. 'Press Release on
August 13, 2019: HKPOP today releases popularity figures of
officials and corporations, and survey findings on anti-extradition-bill
movement commissioned by a newspaper.' 13 August 2019, www.pori.
hk/press-release/2019/20190813-eng.

14 Cheng, Kris. 'Name of Hong Kong police commander handling Yuen
Long attacks removed from public gov't contact list.' *Hong Kong Free*

Press, 23 July 2019, www.hongkongfp.com/2019/07/23/name-hong-kong-police-commander-handling-yuen-long-attacks-removed-public-govt-contact-list/.

15 Footage of Qoser's questioning of Lam is available at: youtu.be/7uqqAmIlRr4.

CHAPTER 8: THE RIGHT TO THE CITY

1 Hong Kong Free Press. '"Hongkongers add oil": Cathay pilot reassures passengers about protest.' *YouTube*, 26 July 2019, youtu.be/EsOh5h-ZT5Q.

2 Lefebvre, Henri. *Writings on Cities*. Edited by Eleonore Kofman and Elizabeth Lebas, Blackwell, 1996, p. 158.

3 Harvey, David. *Rebel Cities: from the right to the city to the urban revolution*. Verso, 2012, p. 4.

CHAPTER 10: THE BATTLE OF SHEUNG WAN

1 Dzenovska, Dace, and Iván Arenas. 'Don't fence me in: barricade sociality and political struggles in Mexico and Latvia.' *Comparative Studies in Society and History*, vol. 54, no. 3, 2012, pp. 644–78, at p. 646.

2 'Three youngsters who start fires: how did moderate protesters become "fire magicians"?' *Stand News*, 22 October 2019, www.thestandnews.com/politics/three-youngsters-who-start-fires-how-did-moderate-protesters-become-fire-magicians/.

3 Hugo, Victor. *Les Misérables*. Translated by Norman Denny, Penguin Classics, 2012, Part IV, Book X, Chapter V, 'The Uniqueness of Paris', p. 901.

4 Leung, Edward, *Facebook*, 29 July 2019, www.facebook.com/leungtinkei/posts/707133229699516. (Translation by the author.)

CHAPTER 11: STRIKE!

1 Xinhua. 'Central government strongly condemns flag-insulting acts by radicals in Hong Kong.' *Xinhua*, 4 August 2019, www.xinhuanet.com/english/2019-08/04/c_138283162.htm.

2 It is sometimes incorrectly reported that tycoon Li Ka-shing owned the Hong Kong Artificial Flower Works. The correct ownership is confirmed in the Chinese-language edition of Gary Ka-wai Cheung *Hong Kong's Watershed: the 1967 riots*, published as *Liu Qi Bao Dong:*

Xianggang zhanhou lishi de fenshuiling. Hong Kong University Press, 2012, p. 39. The fact that Li was not the owner was also confirmed to the author in an email from Corporate Affairs Department, CK Asset Holdings Limited, 17 January 2020.

3   Cheung, Gary Ka-wai. *Hong Kong's Watershed: The 1967 riots*. Hong Kong University Press, 2009, pp. 29, 31.

4   Ibid, pp. 58-59.

5   Ibid, p. 65.

6   Chan, Homes. 'Jailed Hong Kong democracy leader Benny Tai sent to solitary confinement over strike action.' *Hong Kong Free Press*, 8 August 2019, www.hongkongfp.com/2019/08/08/jailed-hong-kong-democracy-leader-benny-tai-sent-solitary-confinement-strike-action/.

7   Kuo, Lily, et al. 'Hong Kong brought to a standstill as city-wide strikes and protests hit.' *The Guardian*, 5 August 2019, www.theguardian.com/world/2019/aug/05/hong-kong-brought-to-a-standstill-as-city-wide-strikes-and-protests-hit.

8   Lam, Jeffie. 'From two-star Michelin restaurant to union organiser, Hong Kong chef's career path is not what he had in mind.' *South China Morning Post*, 26 December 2019, scmp.com/news/hong-kong/politics/article/3043492/two-star-michelin-restaurant-union-organiser-hong-kong.

CHAPTER 12: THINGS FALL APART

1   Agence France Presse. 'China warns Hong Kong protesters not to mistake gov't "restraint for weakness".' *Hong Kong Free Press*, 6 August 2019, www.hongkongfp.com/2019/08/06/china-warns-hong-kong-protesters-not-mistake-govt-restraint-weakness/.

2   Yeung, Chris. 'The fall of the Hong Kong Police Force: a new branch of China's public security machinery?' *Hong Kong Free Press*, 21 August 2019, www.hongkongfp.com/2019/08/21/fall-hong-kong-police-force-new-branch-chinas-public-security-machinery/.

3   Hu Xijin. *Twitter*, 14 August 2019, twitter.com/HuXijin_GT/status/1161312219553882113.

4   Trump, Donald. *Twitter*, 14 August 2019, twitter.com/realDonaldTrump/status/1161325870516264961.

5   Government of the Hong Kong Special Administrative Region,
    11 November 2019, www.news.gov.hk/chi/2019/11/20191111/201
    91111_185151_355.html. Curiously, the key phrase appeared in the
    Chinese version of the government news release, but not in the English
    version.

6   Chan, Holmes. 'Cathay Pacific pilot who went viral for telling
    Hongkongers to "keep it up" no longer with airline.' *Hong Kong Free
    Press*, 21 August 2019, www.hongkongfp.com/2019/08/21/cathay-
    pacific-pilot-went-viral-telling-hongkongers-add-oil-no-longer-airline/.

7   Chow, Chung-yan. 'Hong Kong tycoon Li Ka-shing invokes poetry
    in call for end to protests and violence.' *South China Morning
    Post*, 16 August 2019, www.scmp.com/news/hong-kong/politics/
    article/3023037/melon-huangtai-hong-kong-business-leader-li-ka-shing.

8   Dwyer, Colin. 'Did A Hong Kong Tycoon Hide A Protest Message
    In His Innocuous Newspaper Ads?' *NPR*, 22 August 2019, www.
    npr.org/2019/08/22/753394754/did-a-hong-kong-tycoon-hide-a-
    protest-message-in-his-innocuous-newspaper-ads.

9   Weinland, Don and Leo Lewis. 'Hong Kong's 'Superman' Li Ka-shing
    comes under fire.' *Financial Times*, 27 September 2019, www.ft.com/
    content/062b54b2-e0c4-11e9-9743-db5a370481bc.

10 Ng, Joyce. 'Beijing piles pressure on Hong Kong developers, calling
    on government to seize land being "hoarded for profit".' *South China
    Morning Post*, 13 September 2019, www.scmp.com/news/hong-kong/
    hong-kong-economy/article/3027064/hong-kong-developers-who-
    are-hoarding-land-profit.

11 Lam, Ka-sing. 'New World donates almost a fifth of its farmland
    reserves towards building public homes to ease Hong Kong's housing
    woes.' *South China Morning Post*, 25 September 2019, www.scmp.
    com/business/article/3030317/new-world-development-donates-3-
    million-square-feet-farm-land-ease-hong.

12 Osnos, Evan. 'China Forces the N.B.A. to Weigh Value Against
    Values.' *The New Yorker*, 8 October 2019, www.newyorker.com/news/
    daily-comment/china-forces-the-nba-to-weigh-value-against-values.

13 Twitter Safety. 'Information operations directed at Hong Kong.' *Twitter*,
    19 August 2019, blog.twitter.com/en_us/topics/company/2019/
    information_operations_directed_at_Hong_Kong.html.

14 Twitter Inc. 'Updating our advertising policies on state media.' *Twitter*,
    19 August 2019, blog.twitter.com/en_us/topics/company/2019/
    advertising_policies_on_state_media.html.

15 Pew Research Center. 'China's Economic Growth Mostly Welcomed
    in Emerging Markets, but Neighbors Wary of Its Influence.'
    5 December 2019, www.pewresearch.org/global/2019/12/05/
    chinas-economic-growth-mostly-welcomed-in-emerging-markets-but-
    neighbors-wary-of-its-influence/. The survey was conducted among
    38,426 people in 34 countries from May to October 2019, coinciding
    almost exactly with the period of the Hong Kong protests.

16 Tsai Ing-wen, *Twitter*, 5 November 2019, twitter.com/iingwen/
    status/1191624997028057088.

17 Connolly, Kate. 'Hong Kong activist's visit to Berlin draws anger from
    China.' *The Guardian*, 11 September 2019, www.theguardian.com/
    world/2019/sep/10/hong-kong-activist-joshua-wong-visit-berlin-
    anger-china.

18 Agence France Presse. '"Hong Kong the new Berlin": activist Joshua
    Wong discusses "new Cold War" with Heiko Maas.' *The Local de*,
    10 September 2019, www.thelocal.de/20190910/seeking-support-hks-
    joshua-wong-meets-german-foreign-minister.

CHAPTER 13: A PROTEST OF ENCHANTMENT

1 Cheng, Kris. 'Organisers say 1.7 million joined Hong Kong pro-
   democracy rally against police use of force, as protesters reiterate 5
   demands.' *Hong Kong Free Press*, 18 August 2019, www.hongkongfp.
   com/2019/08/18/breaking-organisers-say-1-7-million-joined-hong-
   kong-pro-democracy-rally-police-use-force-protesters-reiterate-5-
   demands/.

2 Bennett, Jane. *The Enchantment of Modern Life: attachments, crossings,
   and ethics.* Princeton University Press, 2001, p. 5.

3 Abbas, Ackbar. *Hong Kong: culture and the politics of disappearance.*
   Hong Kong University Press, 1997.

4 Lo, Clifford et al. 'Pro-Democracy Banner Hung from Lion Rock Has
   Officials Scrambling.' *South China Morning Post*, 24 October 2014,
   www.scmp.com/news/hong-kong/article/1622971/climbers-hang-
   giant-banner-lion-rock-calling-real-universal-suffrage.

CHAPTER 14: THE END OF SUMMER

1   Emmett, Chris. *Hong Kong Police: inside the lines*. Earnshaw Books, 2018, p. 71.

2   Mahtani, Shibani et al. 'In Hong Kong crackdown, police repeatedly broke their own rules — and faced no consequences.' *The Washington Post*, 24 December 2019, www.washingtonpost.com/graphics/2019/world/hong-kong-protests-excessive-force/.

3   Amnesty International. 'Hong Kong: Arbitrary arrests, brutal beatings and torture in police detention revealed.' 19 September 2019, www.amnesty.org/en/latest/news/2019/09/hong-kong-arbitrary-arrests-brutal-beatings-and-torture-in-police-detention-revealed/.

4   Mahtani, note 2 above.

5   Lee, Francis L.F. 'Our research in Hong Kong reveals what people really think of the protesters – and the police.' *The Independent*, 16 October 2019, www.independent.co.uk/voices/hong-kong-protests-police-violence-public-opinion-polling-support-a9158061.html.

6   Marcolini, Barbara, et al. 'Did Hong Kong Police Use Violence Against Protesters? What the Videos Show.' *The New York Times*, 14 July 2019, www.nytimes.com/video/world/asia/100000006602584/hong-kong-police-protest-video-investigation.html.

7   Yu, Alan. 'Can science offer police a better way to handle protests?' *WHYY*, 14 November 2019, whyy.org/segments/can-science-offer-police-a-better-way-to-handle-protests/.

8   Ta Kung Pao. *We Shall Win! British imperialism in Hong Kong shall be defeated!* Ta Kung Pao, November 1967.

9   'Zhuanli husong "heiyiren", gangtie dianliangguo qingzhong ma?' *China News*, 22 August 2019, www.chinanews.com/ga/2019/08-22/8934910.shtml.

CHAPTER 15: ONE STATE, TWO NATIONS

1   Fong, Brian C.H. 'Stateless nation within a nationless state: the political past, present, and future of Hongkongers, 1949–2019.' *Nations and Nationalism*, 2019; pp. 1–18, doi.org/10.1111/nana.12556.

2   Those aged tenrty-nine and under represented around 40 to 50 per cent of attendees at mass popular rallies, and as much as 70 to 80 per cent at the more radical, wildcat protests. A detailed survey of the demographics of participants in the 2019 protests is reported in Francis L.F. Lee, et al. 'Onsite Survey Findings in Hong Kong's Anti-Extradition Bill Protests.' *Centre for Communication and Public Opinion Survey, The Chinese University of Hong Kong*, August 2019, www.com.cuhk.edu.hk/ccpos/en/pdf/ENG_antielab%20survey%20public%20report%20vf.pdf. Updated survey data is available at *Anti-ELAB Survey Report*, sites.google.com/view/antielabsurvey-eng/.

3   The 3D printing files are available at www.thingiverse.com/thing:3861546.

4   Leung, Hillary. 'Listen to the Song That Hong Kong's Youthful Protesters Are Calling Their "National Anthem".' *Time*, 10 September 2019, time.com/5672018/glory-to-hong-kong-protests-national-anthem/.

5   Anderson, Benedict. *Imagined Communities: reflections on the origin and spread of nationalism*. Revised edition. Verso, 2016, p. 145.

CHAPTER 16: RESIST!

1   Cheung, *Hong Kong's Watershed: the 1967 riots*, p. 85.

2   Hong Kong Legislative Council, Official Report of Proceedings, Meeting of 15th November 1967, p. 476, available at: www.legco.gov.hk/1967/h671115.pdf.

3   Dykes, Philip J. 'Speech Given at the Opening of the Legal Year, 13 January 2020 by the Chairman of the Hong Kong Bar Association Philip J. Dykes SC.' www.hkba.org/sites/default/files/20200113%20-%20Speech%20of%20Chairman%20at%20Opening%20of%20Legal%20Year%202020%20%28Eng%29.pdf.

4   Béja, Jean-Philippe. 'Interview: ex-head of legislature Jasper Tsang says the gov't is weakest player of four in Hong Kong's struggle.' *Hong Kong Free Press*, 16 November 2019, www.hongkongfp.com/2019/11/16/interview-ex-head-legislature-jasper-tsang-says-govt-weakest-player-four-hong-kongs-struggle/.

5   Cheng, Kris. 'Crowdfunding campaign for jailed activist Edward Leung's appeal surpasses HK$350,000 goal within 15 minutes.' *Hong Kong Free Press*, 5 October 2019, www.hongkongfp.com/2019/10/05/

crowdfunding-campaign-jailed-activist-edward-leungs-appeal-surpasses-hk350000-goal-within-15-minutes/.

6   Indeed, scholar Joshua Clover has defined 'riot' as a form of collective action that 'struggles to set the price of market goods' — in contrast with a 'strike', which is a struggle to set the price of labour power. By this definition, looting is the very essence of riot — a collective action which sets the price of goods at 'free'. See Joshua Clover. *Riot. Strike. Riot.* Verso, 2019, p. 14.

7   Ibid, p. 11.

8   MTR Corporation. 'Press Release: Malicious Vandalism at MTR Network Forced Service Suspension on All Rail Lines.' 5 October 2019, www.mtr.com.hk/archive/corporate/en/press_release/PS-2019-10-5-E.pdf.

CHAPTER 17: CITY ON FIRE

1   United Nations (Anti-Terrorism Measures) Ordinance (Cap. 575).

2   RTHK News. 'Independent protest inquiry is essential: John Tsang.' 12 November 2019, news.rthk.hk/rthk/en/component/k2/1491662-20191112.htm.

CHAPTER 18: THE SIEGE

1   Denyer, Simon and Tiffany Liang. 'China says Trump is on "edge of precipice" as Hong Kong rights bill hits his desk.' *Washington Post*, 22 November 2019, www.washingtonpost.com/world/asia-pacific/hong-kong-moves-to-center-stage-of-us-china-showdown/2019/11/21/517aa47e-0bd8-11ea-8054-289aef6e38a3_story.html.

2   Mann, Darren. 'International humanitarian norms are violated in Hong Kong.' *The Lancet,* vol. 394, no. 10214, pp. 2067–68, 7 December 2019, doi.org/10.1016/S0140-6736(19)32909-5.

3   Lam, YP. 'The Siege of PolyU (II): through the sewers, towards the light.' *Stand News*, 4 December 2019, www.thestandnews.com/politics/the-siege-of-polyu-ii-through-the-sewers-towards-the-light/.

4   See generally Arpad Szakolczai. 'Liminality and Experience: structuring transitory situations and transformative events.' *International Political Anthropology*, vol. 2, no. 1, 2009, pp. 141–72.

CHAPTER 19: THE SILENT MAJORITY

1 Cheng, Man Kit. 'For the Record: an enemy of the state.' *Facebook*, 20 November 2019, www.facebook.com/notes/cheng-man-kit/for-the-record-an-enemy-of-the-state/2490959950941845/

2 McKenzie, Nick, et al. 'The moment a Chinese spy decided to defect to Australia.' *The Age*, 23 November 2019, www.theage.com.au/national/the-moment-a-chinese-spy-decided-to-defect-to-australia-20191122-p53d0x.html.

CHAPTER 20: A WAY TO LIVE

1 Pomfret, James, and Clare Jim. 'Exclusive: Hong Kongers support protester demands; minority wants independence from China — Reuters poll.' *Reuters*, 31 December 2019, uk.reuters.com/article/uk-hongkong-protests-poll-exclusive-idUKKBN1YZ0VJ.

2 Government of the Hong Kong Special Administrative Region, Census and Statistics Department. 'Provisional statistics of retail sales for December 2019 and the the whole year of 2019.' 4 February 2020.

3 Lee, Danny. 'Hong Kong protests: traveller numbers at city airport in biggest drop since 2009 as unrest batters tourism.' *South China Morning Post*, 19 January 2020, www.scmp.com/news/hong-kong/politics/article/3046734/hong-kong-protests-traveller-numbers-city-airport-biggest.

4 Hong Kong Public Opinion Research Institute. 'Press Release on August 13, 2019: HKPOP today releases popularity figures of officials and corporations, and survey findings on anti-extradition-bill movement commissioned by a newspaper.' 13 August 2019, www.pori.hk/press-release/2019/20190813-eng.

5 Moody's Investors Service. 'Moody's downgrades Hong Kong's rating to Aa3; changes outlook to stable.' 20 January 2020, www.moodys.com/research/Moodys-downgrades-Hong-Kongs-rating-to-Aa3-changes-outlook-to--PR_415515.

6 Fitch Ratings. 'Fitch Downgrades Hong Kong to "AA" from "AA+"; Outlook Negative.' 5 September 2019, www.fitchratings.com/site/pr/10088391.

7 Chan, Alexandra. '"Buy Yellow, Eat Yellow": the economic arm of Hong Kong's pro-democracy protests.' *The Diplomat*, 13 December

2019, thediplomat.com/2019/12/buy-yellow-eat-yellow-the-economic-arm-of-hong-kongs-pro-democracy-protests/.

8   Cheung, *Hong Kong's Watershed: the 1967 riots*, p. 123.

9   RTHK. '*Fan xiuli shijian you 6 yue 9 ri shang zhou san you 6943 ren bei bu.*' *RTHK*, 8 January 2020, news.rthk.hk/rthk/ch/component/k2/1501678-20200108.htm.

10 Ni, Michael Y. et al. 'Depression and post-traumatic stress during major social unrest in Hong Kong: a 10-year prospective cohort study.' *The Lancet*, 9 January 2020, doi.org/10.1016/S0140-6736(19)33160-5.

11 Video is available at: Jennifer Creery. 'Video: Protesters briefly storm Hong Kong Int'l Airport before being chased away by police.' *Hong Kong Free Press*, 1 September 2019, www.hongkongfp.com/2019/09/01/video-protesters-briefly-storm-hong-kong-intl-airport-chased-away-riot-police/.

12 In the original Chinese it — naturally — rhymed: '*Ma zhao pao, gu zhao chao, wu zhao tiao.*'

13 Pomfret, James, and Clare Jim, note 1 above.

14 Tsang, Steve. *A Modern History of Hong Kong*. Hong Kong University Press, 2004, p. 247.

15 Quoted in Jacques Rancière. *Hatred of Democracy*. Translated by Steve Corcoran, Verso, 2014, p. 60.

16 Cheng, Kris. 'Decision to bar Edward Leung from election "has legal basis," says Secretary for Justice.' *Hong Kong Free Press*, 3 August 2016, www.hongkongfp.com/2016/08/03/decision-bar-edward-leung-election-legal-basis-says-secretary-justice/.

17 Tsai Ing-wen, *Twitter*, 11 January 2020, twitter.com/iingwen/status/1216007345953628162.

All websites accessed 1 February 2020.